FOLLOW YOUR BLISS AND OTHER LIES ABOUT CALLING

FOLLOW YOUR BLISS AND OTHER LIES ABOUT CALLING

Bonnie J. Miller-McLemore

Oxford University Press is a department of the University of Oxford.
It furthers the University's objective of excellence in research, scholarship,
and education by publishing worldwide. Oxford is a registered trademark of
Oxford University Press in the United Kingdom and in certain other countries.

Published in the United States of America by Oxford University Press
198 Madison Avenue, New York, NY 10016, United States of America.

© Oxford University Press 2024

All rights reserved. No part of this publication may be reproduced, stored in a retrieval system, or transmitted, in any form or by any means, without the prior permission in writing of Oxford University Press, or as expressly permitted by law, by license or under terms agreed with the appropriate reprographics rights organization. Inquiries concerning reproduction outside the scope of the above should be sent to the Rights Department, Oxford University Press, at the address above.

You must not circulate this work in any other form,
and you must impose this same condition on any acquirer

Library of Congress Cataloging-in-Publication Data
Names: Miller-McLemore, Bonnie J., author.
Title: Follow your bliss and other lies about calling / Bonnie J. Miller-McLemore.
Description: New York, NY, United States of America : Oxford University Press, 2024. |
Includes bibliographical references and index.
Identifiers: LCCN 2024013789 (print) | LCCN 2024013790 (ebook) |
ISBN 9780190084042 (c/p) | ISBN 9780190084073 | ISBN 9780190084059 |
ISBN 9780190084066 (epub)
Subjects: LCSH: Vocation—Biblical teaching.
Classification: LCC BS680.V6 M56 2024 (print) | LCC BS680.V6 (ebook) |
DDC 248.8/92—dc23/eng/20240412
LC record available at https://lccn.loc.gov/2024013789
LC ebook record available at https://lccn.loc.gov/2024013790

DOI: 10.1093/9780190084073.001.0001

The manufacturer's authorised representative in the EU for product safety is
Oxford University Press España S.A. of El Parque Empresarial San Fernando
de Henares, Avenida de Castilla, 2 – 28830 Madrid (www.oup.es/en or
product.safety@oup.com). OUP España S.A. also acts as importer into Spain
of products made by the manufacturer.

With love
For George, Cade, James, Amos, and those to come

CONTENTS

Introduction: *Double-Edged Callings:* Follow Your Bliss (Blisters)? 1

1. *Missed Callings:* The Road *Not Taken* 17
2. *Blocked Callings:* A Raisin in the Sun 42
3. *Conflicted Callings:* Purity of Heart Is to Will *Several* Things 65
4. *Fractured Callings:* I Do Not Do the Good I Want 87
5. *Unexpected Callings:* With Great Power Comes Lots of *Work* 111
6. *Relinquished Callings:* Riding Off into the Sunset? 135

ACKNOWLEDGMENTS 159
NOTES 163
BIBLIOGRAPHY 189
INDEX 205

Introduction

Double-Edged Callings: *Follow Your Bliss (Blisters)?*

It's funny I've written a book about calling. I've never really liked the word or its companion term *vocation*, often used interchangeably to talk about finding one's purpose in life. They've always seemed like abstract concepts propounded by philosophical theologians. *Or* like an overly pious boast from Christian neighbors sure about their call from God to do this or that, go here or there, sometimes promoting their own good while unknowingly harming others. In general, the Christians I knew gravitated toward one of two extremes, either making sweeping claims about hearing God's call (evangelicals) or dodging the word as a way to frame their lives (progressives).

I fall more in the latter camp. In fact, as I was writing this book, I questioned at times whether I was, indeed, called to write a book on calling! I worried my effort to bring a lofty religious term down to earth was wrongheaded or unorthodox, or my desire to discuss the hardships associated with calling too negative. One friend suggested I simply avoid the word entirely. "Who wants to be told they're not living up to their calling?" she remarked. "The word sounds too revered, esteemed, sacred . . . too laden, too heavy, too burdensome." I couldn't help but agree. There must be better ways to talk about what we should do with our lives, I thought.

And yet I kept feeling tugged Jonah-style toward the very call I resisted, convinced that the superficial views of calling that dominate religious circles and trendy self-help literature are insufficient and misleading. It took me a while to yield, however. In the biblical story, Jonah hears God's call to go to the corrupt city of Nineveh to urge its people to change their wayward ways, but he ignores it until he's caught in a storm at sea, thrown overboard by his shipmates, and swallowed by a whale. Only when spat out on shore does he finally turn his face toward Nineveh.

For me, the "whale" was a small group of wonderful scholars and friends, commissioned by Professor Kathleen Cahalan to study vocation across the life span at the Collegeville Institute on the campus of Saint John's Abbey and University. A practical theologian at the university, Cahalan had learned by directing two previous Institute seminars on vocation that there is little literature or discussion about how callings take different shapes from infancy to old age. She was particularly struck by hearing people say they experienced retirement as a critical vocational turning point, even though it's largely neglected by pastors and theologians as a time for reassessing a calling. She asked her funding foundation for an additional grant to convene a third seminar on vocation at distinct life phases, inclusive of ages we often disregard when talking about calling, like childhood and late adulthood.[1] I was among the small group of pastors, theological educators, and social scientists she invited to join her, all of whom had some history of reflecting on vocation or calling.

My own history was checkered. I stumbled onto the idea of calling over thirty years ago when I experienced the turmoil of trying to follow multiple callings. As a young mother with three small sons and a full-time job as a seminary professor, I felt called to teach and write but also to parent, and like many women before me and others since, I was torn between paid employment and family, struggling to manage both callings simultaneously. When I went to write about the challenge, however—a book I titled *Also a Mother*, subtitling it *Work and Family as Theological Dilemma*—I intentionally steered away from the words *calling* and *vocation*, though I knew they captured well what I meant when I argued that concerns about child care or fair division of household labor weren't just about public policy or even justice in the family but involved bigger questions about *what comprises a good and worthy life* in a society that often emphasizes productivity and self-advancement over care of others. Despite my theological training and faith commitments, I chose instead a phrase borrowed from contemporary psychology—crises of *generativity*.[2]

In essence my book on mothering was a book on calling, not as women's sole destiny, but as one important calling among many. But I wasn't comfortable using the word, and I especially didn't want to get entangled in the confusion surrounding it. Many Christians still assume the only people who are genuinely called by God are those in formal religious or monastic communities—priests, nuns, monks, and so forth. This bias persists despite sixteenth-century claims by Reformers such as Martin Luther and John Calvin and more recent correctives among Catholics and secular spokespersons alike that following a calling is for people in *all* walks of life. Meanwhile, the wider public continues to use *vocation* to refer to skilled training or just one's job, even though calling and vocation have always been expansive words that apply to the two spheres that I had explored—work *and* love.

In other words, I entered the Collegeville conversation with reservations. Don't the words *calling* and *vocation* just get in the way, I thought, when we're trying to talk about the deeper questions of "leading lives that matter," a phrase the editors of a popular anthology on calling opted for as their book title over *calling* or *vocation* for similar reasons?[3] Questions and doubts about the usefulness of religious language actually lay at the heart of the Collegeville seminars. "Is it possible," Cahalan asked as our seminar began, that the religious idea of calling is "beyond repair and too arcane or corrupt ... to be of much good in a contemporary context"?[4]

Not surprisingly, this question hovered in the background as our small seminar group gathered a couple times each year for four years, along with questions such as: Could we find creative ways to overhaul and reclaim calling and vocation as viable theological concepts? What happens to these words when we embed them in time? Would they look different if we thought about them as unfolding throughout our lives, in all its phases from birth to death? How do children, the elderly, and young, middle, and older adults experience calling? Such questions demanded the kind of collaborative learning and space for engagement made possible by the Benedictine setting of Saint John's, with its monastic emphasis on prayer, work, and practices of hospitality, balance, and moderation so basic to Saint Benedict's Rule of Life.[5]

Over time, our reading, conversation, and fellowship led to three significant insights. The very premise we began with—that *callings develop over a lifetime*—was itself refreshing. Most people assume that calling has to do with young adults figuring out their lives. Or they picture it as a one-time summons from God that directs life forever after or draws only a few special people into ministry or the priesthood. By contrast, we assumed from the beginning that a calling doesn't mean we've "arrived" but changes over the course of our lives, taking different forms at different times. It pertains to people "no matter their life situation," as one of the participants put it, arising in all arenas—in our work, relationships, and avocations, not just in our paid careers.[6]

As we explored this basic premise, we gained an additional insight: *Callings are not purely individual matters of knowing and choosing what we alone want or should do but are deeply relational and communal.* They are shaped within and controlled by our intimate relationships and social contexts. For many people, grandmothers play an especially important role as do teachers, mentors, and exemplars. Parents also wield incredible *and* ambiguous influence, and partners, spouses, children, aging parents, stepchildren, and so forth delimit and even dictate whether one can follow a particular calling or pursue a vocation at all. Global forces like climate change and divisive politics as well as social and political parameters surrounding sex, race, class, nationality, and so forth also restrict and sometimes destroy choice and opportunity. Systems that scholars label with sweeping terms, such as capitalism, imperialism, nationalism, patriarchy, racism, and anthropocentrism, can distort callings, misleading us to "serve Wall Street," as one military leader remarked, or other limited and harmful ends rather than the good for which we'd hoped.[7] Even the broadest environment—the climate and natural world—has an impact, as young adults, for example, weigh whether they're called to have children or try to consider their futures in a world threatened by increased drought, floods, heatwaves, and forest fires.

Finally, and closely related to our growing awareness of the earth's fragility and its impact on calling, we realized: *Callings are deeply grounded; they possess a materiality and practicality often overlooked in more theoretical treatments.* Our vocations to work and love evolve amid concrete daily happenings, and our bodies have an especially powerful effect. Their growing and diminishing abilities, their capacity to reproduce or fail to reproduce, and their vulnerability to illness and aging all have immense consequences for callings.

These three assertions, which seldom appear in prominent circles where calling is claimed or studied—whether scholarly spheres, Christian communities, or popular discussions—provided a structure for what became an edited book on the subject.[8] Each chapter assumed that callings are a pursuit for a lifetime and addressed how they are discerned in relationships and depend on the emerging and declining capacities of our bodies at a particular phase of life.[9]

Nonetheless—despite the bold and helpful nature of these three claims—it took one final wave to push me onto the shore of this book. That wave hit me during the seminar when we all read an article about zookeepers.

As part of a growing movement of organizational psychologists and management scholars doing research on paid work as a calling, business professors Stuart Bunderson and Jeffery Thompson wanted to know why people persevere in undesirable jobs and decided zookeepers would make an ideal population to study. Zookeepers are often highly educated and intensely committed but poorly paid with little opportunity for advancement. Their work requires unglamorous, unappealing duties (often classified as "dirty work") like cleaning up feces, scrubbing cages, managing food regiments, and grooming. So why do they stick with their work, Bunderson and Thompson wondered? And what can be learned from talking with them about work as a calling more generally?

From exploratory interviews with twenty-three zookeepers and a follow-up survey of nearly a thousand people from over a hundred zoos, here's what the researchers discovered: When asked why zookeepers do what they do, they seldom talk about following their bliss, although they do express deep love for and desire to be with animals. Instead, they use what Bunderson and Thompson name "neoclassical" words like *duty*, *obligation*, and *responsibility*, reminiscent of classical views of the sixteenth century. The zookeepers describe a calling that stretches beyond pursuit of their own desires or talents to encompass a duty to society and the common good, which they name in various ways, such as the need to contribute to animal care, deepen public knowledge of animal diversity, or preserve animals under threat of extinction. Many see their calling as coming from without rather than within, not necessarily from a divine being but in response to what is "meant to happen," as one person remarked, within the wider order of things rather than a personal choice.[10]

In discussing the findings, Bunderson and Thompson present two critical conclusions: First, in framing calling as a duty and a destiny whose source lies outside the self, zookeepers demonstrate a view that differs dramatically from modern views of calling that emphasize personal life choice and the pursuit of individual happiness. But it was their second, related conclusion that struck me more: "This neoclassical version of calling is a *painfully double-edged sword*—a source of transcendent meaning, identity, and significance as well as unbending duty, sacrifice, and vigilance."[11]

As soon as I read that word, *double-edged*, I was hooked. Deeply meaningful callings are also often painful!

Our seminar group had shared our experiences of calling at various stages of life, and we saw the faltering steps we had each taken to find and follow our callings: how failure arose despite our best intentions; how family expectations and duties restrained and limited our decisions; how social and political realities and dead ends subverted and destroyed our dreams; and how undesired responsibilities landed in our laps. We recognized through our own aging bodies that all callings come to an end, endings that aren't always easy to negotiate. And we also knew from experience that callings centered purely on following our bliss seldom satisfied us, but callings that serve others almost always came with a cost.

We knew all this. But when we sat across from each other at a seminar table with the sun shining over Stumpf Lake outside the large picture windows and discussed Bunderson and Thompson's idea that callings have benefits *and* burdens, the energy in the room changed. Faces lit up, the conversation intensified, and everyone spoke. Suddenly, we had words for a thought we had intuited and touched on but hadn't yet articulated or claimed. Callings are "ennobling" *and* "binding." They come with a "price"—"money, time, physical comfort or well-being" in Bunderson and Thompson's words, but also challenging consequences they don't name like loss, regret, frustration, and failure.[12] To my mind, the idea that *callings cut both ways* needed fuller disclosure and closer examination.

This book was effectively born in that moment. I began to ask questions that I explore on these pages, such as: How can we live out our callings well within the many constraints of life? And how do we remain true to our callings when they are often plagued by mistakes, disappointment, overload, oversight, and conflict? I began to listen to others who were expressing similar concerns: How do we absolve ourselves of guilt for not instantly knowing our "life-calling," for "not 'getting it' right away?," as one of our seminary graduates asked.[13] Or, in the words of a colleague at Saint Olaf College after learning about her Stage IV cancer, "What does it mean to integrate trauma and death into our lives, even to make it part of our vocation, to figure out ways to go on?"[14]

In this book, I try to do some truth-telling. Seldom are callings straightforward or without suffering. We don't resolve them easily or early or all at once. Discerning an inner voice or hearing a higher call from outside ourselves is hard work. Callings conflict and compete for our attention; they are seldom singular or monolithic. Nor do callings rest on our own efforts but instead require the difficult navigation of external demands, unwanted pressures, oppressive social dynamics, and help from others. Sometimes vocation is not where "our deep gladness" meets the "world's deep hunger"—the oft used saying of well-known author Frederick Buechner—but where our *deep sadness* meets the world's deep hunger," as the colleague with cancer suggests. Buechner himself testifies to the pivotal role of his father's suicide in the evolution of his own calling as a person and a writer.[15] Most important, however, these kinds of challenges and hardships are *not* a problem; they are an essential element in a life well lived.

Oddly enough, when social scientists investigate the "dark side of a calling," they often interpret the pain as a *problem with calling* that must be overcome.[16] By contrast, I see the double-sided nature of calling as *a necessary and even good part of calling*, something that can enhance life precisely through its hardship, duty, and even suffering and sacrifice, especially if we talk openly about the challenges. I'm convinced it's better to talk honestly about the hurdles and burdens than to overlook, ignore, or try to avoid them. Early on, I described this project to others as an exploration of the "undersides" of calling, a word often used among Latin American liberation theologians writing from the underside of history and advocating for grassroots theology by those at society's margins. For these theologians, the "underside is not only a source of vitality," in the words of one scholar, but also a resource that grounds us and keeps our theologies from soaring "into lofty ethereality."[17] This need to recognize life's earthiness is also true for *calling*, a word that often tempts us toward grand but untrue claims about our lives. Following a calling comes inevitably with frustrations and complexities that begin in early adulthood and last until our final moments. We don't need "to let go of the term" just because people are "called within difficult situations," a seminar participant remarked in an interview.[18] Instead, we're called to a more complex vision of calling that incorporates suffering rather than overrides it.

People have an understandable tendency to try to mitigate suffering, especially parents on behalf of children and professors and teachers with students. But instead of trying to evade life's tragic situations, we're better off helping each other into and through them. "A life of integrity and purpose," proposes theologian Jason Mahn in an essay on the conflicts inherent within callings, "is more likely to *occasion* . . . and even be accompanied by existential suffering" than to skirt it. Although we should never idealize pain or seek suffering as ends in themselves, they can clarify our commitments and leave space for moral and vocational growth. By contrast, "glibly optimistic and moralistic accounts" of calling, says Mahn, make it difficult to develop the dispositions and strengths necessary to living a meaningful life.[19]

Unfortunately, glib and moralistic accounts of calling abound. Many formal theological discussions speak about calling in language that seldom addresses the needs and hopes of congregational parishioners or people on the street.[20] And where theology fails to go, social scientists are happy to tread. Publications on the concept of work as calling nearly doubled between 1998 and 2008, according to one literature review, and since 2011 the number of social science articles on calling have increased exponentially.[21] However, many social scientists who take up the concept do so without grappling adequately or accurately with its complicated religious history. They often reduce calling to awkward scientific terminology that is almost as off-putting as dogmatic religious assertions and that actually make it more difficult to explore deeper ethical and philosophical puzzles that surround vocation. But most troubling to me, they frequently use the word *calling* in utilitarian and individualistic ways, focusing almost wholly on personal benefits, positive versus negative outcomes, individual choice and fulfillment, and job success.[22]

For the entirety of my teaching career at the intersection of religion and psychology, I have been frustrated when people in popular culture, business, and social science appropriate powerful religious ideas, rituals, and practices without appreciating their moral dimensions or their location in rich and long-standing religious traditions. Here, in the very idea of calling, is yet another case where religious language has great potential to enrich life and serve the common good but has lost its meaning through scientific truncation and secular exploitation. As a person of faith who values religious language and traditions, it often feels as if popular psychology and corporate business have hijacked the notion and then reduced it to pursing one's own personal bliss or job happiness. Even sophisticated renderings of calling, such as Buechner's definition about gladness and the world's needs, get turned into platitudes. The business world has been the most instrumentalist and profiteering, using calling in employee workshops and corporate promotions to entice workers to find happiness in their work, and hence to work harder.[23] But in the longer religious history and many people's lives today, calling has functioned instead as an incentive to consider our responsibilities to other people and to causes outside ourselves, sometimes at great cost to us. Vital moral, religious, and philosophical questions accompany our vocational quandaries even if often overlooked in conventional conversations about work and love.

In a word, calling means so much more than seeking gladness, bliss, or profit. A rich variety of definitions arose as I explored each chapter's challenges and are scattered throughout the book. Among my favorites are: calling as the threefold interaction between joy, talent, and service (with the third aspect deserving more respect and attention); calling as all about time and what we do with the gift of time, an insight that arose as I thought about calling in the face of bodily decline, personal finitude, and human mortality; and, finally, calling as how our living makes us, not how we make a living. I focus on what some Christians distinguish as our specific callings in life, not on what all Christians are called to generally—to love God and neighbor.[24] I also use the word *calling* more than *vocation* as the more widely recognized, comfortable, and common term today. Vocation is too often reduced to a job and what we do to earn money. Calling is a more fluid term with resonance across many traditions for what we're meant to do in life and how we're related to other people, including the divine.[25]

Even here, however, I've had to qualify my favorite definitions. The definition of calling as an intersecting trilogy of desire, talent, and service leaves out an important qualification for discerning and following a calling: income or material survival. Few people can follow their desires, talents, and service and put this matter aside. Only the most privileged can, and calling must not be reserved for the privileged. Sometimes calling is about how we make a living. That said, we still need to resist the encroachment of our market economy, which tempts us to misuse the concept to justify ambitions for personal and financial success.

My primary hope in this book, however, is not so much to redefine calling as to revitalize it in a way that helps you the reader and those you care about cultivate the capacity to bear rather than rush to resolve the ambiguities that naturally accompany our callings.

Honest talk about the undersides will, I believe, help us "resist the temptation to size up" and dispense with every dilemma, to borrow Mahn's words.[26] I consider six dilemmas or three sets of two dilemmas each, organized roughly in chronological order with each pair emerging prominently in early, middle, and late adulthood, respectively: The callings I focus on in the first two chapters (*missed* and *blocked*) often come in early adulthood; those in the next two chapters (*fractured* and *conflicted* callings) usually arise in middle adulthood; and those in the final chapters (*unexpected* and *relinquished* callings) generally emerge in late adulthood. But not always. As I discovered, these dilemmas cross age boundaries, and in each case, people can experience the callings and their related hardships at any time in life. Although the most acute instances of missed callings appear early in life, and retirement is a quintessential moment of relinquishing a calling in late adulthood, in both cases the experiences in young or old adulthood don't exhaust the possibilities. The challenge of deciding which way to go, of leaving one path untrodden to take another, and the difficulty of letting go of beloved callings arise in all stages of life.

Even so, I didn't write the chapters in chronological order but, rather, as I felt drawn to one or another hardship, as my own experience and interests shifted, and I encourage you to follow your own inclination in reading, beginning with the chapter that most interests or draws you in. In other words, the chapters don't need to be read in order. Moreover, because I didn't write them in a linear fashion, you'll see idiosyncrasies in what's happening in my own life: In one of the last chapters, my kids aren't married, my dad hasn't died, I don't have grandchildren, and I haven't retired—all occurrences that appear in the two chapters immediately preceding it. Even though I describe some chapters as closer to the heart of the book than others, I haven't prioritized them. I'm guessing the most important chapter will vary from one reader to the next, depending on where you are in your life and what is bothering you or your kids, partners, or other important relationships. Moreover, even if one of the troubled callings was truly *the* most important for the book and for calling, I still prefer presenting each trouble in the order in which it arises most commonly and poignantly in life.

As this all makes clear, I draw heavily on my life, but I have always liked listening to other people's stories of calling. So, I also tell stories from memoirs, biographies, fiction, friends, colleagues, family members, cultural figures, and everyday people who talk about their callings on public radio, in alumni magazines, and in daily interchanges. I hope the narratives will invite you to fill in your own stories, reading yourself into the book not just in places where you find yourself agreeing but also where I've overlooked valuable illustrations and exceptions. The stories are endless, I discovered, and hence the selected narratives are inevitably limited. Stories are also limited when compared with real life; the telling of a story, says author and activist Wendall Berry, "must begin and end," but a life can't be bound in time because "it does not begin within itself, and it does not end."[27] Even the six places I've chosen don't exhaust the possibilities but only represent where I began and ended. I can imagine other challenges (e.g., unknown callings, undesirable callings), and I hope you can also.

Some stories could appear in more than one chapter. For example, conflicted callings (having too many competing callings) can lead to fractured callings (failures in one area while striving to succeed in another). And a calling that competes in our lives with other equally compelling callings could pertain to both conflicted and unexpected callings (demands put upon us that we don't appreciate but feel called to nonetheless). Fractured callings in early adulthood can turn into unexpected but welcomed callings later in life. Callings that end could easily fall in the chapter on blocked callings (desires, dreams, and hopes for life impeded) or relinquished callings (giving up what we've done and loved). In other words, there is plenty of overlap between chapters.

Finally, each chapter follows a similar pattern, immersing us in the hardships before turning to ways people have navigated them to reclaim the calling anew with enhanced insight and vitality. Chapters often begin with the period of life with which we commonly identify a particular challenge but then turn to other cases that push the usual pattern in new directions. Common themes and feelings appear across chapters: how to hear, know, and discern a call, for instance, and how to live well with grief, lament, anger, frustration, fatigue, disappointment, sacrifice, vulnerability, limitations, closure, mortality, and finitude. Indeed, as the writing provoked my own reflection and engagement with each crisis, I was surprised again and again by the power and place of emotions in the struggle to follow a calling.

Callings are emotional because they are often disruptive and traumatic. They are where we make a way out of no way. They are often what we resist, what we *don't* want, and what we finally take up, a burden or yoke that others help us bear, including help we gain from powers beyond ourselves. Sometimes, overblown claims about following a calling sanctify wrong actions and inflict untold pain on others and the created world itself (a trite but good example—Christians who saw themselves as saviors of the "New World" and regarded nature as a God-given resource to be conquered and subdued). I hope with this book to create space to talk about these complications and the complexities of life in general. For, in a way, calling is just another word for *life* and *how we live our lives. Except*—and here's where it gets tricky—the word carries with it an inevitable and important sacredness, as something ordained or special that we and only we are meant to do or something we're divinely given and compelled to follow. It is this heightened spiritual connotation that often renders the word a freighted concept that hangs over us and weighs us down, leading us to think we can (or must) find the *perfectly* fitting job, the *one-and-only special* life partner, the *ideally balanced* life, the *one-time summons* from God. But if there's only *one* message you take away from this book, let it be that these kinds of expectations are lies that distort life's fuller, richer realities.

· · · · ·

Tired of the popularized misuse of the imperative *follow your bliss* for purely hedonistic purposes, Joseph Campbell is rumored to have finally declared, "I wish I'd said, 'follow your blisters.'" In a series of lengthy conversations with journalist Bill Moyers, later edited down to one of the most popular series in the history of public television, Campbell used the word *bliss* repeatedly to capture the need to stay personally centered amid the inevitable storms of life on what he famously described as the "hero's journey."[28] However, as the self-taught folklorist and literature professor who first uttered the phrase in 1985, never did he anticipate the phrase catching fire as a slogan for finding the idyllic job, the most gorgeous jewelry, or the height of individual enlightenment on self-help book covers, storefronts, Internet sidebar advertisements, and T-shirts. No wonder he had second thoughts.

Given the extent to which the mandate to follow your bliss has filled the airwaves, it's no surprise that the idea even leaked into conversations about calling. Its most damaging consequence, in my mind, arises right here—with the mistaken belief that to have a fulfilling life or to find your one and only purpose and meaning in life, all you need to do is pursue your desire. If you google "follow your bliss," you'll get over eighty-seven million hits, likely more by the time you read this. However, if you search "follow your *blisters*" instead, you'll find at least twelve million citations. In other words, I'm not alone in doubting the pursuit of bliss as a "rule of life" on the same level as Saint Benedict's Rule that has guided monastic communities for centuries.

Follow your *blisters* makes more sense. When Campbell developed his theory about the hero as a universal mythical motif across societies, he envisioned someone who passes through all sorts of adversities in the fight against evil and the pursuit of eternal truths (think *Star Wars*' Luke Skywalker, whom George Lucas says he modeled after Campbell's theory).[29] We should envision a similar path when we think about calling. Following a calling is "not for the faint of heart," as a member of our seminar once concluded.[30] Indeed, the fourth PBS episode of the Moyers–Campbell conversations is actually titled "Sacrifice and Bliss."

Telling the difficult truths about calling—that calling involves bliss *and* sacrifice—provides a revolutionary way to approach it, not as some idealized or glorified notion but as a complicated, ambiguous, and even painful reality that deserves to be understood in all its complexity and glory. Calling carries a lot of weight; it's not always enlightening or helpful. So, it's not surprising we're tempted to lie about it. I imagine I'll continue to use the word sparingly, even after this book comes out. But I hope being honest about the ups *and* downs of calling will open up conversation and help pave the way for living more meaningful and purposeful lives.

Chapter 1

Missed Callings: The Road *Not Taken*

I can picture it as if it were yesterday. My husband Mark and I are sitting in a booth across from our oldest son, Chris, near Vanderbilt, where he's a freshman and we both teach. In order to give him the freedom to settle in on his own, we've treated his departure to school as if he were going out of state, so this was our first chance to hear, face to face, how he was doing. Our unremarkable restaurant meal couldn't compete with our eagerness to learn how his few several weeks had gone.

Vanderbilt hadn't been Chris's only option. A few years before, I'd flown with him to visit a small liberal arts college in Colorado Springs that fit his outdoor interests. But he found its small campus and single dining hall constricting. Vanderbilt, on the other hand, had a spacious campus and, in his words, "lots of cool eating places." While other factors played a part in his decision—strong academics, the beauty of the campus, proximity to where he'd grown up (and we continued to live)—for all practical purposes his decision came down to food—or, more generously, to the elusive leanings that often guide many of our most important decisions.

Hovering over that meal were Mark's and my anxieties, of course. We wondered if we'd done enough to guide Chris in his decision. In contrast to our more relaxed approach, our neighbors and colleagues had taken their kids all over the place to visit schools, and some had fretted over and even restricted their children's choices. Should we have done more research or wielded more influence, I stewed? Was he happy with where he'd ended up? I was both anxious and afraid to hear what he would say.

Part of my worry came from the second thoughts I still harbored over my own college deliberations. "It was raining when we toured Kalamazoo College," my mom always liked to remark any time the topic came up. "I'm not sure *what* you saw in the school but you liked it anyway." With that single sentence, she cast a cloud of her own over my college choice. Behind her skepticism was the fact that Kalamazoo reminded her of her own college, Oberlin, a choice that hadn't turned out well for her.

So, there, in my mind's eye, the three of us sit, ignoring the waiter's "how is everything?" so we can pay better attention to Chris. He tells us about the pre-semester week of rock climbing, spelunking with a student-led wilderness club, and the cool graduate resident on his dorm floor. But then when the meal is almost over, the moment when important stuff often comes up, he says, "Sometimes I wonder if I should have gone to Colorado College," and my stomach turns.

There it was, in pristine form: the road not taken—the pang of living with a decision about which we will *never* be entirely sure. Facing a life-changing choice, we make a decision not just for today or tomorrow but for the rest of our lives, and now we must live forward with it. No one enters adulthood without eventually reaching such a crossroads. Nor without some regret.

Irrevocable Decisions

Over a decade later, Chris still wonders: Did the obstruction of Pike's Peak by fog the day we visited make a difference? For me, there were plenty of rainy days to come at Kalamazoo and more dreary days ahead in a high-pressured graduate program when I wondered if I'd chosen wisely or well. I'd look back and picture the worried students I saw in dorm rooms on the college tour, barely saying hello, absorbed in their studies, and think: My mom was right. I have chosen a life of drudgery. No one was having fun. What was I thinking?

This kind of aching hindsight, so fresh and vivid for young adults, arises again and again throughout life as we try to follow callings. Twenty-five years ago, as Mark and I entered midlife, we faced a question familiar to many couples: Should we move with three young kids for the sake of a job? We had been in Chicago for almost twenty years, since meeting there in graduate school, and we had a network of support for ourselves and our children that allowed us to negotiate demanding jobs. But people told us, "If you're going to move, do it when your kids are young. Don't move teenagers." We deliberated for months before deciding to risk the upheaval. We still talk about what our lives *and* our children's lives might have looked like had we stayed.

Major decisions in middle and later adulthood get dicier because now we're making them not just for ourselves but often for our kids as well. Our decisions also affect others who have become dependent on us—our aging parents, for example, or people we work with. For me, choosing to move meant leaving a close friend who helped me survive early mothering, as well as my first doctoral student to whom I'd pledged support. Mark, a church minister, left all the good people who loved us and our family in a shrinking congregation he'd sustained through hard work. Our experience mimics but pales next to people who have had to navigate harder decisions like staying in or leaving a marriage. I have friends and relatives who weighed that question for years, trying to figure out ways to make the marriage work, before moving out and filing for divorce.

In the restaurant that day, I felt for my eighteen-year-old. I feel for all those making their way out of the teens and through their twenties. Most of my graduate students fall into this camp. Teachers and parents have the mixed blessing of constantly re-experiencing the angst of our own first hesitant moves into adulthood. I know plenty of micromanaging parents who find it difficult not to intervene, determining where their kids go to college, checking out their classes, and even investigating their job prospects. Some parents interfere precisely because we have had to live with our own freighted decisions or poor planning, and we want to spare our kids the pain or agony we've known.

How hard should parents work to steer their kids' lives as they turn the corner into adulthood? How much responsibility do we bear?

Here's the problem: Within our decisions about college, marriage, or moves across the country lie big questions about values *and*, as crucial, far-reaching consequences we cannot predict or control. What neighborhood we choose to live in, for example, says a great deal about our commitments. We can choose a university for its outstanding engineering program (as did my second son) without realizing how much its parochial atmosphere and cut-throat educational approach will affect our well-being and derail us. We cannot begin to see, much less articulate, especially in early adulthood, the meaning and repercussions of our decisions, and yet they are determinative anyway. It is ironic that one of the most important phases of vocational decision-making (first move away from home, first job, first serious relationship, etc.) comes right when knowing what we want is, in the words of youth expert Katherine Turpin, so "elusive, experimental, and even chaotic."[1] Neurological studies tell us that our brains don't even arrive at their full risk assessment capacity until at least the mid-twenties, which doesn't seem fair. Nor does it bode well for our futures. How do we make wise decisions about life when science shows our young brains aren't even done developing?

Some young adults enter the military; others learn a trade, get pregnant, find menial jobs, serve time, go to college, or take a gap year. But we share one thing as we move into adulthood: We reach a turning point in our lives for which we bear responsibility, and the decisions we make have what Turpin describes as "lasting and irreversible consequences." As we move from environments in which we depend on others to those in which others begin to depend on us, big vocational questions "press in" like a "gift and curse," she observes.[2] Missed callings are not unique to this stage, but they are experienced acutely on the brink of adulthood. Understanding them at this juncture sheds light on later encounters. If we're lucky or savvy, we get better at predicting the disappointments and compensations. But, for all of us, at all sorts of life phases, determinations to go one direction and not another carve out a stream into which the tributaries of future callings will have no choice but to flow. In short: Things get serious.

Thus, over forty years ago, before I knew what I was doing, I chose academics over sororities, and studying over partying, and I still wonder about it. I had had enough of petty high school dynamics in my hometown—who to sit with in the lunchroom, what outfit to wear, which popular people were hosting parties. And I had to admit, I liked studying. But these thoughts were about the extent of my self-awareness. On the whim of a rainy day, I chose a small liberal arts college with a heavy emphasis on academics, and I'm still slaving over books.

In a word, the road into and through adulthood is littered with the casualties of ambiguous decisions. These moments crystallize in young adulthood, but they don't end there. We experience the pang of living with weighty decisions as we make choices that are determinative about who we will love, where we will live, and how we will make a living or spend our time. Missed callings are one of the earliest vocational challenges, experienced poignantly in young adulthood but returning throughout life. Probing the sorrows and looking for ways to navigate the losses, as I do in this chapter, comprise essential steps in grappling with the hardships of callings often ignored by popular uses of the term.

I can't remember what we said to Chris that day. If we didn't get it right, we had plenty of other opportunities. Similar moments arose for our middle and youngest sons. These musings—"What would have happened if I had chosen otherwise?"—may seem trivial, but they reveal a struggle all of us go through on the road to calling. How do we live forward with what we've left behind, the selves we've inadvertently "murdered," to borrow Williams James's pointed words?[3] I hope Mark and I explored what was behind Chris's remark—what doubts or discontents, joys or hopes. By our second and third sons, we had a better idea of what to say: No decision is perfect, some are not so good, but no matter how hard you try, you will leave behind a string of untrodden paths, and that's okay. Navigating these irrevocable decisions is a pivotal marker of the turn into adulthood.

The Road Not Taken

Some poetry experts suggest that American poet Robert Frost enjoyed fooling his readers. It's a perception he himself occasionally encouraged. His playfulness and brilliance are nowhere more on display than in his famous poem "The Road Not Taken." He composed it to humor a hiking companion and poet, Edward Thomas, who frequently vacillated about which wooded path they should take and then rued what they might have missed on the road not taken. When Frost sent the poem to his friend, however, Thomas read it as an ode to bold choices and got upset when Frost told him he was just poking fun at human indecisiveness.[4] Readers wouldn't get the joke, Thomas warned.

And Thomas was right. The poem has been incredibly popular but *not* so much because of its wittiness about our equivocation before decisions. I'm one of more than four hundred authors in just the last thirty-five years who have used the poem in a title, subtitle, or heading. But the vast majority interpret the poem as Thomas did—as a celebration of courageous choices. This is nowhere more apparent than the title of M. Scott Peck's bestselling self-help book, *The Road Less Traveled*, which runs roughshod over Frost's own more rueful title, "The Road *Not* Taken." This (mis)titling is likely one reason why the book sold over seven million copies. People like the idea of being a bold and daring traveler who takes the road *less traveled*, and less so someone who regrets the road *not taken*. By the time we get to the last line, we forget that the "less traveled" road glorified there is the same road the storyteller admits earlier as "equally" traveled, the two "worn . . . about the same." Instead, we routinely identify the poem as praise for the daring nonconformist, the free-spirited thinker who marches to the "different drummer" of Henry David Thoreau's *Walden* (a work Frost admired). We picture a heroic (white male?) subject who picks the unbeaten path and is better off for his shrewd choice.

Why do so many people read the poem as a tribute to the triumphant adventurer? Perhaps it's because we want to avoid the sustained indecision of the first three of the poem's four stanzas and the irresolvable ambiguity that surrounds our own decisions (especially in young adulthood). We're narrative creatures, after all, who like happy endings. We want so badly to put a positive spin on things. We like tidy resolutions. We want to believe that even the choices we aren't sure of will work out. Good life stories, as psychologists and literary theories like to say, resolve conflict.[5]

But what if we *have* taken the wrong path? What if we had gone the *other way*? Although literary critics have debated the meaning of Frost's poem for decades, I'd like to linger with the ambiguity and regret at the poem's heart.[6] The route we choose is only "*perhaps* the better claim*," as the narrator admits. We'll never know for sure. Looking back, we say it's better; we iron out the bumps in the retelling; we tell ourselves we're saving the other way for another time. But "way leads on to way," and we won't come back this way again, as the narrator acknowledges. Staying with the discomfort in the poem helps shed light on the plight of missed callings.

With a Sigh

Fifteen master's students and two faculty members—myself and another woman—were gathered around a long seminar table in a downstairs classroom at the Divinity School for a conversation sponsored by our Office of Women's Concerns and Graduate Department. The students had asked the two of us to talk about pursuing a Ph.D. and entering the profession of teaching in religion. We spoke about some of the hurdles and strategies and shared how our own lives had taken unforeseen twists and turns on our way to our current positions. My colleague across the table had just told the women, most of whom were in their mid-twenties, that if she could go back, she would have done a doctorate in early Christian history rather than systematic theology. And then, without censoring my words, I blurted out (a little flippantly), "If I had it to do over again, I would have been a forest ranger."

I wasn't entirely kidding. Academicians, I told the aspiring young women, spend an inordinate amount of time indoors by ourselves with books and, nowadays, in front of a computer screen. I didn't want to convey the wrong message: I love what I do; I've felt unquestioningly called to the writing/teaching life; and, for those who love ideas, the academic world is wonderfully engaging and flexible. Women face enough discrimination and discouragement about their intellectual gifts without my meddling. At the same time, countless students in our master's degree program have ambitions for doctoral study, and, before these folks abandon some other call of the wild, I try to be ruthlessly honest about the hours and hours ahead of what some would call a real slog. There are certainly times when I'd like to throw the whole academic thing over and get into the greater outdoors.

If we're honest, we tell our vocational stories like the narrator of "The Road Not Taken"—*with a sigh*. Earlier, my colleague had talked about her undergraduate major in music and her aspiration to focus on religion and the arts until she ended up in an institution where none of the faculty had any such expertise. In figuring out your life, she implied, you inevitably give up dreams and, for all sorts of reasons, leave behind a trail of paths not taken.

No wonder the nineteenth-century existentialist Søren Kierkegaard made decision *the* turning point in his stages of Christian faith between the "aesthete" who indulges endless possibilities but is unable to move and the "moral actor" who dares to "cut off" options in order to go ahead and commit—the Latin meaning of *decide* (*de*, "down from" and *caedo*, "cut," or to "cut off"). Kierkegaard is especially good at capturing the tyranny of choosing through the voice of the aesthete:

> If you marry, you will regret it; if you do not marry, you will also regret it; if you marry or if you do not marry, you will regret both; whether you marry or you do not marry, you will regret both. Laugh at the world's follies, you will regret it; weep over them, you will also regret it; if you laugh at the world's follies or if you weep over them, you will regret both; whether you laugh at the world's follies or you weep over them, you will regret both.[7]

After a few more vacillating refrains, the aesthete concludes, "If you hang yourself, you will regret it; if you do not hang yourself, you will regret it... whether you hang yourself or you do not hang yourself, you will regret both. This, gentlemen, is the sum of all practical wisdom." Or in another translation: the "essence of all philosophy."[8]

For Kierkegaard, only the aesthete gets stuck with regret. The pleasurable life, he argues, is inherently unstable, unforeseeable, and risky. If pleasure is our only criteria, we cannot decide anything because all options have a modicum of gratification. Living only by what we like or don't like and not according to what is good, right, or beautiful leads to dead ends. Simply put, to become a mature self on Kierkegaard's "stages on life's way" requires cutting ourselves off from equally desirable courses of action.

In my view, however, no one, not even the moral actor who chooses according to higher aspirations, escapes the ambiguities of living our callings. Loss and regret are endemic to following a call, even if popular spokespersons on calling seldom mention them. Unfortunately, the indexes of blockbuster books on calling have entries on love, lust, greed, and much more, but little on remorse or grief. A massive anthology of Christian classics on calling, for example, doesn't list grief, loss, regret, or remorse. It has a reference for sacrifice, but it refers to an excerpt on martyrdom, as if calling only exacts a price for those in dire situations.[9]

But loss and regret permeate our vocational lives. No matter how long we stand at the crossroad, no matter how hard we peer down into the "undergrowth," as Frost writes, we cannot travel both roads and still "be one traveler." Integrity—to be whole—requires decision, and with decision comes loss and grief. There is, in other words, pain internal to calling that grows out of the very nature of discernment.

Learn to Count Your Days

It wasn't until I was teaching a unit on care of the dying that I suddenly recognized I was grieving. No one had died. What was my problem?

Mark and I had moved to Nashville after nearly twenty years in Chicago, and I thought I was adjusting. But I was sighing. A lot. Then I read my lecture notes. Years ago, as World War II ended, psychiatrist Erich Lindemann published an influential journal article on the "Symptomatology and Management of Acute Grief."[10] He included repeated sighing among the many physical signs. Until that moment, I hadn't noticed my "deep expiration of breath," or how much I missed my home, friends, and former way of life. Now a classic in posttraumatic stress disorder literature, Lindemann's conclusions were based on a study of a Boston nightclub tragedy, the Cocoanut Grove fire of 1942, which killed nearly five hundred people. Grief, he discovered from his interviews, is a physical experience, a "definite syndrome with psychological and somatic symptomatology."[11] Increased sighing is one of the telltale signs alongside tightness in the throat, shortness of breath, stomach upset, exhaustion, restlessness, and irritability. His essay made a profound impression on clinicians and beyond because it offered reassurance: These symptoms are completely *normal*. The "tendency to sighing respiration," he observed, "was most conspicuous when the patient was made to discuss his grief."[12] We exhale our sorrow.

Lindemann isn't the first psychologist or Frost the only poet to notice our sighs. "Our years come to an end like a sigh," wrote the psalmist centuries ago in a lament sometimes read at funerals. In the *New Oxford Annotated Bible*, Psalm 90 is identified as "A Prayer of Moses, the man of God," the man who performs mighty acts, liberates the Israelites from the Egyptians, and brings the Ten Commandments down the mountain to his people. But he is also the man who never makes it to the Promised Land, dies on the other side of the Jordan, and is told by God that he will only see the reward "from a distance" (Deut. 32:52) because of a failure of faith. And he's a man who seems incredibly faithful and undeserving of this punishment. But in his prayer, Moses recognizes his sins, God's wrath, and, notably, life's brevity and God's vastness. "A thousand years in your sight are like yesterday when it is past" (Ps. 90:4a). Humans are "like grass that is renewed in the morning; in the morning it flourishes and is renewed; in the evening it fades and withers" (v. 5b–6). To gain a heart of wisdom, the psalmist instructs, learn to "count your days" (v. 12a).

We associate grief and mourning with the death of loved ones, its most acute form. But since loss is a constant—something I experienced starkly as a young parent—it helps to recognize the pervasiveness of *mundane grief*, the daily sorrows that accompany day-to-day living.[13] All parents "begin losing their children as soon as they are born," observes historian Anne Higonnet.[14] In a peculiar thought I tried to suppress when pregnant, I realized that the one I was bringing to life must also face death. Other mothers, I later learned, have a similar foreboding. Then once born, parents must gradually let go of the children gifted them, leaving them with caregivers, letting them fall off couches and slides, and watching them climb on school buses and planes. "My momma always said, 'Death is a part of life,'" Forrest Gump says in the epic film. "I sure wish it wasn't." I do too. The film appeals because it touches poignantly on ubiquitous loss—loss of dreams, loss of bygone times, loss of physical and mental potential, and loss of our mothers and partners.

A first step in responding to the quotidian grief that pervades discerning and following a call, then, is simply recognition and support. Pastoral theologians Kenneth Mitchell and Herbert Anderson break down loss into six component parts, gleaned from over a thousand statements they collected from those bereaved: *material* loss, such as the disappearance of a loved object, often the first loss experienced as children (a toy, a blanket, a pet); *relationship* loss, also common in childhood when a parent leaves, a friend moves, a grandparent dies; *intrapsychic* loss, such as the demise of an image of ourselves or our aspirations, often encountered as we enter adolescence; *functional* loss of physical capacities starkly felt in middle and late adulthood; *role* loss when we leave home, change jobs, retire, and so on; and *systemic* loss where we lose an entire network of connections with a move, divorce, or other major change.[15] A colleague, Melissa Kelly, adds a seventh type persistently overlooked in popular grief literature—grief *"born of injustice"* or loss from inequities that are preventable and deeply destructive.[16]

Following a calling may involve loss in all seven areas across life, but unfortunately the great modern theories of human development struggle to make a positive place for loss, closure, and letting go. Contemporary psychologists, such as James Marcia, have tried to update Erik Erikson's well-known life cycle theory of the 1950s by adding intermediary steps to nuance his stark opposition between poles at each adult stage, such as identity consolidation versus diffusion in adolescence, intimacy versus isolation in early adulthood, generativity versus stagnation in mid-adulthood, and integrity versus despair in late adulthood. Marcia tries to make room for greater variance in success or failure at each stage by inserting different styles of resolving the life crisis. He names one of these styles *foreclosure*. But he describes it as a negative, defensive, and unsatisfactory pattern in the adolescent search for identity and, consequently, turns it into an immature and regressive response. The person who forecloses options in late adolescence is more likely, Marcia says, to lack "self-reflective depth" and hence less likely to "become intimate in young adulthood, generative in middle age, and integrated in old age."[17] This characterization fails to carve out a positive place for the kind of endings or closures that aren't premature or rash but fitting and necessary in adolescence and beyond.

To follow a calling, we must cultivate hearts capable of living with indeterminacy, ambiguity, and conclusions, not just at the beginning of adulthood but also at life's end. Even at the end of life, or even more so at life's end, we often try to dispel loss. For decades, physicians, psychiatrists, and medical ethicists have lamented the denial of death that pervades medical science and popular culture. Only when accompanying his own father through the throes of spinal cancer does physician Atul Gawande, also a well-known editorialist and author, question the life motto he inherited from his father: Never accept limitations that stand in your way. For decades, this mandate has warped medical judgment about treatment, he suggests, even when life is clearly ending. Gawande uncovers research that confirms a peculiar paradox well known to those familiar with Christian gospel reversals (e.g., that giving up your life for Christ's sake will save it): Those who stop treatment and enter hospice often experience less suffering and live longer. Indeed, intensive efforts to ward off death—radiation and chemotherapy, surgery, defibrillation, intubation, and so forth—can make people worse rather than better, substantially diminishing their quality of life and leaving family members more distraught. Simply talking about loss, hospice, and life priorities leads to less suffering, better connections with others, and, most surprising, longer lives. In other words, we have to "come to terms with limits," Gawande says. The challenge in aging and dying is not that different from the challenge of early adulthood: "when to shift from pushing against limits to making the best of them."[18]

"We won't ever do another long drive like that again," my mom said as she and my dad braved one more closure in their late eighties. They had just returned from a long road trip, visiting childhood homes in Iowa, family gravestones, and the university medical complex that had honored my grandfather's years of service by hanging a beloved picture of the Iowa Hospital Tower given to him by my grandmother. My parents' world would continue to shrink.

In other words, rather than talk about closure only as *foreclosure*, we need a constructive place for it. Closures mark our entry into adulthood, and they continue until we die. Adulthood requires acknowledging missed callings and living with limits and endings. In the best of circumstances, pursuing our callings involves letting go of regret so we can be most fully where we are.

Sleeping with Bread

During World War II, orphaned children in refugee camps couldn't sleep through the night because they were terrified of waking up hungry and homeless. Those who cared for them were at a loss. What could they do to comfort them? Finally, someone suggested giving each child a loaf of bread to take to bed. And that was enough.

Good processes of discernment are like "sleeping with bread," say Dennis Linn, Sheila Fabricant Linn, and Matthew Linn, allowing us to "hold what gives us life." With the story of refugee children, the Linns begin a beautiful book, *Sleeping with Bread*, on the Ignatian practice of discernment.[19] In the 1500s, Ignatius of Loyola, a Spanish priest and theologian who founded the religious order of the Jesuits, developed a process of prayerful deliberation, *The Spiritual Exercises*. In the centuries since, many people have found his *examen* or process of contemplative examination useful.

Many of us lack effective processes for discerning and deciding. I struggle with making decisions and, as is true for many religious people, with listening for God's voice and finding ways to know I've heard it. Once when I was grappling with a major decision, a therapist friend suggested I draw a picture of my dilemma or have an imaginary conversation with it, but both exercises felt contrived, even if they sparked some right-brain creativity and circumvented overthinking. I have also tried pro and con lists. But mostly they just reveal why I'm stuck in the first place, with the cons simply the inverse of the pros. The list helps only if it paves the way for conversation with friends or reveals the deeper values behind my itemization. In short, the list helps when it is connected, even indirectly, to richer practices of self-reflection, familiar within religious communities.

Religious communities have cultivated processes of decision-making for centuries. Quakers, for example, have well-defined guidelines for "clearness committees" that have helped people determine what to do in all sorts of situations. People agree to sit together in silence, invoke God's spirit, let the person talk, ask elucidating open-ended questions, and see what "clearness" emerges with communal receptivity and support. This practice grows organically out of deeper Quaker commitments: respect for the power of silence and divine presence; profound trust in the Holy Spirit's movement; and identification of community as a crucial space for divine reception.

When I first looked up the Linns' book on Amazon, it was hard to take the slim paperback seriously. It looked like a children's storybook. The blue and pink cover shows a young boy in bed cuddling a bread loaf with the moon and stars twinkling overhead. Colorful pastel pictures of smiling kids, bread bakers, streams, flowers, and trees illustrate the written material. Yet, on closer reading, I was amazed at its depth, wisdom, and clear distillation of the examen. For many years, each author has concluded the day in the same way—by turning their awareness to God's presence and spending several quiet minutes pondering two questions: For what moment today am I most grateful? For what am I least grateful? After twenty-five years of hosting retreats in forty countries, the Linns concluded that these two questions "are the most helpful way for people to find direction for their lives."[20] They offer other adjectives to frame what Ignatius called "consolations" and "desolations"—when did I feel most alive, loving, happy, or connected, and when was I drained, unloving, sad, or alone? Consolation is "whatever helps us connect with ourselves, others, God and the universe. Desolation is whatever disconnects us."[21]

Grappling with these questions transformed Ignatius's life, and use of the examen daily, annually, and before life's small and large crossroads has altered lives in the centuries since. These queries can help us discern our calling at both mundane and momentous points in our lives. We need to pay special attention to feelings, a challenging practice of inner assessment sometimes distained and often neglected. Feelings of consolation give "rise to life, love, peace, joy, creativity and communion," according to Ignatian scholar Frank Rogers, while feelings of desolation lead to "despair, confusion, alienation, destructiveness, and discord." We might live for a reflective period with each side of a decision, he suggests, and then ask ourselves, "Which choice gave rise to the deeper feelings of consolation"?[22]

We can also transpose these questions to engage young people in fresh ways. Adults often ask children and youths, "What do you want to do when you grow up?" But if we really want to connect to young people and help them figure out their lives, theologian and education scholar Katherine Turpin suggests, we should ask different kinds of questions: "What are you doing when you feel most fully alive? What are you doing when you feel most connected to other people? What moments have made you feel proud of what you are able to contribute to a group or project?" Or even "what breaks your heart about the world?"[23] We can hear an echo of Ignatius's queries about consolation and desolation within Turpin's questions. Such questions open space for conversation and disrupt the false impression that following a call is about finding that *one true thing* to do. They also deflect the anxiety that many of us carry about our kids' future and our own uncertainty about what we've done or failed to do with our lives.

Communal and individual processes are crucial not only for discerning a calling but also for pursuing it through its inevitable doubts, losses, and ambiguities. We can see in different religious practices a common movement through similar steps: self-examination of inner thoughts and desires; tuning in to higher causes and voices through prayer, nature, or community gathering and worship; trying on a choice and assessing it by its fruits in our lives and those around us; and continued self-reflection and trust in the support of those around us.

However, vocational insight and clarity can also come unexpectedly in *kairos*-like epiphanies. One day, in my mid-twenties, as I walked out of a university medical complex where I was doing a chaplaincy internship, I suddenly knew with a clearness and certainty that had eluded me for months: I didn't want to spend the rest of my life as a hospital chaplain. The realization came precisely when I was *not* thinking about the dilemma of what to do, a question I had deliberated for months. Several years later, as my plane took off for New York City where I would meet with a research mentor, I saw in a flash that I wanted to quit the small pastoral counseling practice I juggled alongside teaching so I could get going on a book on mothering. I had dwelled on the decision of paring back my overloaded schedule for a long time. But suddenly it seemed obvious. My children were growing faster than my clients, I felt compelled to capture what I knew from inside mothering, and the work was best done right at that time.

In each case, my reasons felt elusive. But for all practical purposes, my chaplaincy and my counseling careers ended in these singular emotive moments. I had belabored the dilemmas for months; talked with friends, spouse, and clinical supervisor; demanded to know, perhaps before I was ready. In retrospect, I see how these conversations and my own self-reflective effort led to moments of crystallization. This labor plowed the ground, *but* it ultimately didn't achieve results. I can also come up with legitimate reasons behind my sudden intuitive sense about my calling. But the processes and rationales are clearer only in hindsight. Instead, I discovered what to do with clarity and precision in a moment of revelation that came exactly when I was *not* forcing it.

Living in Vocational Liminality

"I'm about to finish course work," one of my advisees burst out, "and I have *no* idea what I'm going to do with my life. I need to know *now*." I field these kinds of anxieties regularly. The conversations take all sorts of directions, but I find myself sharing certain stories and thoughts again and again.

Doing a degree, I say, automatically puts you into the awkward place of *liminality*, a term used by twentieth-century anthropologists to describe the middle phase of rituals when initiates have left the safety of their previous world but have not yet moved into a new role and place. The word captures the angst of living suspended between who you were when you entered the degree and where you are going next, a state that Victor Turner described as "betwixt and between."[24] I could identify with my students; I remember my impatience in my twenties as I watched peers move into jobs and relationships while I spent years stumbling along in an interminable graduate program, unclear where I was headed. I got tired of living suspended with so much undecided. I see the same vocational fatigue in my students and kids.

Turner took the term *liminality* from a forerunner in anthropology and tossed it "like a pebble into the pool" of his data, and it "spread rings" across a wider range of activities than he ever imagined.[25] The word comes from the Latin root *margin*. Anthropologists who have studied *rites de passage* or rituals of transition that accompany birth, puberty, marriage, and death suggest that the initiate moves through three phases—separation, margin or *limen*, and incorporation or re-entry. Essentially, when people enter rituals, such as puberty rites or weddings, they leave behind established norms and social structures (preliminal) and cross a threshold into a middle phase of transformation (liminal) that prepares them for return to values and expectations of the community (postliminal).[26] In liminality, the initiate stands on the brink and has nothing—"no status, property... rank or role."[27] In puberty rites, for example, one is neither youth nor adult; in marriage rites, one is neither single nor wed. The person is in a position of "sacred poverty," in Turner's words, a place of "ambiguity and paradox, a confusion of all the customary categories."[28] In a way, the practice of a honeymoon provides exactly the kind of sanctioned transitional space to grow accustomed to new roles and patterns, not only for the couple but also for the couple's extended relationships.

Liminality is a better term, I believe, for suspended periods of discernment than *moratorium*, a word popularized by Erikson that carries moralistic connotations of escapism, dilettantism, and dabbling. He used the term to describe his own period of wanderlust, but it might be better described as *liminality*. In the 1920s, he roamed Germany and Italy for several years as a young artist before settling into the role of child analyst with the emerging psychoanalytic movement. The experience of being "neither here nor there" is intensified in the spaces so many young adults occupy—transitional jobs, higher education, internships, living together, short-term mission work, Teach-for-America, and so on. But liminality also crops up in other phases of life, such as when we consider marriage, navigate divorce, enter retirement, or endure chronic illness. My husband and I anticipate another period of liminality up ahead as we end our jobs but don't know yet where we'll live and how we'll spend our time. When sustained for protracted periods of time, liminality is especially discomforting.

As a graduate student, I wanted instant clarity, a voice from the clouds telling me what to do. Now I see I needed patience. We should not expect instant clarity or immediate comfort, as experts on spiritual discernment often say, even though our culture entices us to believe in infinite choice and immediate results. Discerning a call takes time, patience, and practice.

So, I invited the dismayed student in my office to try to live as peacefully as possible within the unrest. Clarity will come. Do not expect a coherence that eludes us. You cannot force revelation or decision; sometimes we must wait for them to come to us.

Know Your Ancestors

Last summer when my parents downsized their home of twenty-five years, the question of what to do with Myrtle arose. Myrtle Alice Lee McAdow inhabits a colossal gilded frame that resided in my parent's spare bedroom next to other unnerving photos of ancestors, looking down on anyone who dared to sleep under their gaze (my son's friends opted for the living room). The vaulted ceiling accommodated my great-grandmother well. But I couldn't imagine her three-by-three-foot portrait in our house. "Definitely not in our bedroom," my husband said. I agreed. "Nor in our entryway," he added (which I *had* considered).

Then, during a week of sorting, packing, and throwing out, my dad told me more.

I knew part of the story because I had already received a pearl-covered album that my grandmother, Myrtle's daughter, had passed on to me. Inside its ornate clasp and thick gold-edged pages were several college graduate photos. In the front, she had tucked a card on which she had explained in meticulous handwriting, as if for museum display, "This photograph album was a gift to my mother when she was graduated from Eureka College in 1894. The pictures show how college youth of that day looked." They sure do. The men in the sepia photos sport thick cravats and broad lapels; the smaller handful of women wear high-necked filigree gowns. None of them smile; whether due to protocol or shutter speed, I don't know. Myrtle is one of only five women in the class of seventeen, and she and her four friends represent the small minority of women admitted into higher education at that time.

Here's what I didn't know until my parents' move: My great-grandfather, Samuel McAdow, an Iowan farmer who hadn't finished high school, had scrapped together what little money he had, bought the immense frame, and given the portrait to his wife Myrtle, so proud was he of her accomplishment. Now I was hooked, line and sinker.

That's how Myrtle came to rest in our dining room. From the corner, she stares at her framed needlepoints on the adjacent wall next to furniture she once used. The placement isn't perfect, but it works. I have taped my own museum note to the back in case no one remembers how she moved in and where she should go (because who will want her next?): "Myrtle Alice Lee, Eureka College, 1894, graduation photo, framed by her husband, Samuel McAdow, at quite some expense for an Iowan farmer of small means and minimal education." With an asterisk: "If you don't want Myrtle, donate her to Eureka College archives." On occasion, when I turn off the lamp on the table beneath her picture, I look up and say, "Good night, Myrtle."

"Which of your ancestors ordained you?" I ask students, drawing on the words of rabbi and counselor Edwin Friedman, who wrote a savvy book about family systems in congregations.[29] He's talking to those going into the ministry, but the question can be extended to anyone deliberating a calling. The more clarity we have about our position in our family system, he says, the more we can "learn to occupy it with grace and 'savvy' " and the better we will operate in similar systems, whether congregation, workplace, or family. As he puts it, "Anyone who works to gain more *differentiation of self* in his or her family of origin will find that the way one thinks and functions within his or her vocation is affected."[30]

Friedman uses an interesting word here, first articulated by prominent family systems predecessor Murray Bowen— *differentiation*. Its definition contains a paradox that unites individuality and community: the "capacity to be an 'I' while remaining connected," in Friedman's words. More specifically, it's the "capacity of a family member to define his or her own life's goals and values" in relationship to but "apart from surrounding togetherness pressures."[31] In a word, the more we grasp how multigenerational forces shape our decisions, the greater "our flexibility to function within the parameters of our 'calling,'" he suggests, and the more we "reacquire our profession for our own."[32]

Knowing about Myrtle doesn't explain why I do what I do, but it does go a long way in understanding some of my motivation. A great-grandmother who earned a college degree when very few women were allowed into higher education, followed by two grandmothers (my mom's and my dad's mothers) who graduated from college when it was still uncommon, makes my doctorate a whole lot less surprising. I took up a mantle that I didn't even know was being handed to me until I did my family systems tree.

I asked the befuddled student in my office, confused about future directions, why he pursued a seminary degree. "My parents believe in higher education," he answered, "and people in my home church where I began preaching at an early age assume I am going into ministry." He felt a pressure to excel, he said, not just for the sake of his parents and church but, as a young Black man, "for my race." He had gifts for ministry, but as he said, "I don't really want to preach or lead a congregation; it just doesn't feel right." He had dreamt of preaching, "but the dream doesn't really feel like mine." What would he do if he felt no pressure, I asked? He didn't hesitate: "Something in clothing design" (smiling). He was one of the best-dressed students in the school. I suggested letting people know about his thoughts and exploring what it might take to consider that call. Now, looking back, I wish I'd encouraged him to think more about his family and social position. Knowing where we stand can help us *refuse* the ordinations that our ancestors sometimes foist upon us. Reflecting on wider social patterns can also help us adopt a critical stance toward destructive systems that sometimes misshape callings. Ancestral callings and political pressures shape vocation more than we realize, and their influence bears down especially hard on the big decisions and on some people more than others.

We assume our choices are freely willed, but they are often shaped by circumstances beyond our own telling. Our culture places so much weight on individual choice, and some people even reduce calling to a personal decision when, in reality, all callings are shaped and even determined by forces outside ourselves, as the next chapter on blocked callings forcefully reminds us. But for now, simply recognizing that inherited conditions and communities bind *and* liberate our callings can enrich our discernment.

Redeeming the Path We're On

Okay, now for happier endings than regret and sorrow: redemption despite loss.

First, loss: The heartbreak of the *road not taken* is partly what has arrested readers of Frost's well-known poem even if we don't realize it. *Two roads diverge*—the poem's very first words. We can't have it both ways. We know this. We rule out, cut off, let go, and take one road, not another. Our calling is forever a bit uncertain, even with the best discernment.

Then, like an act of grace unnoticed, the *road not taken* becomes the *road less traveled* "that has made all the difference" in the poem's parting words. Here's the poem's stumbling block *and* its genius.

Buried in its fourth and final stanza is a twist, a second truth, a bonus that has assured the poem's appeal. The road taken is refashioned as unique, wise, right. In the send-off, the narrator turns wistful misgiving about life's thresholds into gain, freeing readers from regret. Reinterpretation of one's path from the vantage point of accrued wisdom becomes the poem's redemption, our redemption. No wonder we love this poem. Readers are happy to follow the sleight of hand.

Or is it a sleight of hand? Perhaps Frost isn't poking fun at how we reconstruct our life story to justify or glorify our decisions. The poem allows for, perhaps even invites, a rebirth. For, hidden within it are *two* stories—the road not taken *and* the road less traveled—that "revolve around each other," to use critic David Orr's words, "separating and overlapping like clouds," crossing over and rescuing each other in a way that makes both interpretations plausible.[33] In the first three stanzas, the narrator invites us to re-experience the tensions and complexities of having to decide. God doesn't speak to most of us in a crystal-clear voice.[34] Instead, we live forward with the relentlessly mixed choices we've made.

But, as the last stanza makes clear, the poem and life itself are less about good or bad decisions, valiant or ordinary paths, than about the simultaneously arduous and potentially joyous lifelong endeavor of pursuing, sustaining, and reinterpreting our callings. Over time, negative and positive accounts of our lives circle around, entwine, and convert each other. Saying no to one way in life allows us to a say yes to another, putting the no into the context of a larger "life-affirming yes."[35] Or, as a friend once said, "If you can't say no, you can't live the yes. In fact, what you say no to is as important as yes." This, in my friend's eyes, is the heart of the Christian story: "The empty tomb is the biggest 'no' and so the biggest 'yes.'"

Forty years ago, when my husband and I visited my in-laws, my mother-in-law brought out two old boxes and said to her son, "Here's the rest of your stuff." In other words, "You're married. Clear this out." With three sons of my own now, I understand (we have an attic full of baseball cards, Star Wars ships, stuffed animals, DVDs, one drum set, and a Hammond organ).

As Mark sorted through the boxes, he pulled out a photo that caught my attention: a shot of fifty high school kids at a church camp that he attended in Northern Indiana.

"There I am," he said as he pointed.

"*You're* in this picture?" I asked.

"Right there, second row left."

I was also in the picture. Second row right. I knew it immediately. The moment the photographer snapped the picture a boy behind me pulled one of my pigtails. You can only see my center part.

That we were both at the same church camp a decade before we met in graduate school was uncanny. A fortuitous coincidence? Our unique destiny? Maybe both. Sometimes, it's all in how we tell the story. We need to assure ourselves that we have chosen well and ever so uniquely. But sometimes, just sometimes, we receive validation of a calling long after the decision we made. Or at least that's the grace that Frost and life itself promise. Our lives make sense when seen anew "somewhere ages and ages hence."

Chapter 2

Blocked Callings: A Raisin in the Sun

"I got a feeling I ain't going to be here long," C. J. told his girlfriend not long before his death. He was killed one winter night while out on a ride with his cousins when a train hit their car, not coincidentally in a predominately Black county where the warning system was unreliable at best. He's one of five young men whose deaths author Jesmyn Ward chronicles in her searing memoir *Men We Reaped*. Borrowing Harriet Tubman's words for fugitives fleeing slavery felled among the crops, Ward memorializes rural Mississippi friends, relatives, and a brother who died violently in the span of four years, their prospects "pinioned beneath poverty and history and racism."[1]

Follow a calling? Hell, life in the rural south for men like C. J. was "like walking into a storm surge," Ward says. Seen as a problem in a school system that didn't care and surrounded as he was by unemployed men—men who were fired from or quit minimum wage jobs that didn't even cover basic needs, men who resorted to selling drugs when dead-end work didn't pan out—C. J. didn't stand a chance. "Maybe he looked at those who still lived and those who'd died, and didn't see much difference," Ward writes, so he stopped caring and talked instead about dying young.[2]

Here in its rawest form is blocked calling. In fact, for C. J. and his peers, the term *calling* seems a bit pointless. Calling for these men is not just impeded; it's cut dead. Maybe *obliterated callings* is a better way to put it.

Simply put, *blocked calling* refers to a hope or aspiration indefinitely deferred, ambushed, or denied because of circumstances outside our control. Blocked callings differ in their severity, but even those with money and opportunity encounter barriers that impede them. Blocked callings fall along a continuum from minor hopes crushed to major pursuits destroyed. We live by someone else's expectations; we can't do what we want; we're stymied by injustice and discrimination. By contrast with missed callings, blocked callings come from forces beyond our influence. If missed callings are about an overabundance of choice, blocked callings are about little or no choice. They are not paths we've discerned and decided against; they are dreams, desires, and hopes dashed by insurmountable and sometimes horrendous obstacles. Missed callings spark regret; blocked callings bring anger, resentment, bitterness, and despair. They are the *underside* of the *undersides* of calling.

Does It Explode?

When I first considered blocked callings, I immediately heard poet Langston Hughes's words—"what happens to a dream deferred?" To my ear, his poem "Harlem," better known as "A Dream Deferred," decries callings not just deferred but horribly thwarted. He uses the word *deferred* with tragic irony to underscore the torment of a hope hanging tantalizingly before his audience, visible but forever withheld. The visceral images in his short poem punctuate the fallout of extreme deferral—"does it fester like a sore . . . stink like rotten meat . . . crust and sugar over like a syrupy sweet . . . sag like a heavy load. *Or does it explode?*" A Harlem Renaissance writer and activist, Hughes wrote the poem in 1951 in the shadow of the 1943 Harlem race protests provoked by the shooting of a Black soldier by a White police officer, an act of unwarranted violence and racism still sickeningly familiar to us today.

Dreams differ from callings, of course. Callings are more concrete and focused; they involve a way of life, a way of making a life, and the way our lives make us. But dreams share with callings a hopefulness, a yearning for a promising future. Dreams inform our callings, and when dreams are denied, callings can dry up, fester, and explode.

A "dream deferred" holds many meanings for Hughes and his readers—a yearning for "individual achievement," in the words of one commentary, and "the promise of Harlem, and America's supposed equality."[3] On the surface it appears that Hughes discovered his own calling with ease. He declared his aspirations to be a writer in grammar school, published his first book of poetry while a college student, and became a leading figure in the Harlem Renaissance in his mid-twenties. But, like any Black man in his time, he knew deferral intimately. In a famous 1926 essay, he likens his life to an impossible climb up a racial mountainside defying relentless pressures toward whiteness.[4] To follow his call, he paid what his assistant described as "an enormous creative toll."[5] For rejecting White stereotypes *and* the Black temptation to camouflage his community's foibles, he was ignored by Whites, attacked by Blacks, and criticized from every angle as too simplistic, too radical, too conventional.

Hughes's rumination on what happens to a dream deferred took on new life through playwright Lorraine Hansberry's imagination. She used his words in the title of her 1959 portrait of racial discrimination on Chicago's Southside, *A Raisin in the Sun*. The play's protagonist Walter Lee Younger Jr. seethes under the racism and classism that crush his hope for a more expansive life beyond chauffeuring White people (it "ain't no kind of job," he says) and the attainments his mother wants him to settle for ("a job, a nice wife, a fine boy"). Like C. J., Walter experiences the future as a "big, looming blank space—full of *nothing*."[6] His mother refuses to let him use a large insurance payout from his father's death to invest in a liquor store, an ill-conceived plan driven by illusions about wealth. His ensuing fury unsettles an already strained Black family and becomes the focal point of conflict across generations, gender, class, and race.

Hansberry understood these vocational furies well. The first Black artist to have a production on Broadway, she wrote *The Raisin in the Sun* at age twenty-six, drawing on her experiences growing up in an illustrious Chicago family that fought legal battles over housing and other forms of racial discrimination. Like Hughes, Hansberry lived amid contradictions. As one observer says,

> she achieved literary celebrity but called herself a "literary failure," was supported in a marriage that ultimately collapsed, resisted her family but didn't denounce it, became an icon of the civil-rights movement that she relentlessly criticized, and wrote a masterpiece only to watch as it was widely misunderstood.[7]

She also faced gender stereotypes and inequities. Some critics suggest that Walter's sister Beneatha is Hansberry's alter ego. Beneatha refuses to live a life constricted by sexism, heterosexism, racism, and classism. By pursuing medicine and resisting marriage, she bucks convention, including religious beliefs that give God "credit for all the things the human race achieves through its own stubborn effort."[8]

Hansberry's race location was further complicated—or as people often say today, it "intersected" with—her perceived gender and sexual identity.[9] In *A Room of One's Own*, literary genius Virginia Woolf recounts the history of women born with gifts doomed to a life of strife.[10] Being deprived of a room of one's own—a literal and symbolic sign of support— jeopardizes callings. Over history, women have born, bred, fed, washed, tended, and raised the generations while being deprived of the means to follow any other calling—space, time, energy, money, circumstances, permission, choice, education, travel, and, as Woolf makes clear, both uninterrupted solitude and what others have called the *angel in the home* who seamlessly oversees daily life.

A biographical film *Camille Claudel* about the nineteenth-century sculptor brings to life the disheartening pattern of women whose artistic creativity is stolen by the very men they've loved and supported. As a child, Claudel made forms out of mud and stones. But when she pursued her love of clay, she faced hurdles that have tormented women before and after. Few art academies of the late 1800s accepted women. Gender discrimination, intensified by the sensual nature of her work, sabotaged funding for the costly processes of her chosen medium, bronze sculpturing. And when she was only nineteen years old, her forty-two-year-old artistic mentor Auguste Rodin became her lover, attached his name to her works, and surpassed her even as he fed off her talent. When she insisted on recognition, their relationship fell apart, and she struggled to sustain her art amid poverty and isolation. Only her father supported her gifts, but he died prematurely. Her mother detested her aspirations (she wanted a boy). Together with Claudel's younger brother Paul, a poet anxious to protect his own reputation, Claudel's mother committed her to a mental hospital in 1911. Whether institutionalized under false pretenses or for paranoia (symptoms that seem justified given Rodin's theft and her family's antagonism), Claudel's life ended in obscurity. We know about her gifts only because they've been memorialized in film and through a museum established in 2017 in her small hometown of Nogent-sur-Seine, France. Paul's granddaughter wrote the book that inspired the film, perhaps in hopes of assuaging the family's guilt and contesting the forces of history.[11]

Social obstacles and insidious biases deter and damage callings in small and profound ways. A Korean American peer once told me he never "felt a sense of freedom in my 'choosing' when I arrived at 'two roads'" because of his conservative religious background and social location. His life course was dictated, "done in certain ways because I believed I had to do them in those ways." Another colleague confessed she had always wanted to be a parish minister but had given up her "first love" because she refused to put her partner in a position of stress. On a different occasion, a young lesbian doctoral student remarked to a scholarship committee on which I sat, "Growing up, I didn't even know women could be ministers. I went to college to get a husband." She continued, "And *I hate the language of vocation and call.*"

No wonder. The language often overlooks those whose callings are socially rejected. Our divinity school welcomes people whose religious traditions forbid their call because of their sexual identities or their female gender, and many ministry students work hard to surmount impediments, experiencing a call to ministry only to have it revoked by their community or superiors. Doctoral graduates, especially White men, feel called to teach but struggle to find jobs in a tight market and an academy that is rightly rectifying long legacies of injustice. My mother-in-law loved teaching high school Latin in the 1940s and 1950s but was forced by law to quit when she became pregnant. Although my own calling benefited from a widespread push to hire women in the 1980s, I know the convoluted path on which I trod. I stand in a line of women granted college degrees, going back to my great-grandmother, but I have always thought that one cause behind my grandmother's depression was restricted options. What were these educated women to do with their learning? Supporting husbands and teaching women French in a basement, as my grandmother did, had its limits. When I began graduate school, I didn't have the faintest idea of what I might do, and there were few women ahead of me to emulate.

These stories reinforce a premise that undergirds this book: Calling is not an autonomous personal choice so much as a communal and political matter, supported or destroyed by religion, prejudice, and the market. Yet, as an author of a singular book on "calling in context" emphasizes, popular treatments of calling seldom acknowledge how much social location and economic power shape calling, whether we live in Malaysia or the United States, attend a Reformed or Pentecostal church, or face discriminations of color, class, gender, sexuality, ability, age, and so forth.[12] Blocked callings are never restricted to one individual or an isolated party. They are ultimately family and social affairs.

The "hard economies of a family, a town, a region, a country, a world were shaping ... what I would or wouldn't have a chance to make of myself," writes memoirist Sarah Smarsh in her story about growing up poor in the richest country on earth.[13] She didn't realize the extent of her family's poverty until she got to college. America doesn't talk about class, but in her rural world thirty miles west of Wichita neither personal choice nor natural talent determined one's calling. Her father, a fifth-generation Kansas farmer, picked up odd jobs in construction when wheat prices fell; her mother, born into a long line of teenage mothers, eventually turned a flare for home decor into a real estate job—work that neither parent would have chosen given other options. There's a myth behind the American Dream and popular ideals of calling that suggests the working poor end up where they are "because it's all they're suited for." But Smarsh protests, "what put us there ... was birth, family history—not lack of talent for something else."[14] Her goal: to break the cycle she had been handed.

"I don't want to waste my life," remarks Cristina Reveles, but she has had little choice in her calling.[15] Fifteen years ago, she immigrated from Mexico with her husband and infant son Brayhan, hoping to avoid a divided life in which her husband would have traveled to the United States for work and only returned home once a year. Parents at Brayhan's school noticed her talent for organization and community service and naively suggested she run for the school board. But to keep secret her son's status as a noncitizen, she turned down one opportunity after another and focused instead on rendering her family's apartment in a decrepit complex a well-kept home. "Sometimes I feel like a pretty bird in a cage who picks up scraps and tries to make the cage more beautiful," she told an interviewer. Her son Brayhan also faces daunting prospects. Having arrived in the United States as an infant, he is one of thousands of DACA recipients (Deferred Action for Childhood Arrivals) who have grown up here and graduated from high school but now stand on fragile legal footing. Politics around DACA have placed approximately 665,000 young people in vocational limbo, creating, in essence, a deferral of monumental proportions.

Less Dire Obstructions

As extreme deferrals underscore, calling is not a special message hand-delivered by God or a profitable job. It is a deep desire, a driving force, the impulse for a fruitful life granted to all living beings, whether received as a divine gift or perceived simply as part of life's vitality. Talent and desire undermined by poverty, prejudice, and lack of opportunity are a waste and tragedy, made more appalling because the causes lie within larger systemic patterns. When we ignore the impact of deprivation across generations, we risk turning calling into a luxury reserved for the elite.

Less dire, even banal, obstructions abound too, however. Years ago, when a first-grade teacher invited my son's class to dress up in what they wanted to become, he went to school in his dad's wide-brimmed fedora, red bandana, and flannel shirt as Indiana Jones. We didn't disabuse him of the idea that boring but handsome archeology professors (played by Harrison Ford) have adventuresome side lives as treasure hunters and action heroes. But, as he donned his outfit, we did repeat "archeologist," a career more in line with what we thought his teacher would want to hear than "grave robber" or "movie star." Recently, this same son, now in his thirties, retrieved his middle school yearbooks from our attic to show his sixth-grade math students how he looked at their age. One volume listed the dreams of each person in his class. Next to his name: NBA player.

Many of our early aspirations are driven by popular culture and indefinitely deferred because they are fantastical and unrealistic. But most impeded callings fall in the wider middle ground between inconsequential and profound. Sometimes our aspirations get stalled by competing callings like having kids, caring for parents, or following a partner to a new job. An April 2017 report from the US Census Bureau reveals a postponement among young adults ages twenty-five to thirty-seven of three major milestones that often mark adulthood and calling—independent living, marriage, and childbearing. The number of young adults who reach these markers dropped from forty-five percent in 1975 to only twenty-four percent in 2016.[16] Many young adults today put off various callings of work and family until they are older and more economically secure. Of course, when young adults enter midlife without a companion or have trouble conceiving, these postponements can turn into more painful deferrals.

Some blocked callings slip away without fanfare. "I missed some kind of call to be something more than a mediocre high school English teacher in a little dirt-blown town," Louis tells Addie one night in Kent Haruf's final novel *Our Souls at Night*. Two widowed adults, Louis and Addie scandalize their neighbors in an imaginary town on the windswept Colorado plains when Louis crosses the street and spends lonely nights lying in bed with Addie examining their lives. He tells her about his aspirations to become an author. He wrote poems around the edges of his high school teaching job, "pitiful stuff really" that brought ample rejection letters. But then a child came along, and his wife didn't appreciate the time he spent away or dreams he had that were bigger than her own. When Addie encourages him to revisit his desire to write, he observes, "I think it's past my time for that."[17]

"Who does ever get what they want?" Addie ruminates. "It doesn't seem to happen to many of us if any at all." Life is mostly "people bumping against each other blindly, acting out old ideas and dreams and mistaken understandings." Her own hopes were vaguer that Louis's. She thought she wanted to teach but got pregnant, quit school, and never got back to it. When Louis asks her why not, she admits teaching wasn't all that appealing, "just what women did," she says. "Not everybody finds out what they really want."[18]

Haruf himself faced frustrations and hurdles with his own calling as a novelist that he plays out through the characters in his novel. Married with three small children, he taught high school and then built grain bins when he couldn't find a teaching job. "Then that construction job ended, and for three months I milked cows," he recounts. "I felt tremendously thwarted. I felt desperate for time to write, yet I wanted to be a decent parent, so I had to make some kind of living. . . . I was working as hard as I could physically and making very little money . . . and I still couldn't write."[19]

Many people live with a kind of suspended deferral. My dad served nearly four decades as a university student health doctor. It looked like he followed a call without hindrance, but his bookshelves suggested otherwise. They held books of two sorts: thick treatises from his medical degree *and* religion books—yellowed volumes from a college religion course, a Bible from baptism at twelve, and prayer books for elders at the communion table. His paternal grandfather and great-grandfather were American Baptist ministers on eastern Iowan farmland, but he followed his dad into student health. I didn't think much about his vocational tensions until he died, despite my mom's occasional musings about his divided bookshelves. But in a pastoral visit prior to the memorial service, the minister asked my family to choose one-word adjectives that captured who he was. When we described him as faithful but completely non-pietistic, reticent to talk about his beliefs (the language of calling and God's will especially put him off), the minister asked, "Then how did he convey his faith to you?" So, my brother told *The Story of the Other Wise Man*, a quintessential tale of deferred and blocked calling if there ever was one. Our father had read Henry van Dyke's late-nineteenth-century novella to us on a few Christmas Eves from a tattered copy, methodically abridged by his mom. Artaban is supposed to join the three Magi on their journey toward the star, but he's repeatedly delayed. The other wisemen depart without him, and he never catches up. He doesn't make it to the manger, and over the next thirty years, he is always one step behind Jesus, all the way to the cross.

Did my dad favor this story, I wondered as my brother retold the story to the minister, because he too lived a life of quiet deferral? Artaban never makes it to the cross, and, in a way, neither did my dad. My dad didn't just defer a ministerial vocation; he also put off difficult questions about faith and Jesus. A humanist as much as a Christian, he saw Jesus as a good man and suspended claims about divine birth and bodily resurrection that went against modern science. These questions about the Christian life troubled my dad more than questions about his job, and more so as he aged and watched a world in turmoil and his friends decline and die.

In a word, blocked callings come in all shapes and sizes. They pertain not only to what we do to make a living but also to what we believe and how we understand our place in the curious universe around us. Many of us suspend such questions and the callings within them because they are so hard to answer and to follow.

When Callings Are Thwarted

My dad did not suffer much, however. Neither did Haruf or his fictional characters. Nor have I, not in the way many people have. But perhaps we can learn from more dramatic instances of obstructed callings what it's like to abide in their shadow and how to live well nonetheless. Instances of extreme deferral put a serious ethical quandary in front of us: What happens when callings are thwarted and deranged on a massive scale? How do we address such widespread systemic destruction of vocational hope? If we can understand our small individual pain, then perhaps we can grasp the suffering of those whose callings are shattered and do something about it.

So, what happens to us when callings are thwarted? Whether obstructions are small or large, temporary or permanent, the patterns are often similar: *anger, frustration, discouragement, rage, self-hatred, depression,* and *despair.* The range of responses is also related: *defiant survival, visibility, radical self-love, affirmation, recompense,* and *hope across time and generations.*

In a remarkable instance of scientific understatement, researchers suggest that thwarted callings lead to "negative outcomes."[20] It's hazardous to have a sense of calling, they conclude, if opportunity is denied or we're trapped in a job that is not our calling. Hughes's poem states the consequences in more visceral terms. Line by line he ticks off the outcomes, ending the poem with an italicized question that dispels any lingering doubts about the damage: *Or does it explode?* The sentence is not a final query; it's an accusation. Quite simply, dreams deferred too long at too great a cost blow up, not just in front of an individual's face but in the history of a people.

Walter "always [has] in his voice . . . a quality of indictment," Hansberry instructs in the play's opening direction. Walter's fury hangs like a cloud over the family as they bicker over how to use the money from his mother's deceased husband. When George, Beneatha's preppy suitor, accuses Walter of being "wacked up with bitterness," he replies, "Bitter? Man, I'm a volcano."[21]

Rage is distinct from anger in both origin and velocity. It erupts out of what mid-twentieth-century founder of self-psychology Heinz Kohut describes as narcissistic injury or wounding—a severe ontological blow to personhood and humanity. After the fatal shooting of eighteen-year-old Michael Brown in Ferguson, musician Lauryn Hill began a protest song with this line: "Black rage is founded on two-thirds a person." The lyrics turn the flowery melody of "My Favorite Things" into a dirge detailing the end products of violence, poverty, and injustice: wounds to the soul, self-hatred, denial of self. Because blocked callings cause such a primal injury to our very being, the rage knows no bounds. It cannot be dispelled "via successful action again the offender," as Kohut says.[22]

Pastoral theologian Greg Ellison borrows a nineteenth-century phrase from psychologist William James—"cut dead"—to get at the devastation of such wholesale denial. "If no one turned around when we entered, answered when we spoke, or minded what we did, but if every person we met 'cut us dead,' and acted as if we were nonexistent things," James says, "a kind of rage and impotent despair would before long well up in us." Some societies punish their members, anthropologists observe, through excommunication and ostracization, refusing to see or hear them, erasing them entirely, and rendering them as good as dead. To be cut dead leads to "inner turmoil and externalized rage," Ellison argues.[23] His book on young Black men is an extended investigation into the consequences of frustrated callings. Muteness and invisibility inflicted on Black men—not seeing or hearing them for who they are or could become—thwarts fundamental human needs for control, meaning, self-esteem, and belonging, he says. Silenced and unseen, people dry up; fester; stink; sag; *explode.*

Kohut's own path as a White European male seems straightforward enough, his narcissism well rewarded by a school of admiring followers that grew into a recognized psychoanalytic approach. But his familiarity with narcissistic injury has a deeper source than he acknowledges. One of his primary biographers followed a trail that Kohut left behind in which he masked and repressed his Jewish heritage, hinting at a profound racial insecurity as a US immigrant in the shadow of the Holocaust.[24] His early writings on the heroism of Nazi resisters and the self-pathology of Hitler reveal an intimate, if hidden, battle to protect himself from extinction through a theory and therapy directed explicitly at shoring up self-cohesion.[25]

Hughes's poem ends in explosion but on the way to erupting contains penultimate outcomes related to self-esteem that Kohut understood well—*discouragement, depression, despair,* and *self-*

loathing. Callings deferred "fester . . . stink . . . sag like a heavy load" and make people sick in a basic and immediate way. Here Hughes echoes biblical wisdom—"hope deferred makes the heart sick" (Prov. 13:12a). Although the Freudian truism—*depression is anger turned inward*—may not be empirically valid, it still fits our experience. Depression immobilizes and arrests desire, leading to what nineteenth-century philosopher Søren Kierkegaard described tellingly as a "sickness worse than death." This sickness is certainly true for many women who internalize the misogyny that surrounds them. Whereas society has routinely condemned men to jail, it has historically pushed women into psychiatric hospitals. Claudel ended her life in a mental institution; my grandmother received electric shock treatment. These are dramatic instances, but in societies where women face violence and abuse, reduced wages, glass ceilings, high poverty rates, damaging media images, distorted beauty standards, and the double duty of employment and household labor, depression is a normal rather than abnormal response, "an adaptive reaction to a destructive culture," as one pastoral theologian argues, "a survival strategy" according to a feminist therapist.[26]

Self-hatred and shame also afflict the poor. Although the word *poor* literally means *without money*, it also connotes *bad*, Smarsh observes, as in "poor health" or "poor test results." Not surprisingly, "Many of the people who raised me believed themselves to be bad. I know because they often treated me like I was bad."[27]

This "sense of lack," however, is a "feeling that knows no social and economic boundaries," Smarsh argues.[28] It can impede callings in all sorts of places. Even though Ward focuses on five men who died too young, the constricted callings of women who mourn and endure also haunt her account. Whereas Ward's father walked out on his family, her mother had no time for wanderlust, no luxury of a youthful "moratorium," to use the romantic phrase of life cycle expert Erik Erikson. Instead, from early on, even as a child, "her vistas were the walls of her home." She "did what her mother did before her, what her sisters did, what her aunts did"—bore the weight of the family. The oldest of seven in a fatherless household, she raised her brothers and sisters while her mother worked two or three jobs to support the family. When she became a mother, she sought work as a laundress and a housekeeper so she could be home for her children's homework, bedtime, and the next morning's tasks. She forgot the "meaning of possibility," Ward says, "like the women in my family before her."[29]

Of course, depression and despair are not unique to women. When Ronald Wayne Lizana ended his life, telling his girlfriend over the phone that he loved her and then shooting himself, Ward grappled with the darkness, the "conviction of worthlessness and self-loathing" that she saw spreading like a contagion across her people. She didn't know all Ronald's "demons," but she recognized the distress that led him to think "it would be better if he were dead." With his suicide, she realizes: "the same pressures were weighing on us all." Her whole community—the extended network of family and friends all the way back to her enslaved ancestors—suffers from "a lack of trust" that erodes self-worth "until we hated what we saw without and within."[30] When she checked out mental health statistics, she discovered a high percentage of Black men with depression, and the statistics are likely an "underestimate due to lack of screening and treatment services." Lack of services makes men more susceptible to "incarceration, homelessness, substance abuse, homicide, and suicide."[31] Fifty years earlier, in a controversial bestseller, *Black Rage*, psychologists William Grier and Price Cobbs surmised as much from their psychoanalytic cases amid the race unrest and civil rights movement of the 1960s.[32]

Living (Well) Despite Limits

So, how do we get out from under the shadow and condemnation of deferral? As with the other undersides of callings, there are no simple answers. Blocked callings depress and infuriate in a unique way, more so when they result from centuries-old patterns of denial and destruction. Some of the negation is overcome with time—we make a way, we find something else to do, we work for social justice. But it is seldom entirely dispelled. Doors shut, others don't open, and the ones that do sometimes lead down unfortunate paths. So, with blocked callings, it's less a matter of discerning choices than surviving amid unwanted and difficult circumstances and maybe, just maybe, living well or even thriving despite the limitations.

Sometimes the first step is *to survive*, as theological educator Patrick Reyes argues. A spokesperson on calling, he grew up in one of the most underserved communities in the country, a gang-and-violence-infested Chicano neighborhood in Southern California where forces toward death were strong. "*I should not be alive*," he testifies, "*But here I am.*"[33]

Reyes sees his survival as a call to help others reinterpret calling. God calls you to survive, he tells the underclass, the fieldworker, the gangbanger. Vocation, he insists, is "not about finding your dream job, our first call to ministry, or the like. It's about being called to live.... Living is our primary vocation."[34] *Cut dead but still alive*—that's the full title of Ellison's book.

Reyes's testimony has authority, especially for those in similar places. Like C. J.

C. J. "never talked like the rest of us," Ward recounts, "never laid claim to a dream job. He never said: *I want to be a firefighter.* Never: *I want to be a welder.* Neither: *Work offshore.*" No, his desires were basic: "*Live good*," he said to his girlfriend. Then Ward underscores the simple four-letter word—*Live*—letting it hang there.[35]

For all of us, sustaining a calling in the face of deferral and obstruction requires an external *affirmation*, inspired and upheld by *visibility*—by being seen, heard, attended to, recognized, affirmed, respected, and supported. To survive when others don't see, hear, or respect us also requires a corresponding internal strength, resilience, courage, and, yes, what Kohut calls healthy or mature narcissism. One of his huge contributions to modern thought was his insistence that narcissism or *self-love* is not inherently bad but a basic human need that goes back to our childhoods, a need to be seen, affirmed, and admired that can, under harmful conditions, turn into an obsessive drive for unrelenting attention. Contrary to a Christianized culture that has praised self-sacrifice and castigated selfishness, Kohut contends that there is a difference between *mature* and *immature* narcissism, between the rudimentary all-consuming appetite to be the center of the world that we display as children (and see in childish adults, some with immense power to wreak havoc in the world) and the more developed and appropriate desire to be appreciated, valued, esteemed.[36] *"You are priceless,"* Smarsh finally tells herself, challenging the society around her that predicates worth on wealth. "Your worth," she writes in the final pages of her memoir, is "unto itself." Her life work, she grasps, "was to be heard," and her book provides an obvious forum for that.[37] Simply put, mature narcissism is knowing one has been seen and heard and finding constructive ways to sustain self-worth and life as a whole.

In counseling men transitioning out of prison in Uth Turn, a rehabilitation program in Newark, Ellison worked hard to make the young Black men *seen* and *heard*. He identified with their plight. However, one week, right when he thought he was being empathic, his advantages of education and class blinded him. He told the group that he had witnessed his own friend's murder in high school, and in response he chose "conflict mediation" over violence. "Bullshit," exploded Thomas, an otherwise levelheaded participant. What did Ellison *really* know when he claimed, "life's difficulties aid in the discovery of purpose"?[38] Easy for him to say.

There is so much to learn from Ellison here: first, the extent to which all of us must go in listening to others, especially those whose callings have been decimated by forces beyond their control. Grasp the shallowness of our perspective and listen. Be moved from self-righteousness to genuine empathy. That's what Ellison models in a second move—his honesty in admitting his blindness as an insider who still struggles to learn and listen from his outsider position. Third, he makes clear the righteous place of anger and rage. The "logic" of Thomas's posturing, Ellison explains, follows a basic rule: "If you disrespect or ignore me, I will hit you (i.e., with my fist or my gun) and you will 'see me now.'"[39] *See me now.* Visibility through aggression. Not optimal but, if all else fails, necessary. *Be seen or die.*

Rage is an important starting place in hearing and proclaiming a calling obstructed or destroyed. For the young men with whom Ellison worked, rage is a survival skill, protecting people from self-demise, even if sometimes ineffectively. It is an understandable response to erasure and a positive, not a negative, sign. It reveals that the person hasn't given up, and it can potentially provoke constructive developments. "Borne out of brokenness . . . its ultimate aim is wholeness," Ellison notes.[40]

To sustain wholeness in the face of denial, *community* matters. Reyes first heard God speaking through a principal at an all-boys Christian Brothers school. He arrived at school one morning in a turtleneck, worn to hide bruises from his stepfather's blows but against dress code. The principal called him in and, somehow, instead of penalizing him, grasped his situation even though Reyes was unable to say anything about it. Profoundly formed by the Christian Brothers' mission of educating and serving the poor, the principal provided sanctuary, assuring the twelve-year-old that he would "always have a home there at the school and with the Brothers."[41] In a similar fashion, Smarsh called the public school teachers who "noticed I was smart" the "defining intervention" of her life.[42] She also found sanctuary in the humble homestead and wild wheat fields on the 160-acre property of her maternal grandmother Betty and her seventh husband Arnie. God didn't provide a "job description," Reyes reflects, "but God did provide mentors, guides, leaders, role models, loved ones, and experiences through whom and through which I could hear God's voice calling me into new life."[43] Without this community calling, he wouldn't be here today, he testifies.

Grandmothers, it turns out, figure big in many calling stories. Reyes likens his to a "mother tree" sustaining him through underground roots that connected him to his ancestors and life around him.[44] He also heard a call from a college roommate whom he had abandoned when the friend started trafficking drugs. After an incredibly alienating year in graduate school, Reyes returned home to his migrant farming community in Salinas, California (considered the second-least-educated US city), to apologize and tell his friend he was giving it up. "That is bullshit," his friend replied, "If you come home, I won't forgive you.... Don't let those *putos* get to you."[45] Just the words Reyes needed. A hope deferred brings pain, yes, "but a desire fulfilled is a tree of life," as the author of Proverbs promises (13:12b), with people as branches and limbs.

As this suggests, addressing blocked callings isn't just something for us to manage by changing our attitudes, but a national and international cause of megaproportions. Since many thwarted callings result from economic and cultural distress, they require *recompense* on a broad social scale, wrongs righted by material remediation and political intervention on behalf of structures that undergird individual callings. *Recompense* means *to make amends for loss or harm*. Biblically, the term evokes images of Jesus's parable, retold in Luke's Gospel, about the vineyard owner who throws a banquet for the poor and disabled who cannot give in return. Political debates about paying back huge debts accrued by the massive injustice of historical oppression in the Americas—land and lives stolen from First Peoples and Africans whose sweat, blood, and lives built the early US economy—are also debates about reparation for stolen and obliterated callings.

For those at life's margins, oppressed by various powers that be, the offering of hope can be misleading. Those in power can hold out assurance of justice that simply sustains the status quo. We should reject false promises that do nothing to change the realities of poverty and oppression. Social ethicist Miguel De La Torre makes an important argument for the value of "embracing hopelessness" for those on the underside of history who are often misled by illusive pledges. But it's important to recognize, in De La Torre's words, that "the hopelessness I advocate is not disabling; rather, it is a methodology propelling the marginalized toward liberative praxis—even if said praxis might lead to death in a desert."[46] His advocacy for hopelessness is, in other words, actually a call to defiance and resistance.

Nonetheless, sustenance in the face of blocked callings can still come in small ways by cultivating *hope across time*. "I felt as though I had a little flame of talent, not a big talent, but a little pilot-light-sized flame of talent," author Kent Haruf tells graduate students. "And I had to tend to it regularly, religiously, with care and discipline, like a kind of monk or acolyte, and not to ever let the little flame go out." His breakthrough novel didn't happen until midlife, after he had been writing "as hard as I could for almost twenty years." He landed a teaching job and wrote in the summers. Looking back on his late-blooming career, he concludes, "If I had learned anything over those years of work and persistence, it was that you had to believe in yourself even when no one else did."[47]

Haruf's final book, *Our Souls at Night*, grew out of a second marriage, what he calls a "late-life gift."[48] His new wife helped him finish the novel before he died. It's a "book about us," he told her.[49] Like Louis and Addie in the novel, he and his wife often ended the day talking quietly together in bed. In other words, keep fanning the flame, Haruf suggests. Learn when to fight, when to give in, and when to find a calling where you are. And when in doubt, find collateral help.

Sometimes addressing obstructed and destroyed callings cannot happen in our lifetimes, and we must *hope across generations*. Both Hughes's and Hansberry's fathers died as exiles in other countries, disillusioned by US political hypocrisy. Where their parents had given up, Hughes and Hansberry threw themselves into creative means of fomenting transformation. They both provide an instance of what writer Barbara Kingsolver means when she observes that "anger and bereavement, throughout history, have provided the engine for relentless struggles for change."[50] While Hansberry's father and uncle fought injustice through the courts, Hansberry turned to the power of the word. Shortly before she died of cancer at the young age of thirty-four, she left the hospital to encourage the young winners of a national writing contest to keep making their truths known. Long before others designated Black as beautiful, she told her audience, the next generation of writers, that she could think of "no more dynamic combination that a person might be" than "young, gifted, and black."[51] A PBS documentary on her life, "Sighted Eyes/Feeling Heart," draws on her claim that "one cannot live with sighted eyes and feeling heart and not know or react to the miseries that afflict this world."[52]

Ward leaves her brother's story until last. His death seems especially meaningless. While she was bent on getting an education, her brother Joshua Adam Dedeaux was working extra hours as a nightclub valet. When he was rear-ended on his way home from work by a drunk driver going eighty, he tried to counter the impact, but "there was so much momentum," not just from the car but from "histories and pressures moving all at once that my brother could not stop."[53] But Ward finds a way to push back. She dedicates her memoir to him. At once lament, brave testimony, and cry of protest, her book executes justice by raising consciousness and spreading the word.

Sometimes we make our way back to our more fantastical callings of childhood by another way. Although my son-cum-Harrison-Ford never ventured into strange lands to fight adversaries over precious objects, he majored in anthropology and philosophy and now teaches fourth graders at an outdoor-friendly "School in the Woods" and goes adventuring in the summers.[54] We might say that some of my son's inflated ambitions panned out in a remote, transmuted way.

Sometimes blocked callings turn out to be simply interrupted callings. Although young people who postpone certain markers of adulthood may face challenges getting into the housing market, conceiving children, or acquiring economic stability, many return to these callings later with greater maturity and integrity. Some interruptions do little lasting harm and have advantages.

Sometimes, others carry on where we leave off. It was youths and young adults who spearheaded the civil rights movement, putting into practice at considerable risk the ideals of their elders. When I asked an African American colleague how she knew so early in life that she wanted to be a professor, she told me about her mother. Her mom had had academic *and* athletic scholarships but gave them both up for marriage, managing to return to school years later as her twelve children grew. From an incredibly young age, my colleague knew with unusual clarity, perhaps from watching her mother, that she would earn a doctorate. Sometimes, "our callings have a way of catching up to us," writes Mark Schwehn. The son and grandson of parish pastors, he had resisted pressures as a young adult to go into ministry only to raise two children, both of whom are now ordained and serve churches, carrying forth a calling he'd turned down.[55]

I see similar family patterns in my own life. It's possible that my dad's suppressed interest in religion and my mom's refrain about the two sorts of books on his shelves inadvertently drew me where he didn't go, earning a degree in religion and doing ministry and teaching. And even though I never found a viable path into the woods as a forest ranger, one of my sons is an environmental arborist, preventing fires through forest mediation and conservation; another teaches at a school that immerses kids in the surrounding ecosystems and invites them to become naturalists; and all three spend considerable time outdoors, hiking, biking, rock climbing, and so on. And I never realized until gathering information for my dad's obituary how much time he spent in avocational "ministry," leading boards and committees of local and national nonprofits and serving community ministries and a local congregation. In a folder of poems and quotes he labeled "funeral ideas," I found a quote from a Quaker theologian that became the lead line of his obituary: "We have made at least a start on discovering the meaning of human life when we plant shade trees under which we know full well we will never sit."[56]

As the Story of *The Other Wise Man* closes, it looks like Artaban has failed. He is waylaid again and again by the needs of others in his attempt to catch up with Jesus, and he has given the last of his gifts, "a pearl of great price," to ransom a young slave from bondage. But, as he lies dying, his primary life's aim and desire unmet, a peace descends. He had "been true to the light that had been given to him," the narrator tells us. In fact, he had seen Christ in caring for "the least of these," says Van Dyke as he rounds out his morality play.[57] The moral might seem a little schmaltzy, but perhaps in meeting the demands that arise on our way, in making a way out of no way, we discover our calling.

Chapter 3

Conflicted Callings: Purity of Heart Is to Will *Several* Things

"When are you going to *quit working*?" my husband Mark asked. His question sounded innocent enough, but I knew from his tone that he didn't mean "quit for the day." No, he meant for life. I was retired after all. But before joining him for dinner, I had been absorbed in my upstairs alcove, laboring over this book. In fact, I'd spent the last several months glued to my desk, the ding of a saved Word document accenting the passing of the hour. So, his question felt more like a demand or reprimand than a genuine query. And he was right: For two years since my final paycheck, my daily pattern had looked a lot like when I was employed. Upon retirement, I had received a two-year research appointment, and I'd spent much of that time trying to finish up some advising, editing, and writing. When was I going to wrap it all up? Will there just be something else to write when I complete this book? When *will* I stop?

Until that moment I figured I was beyond conflicted callings. After all, I'm officially done with work, my kids are grown, and for all practical purposes I'm well past the acute phase of middle adulthood in which the demands of work and home multiply and pull us in so many directions. But then in my own backyard, I faced a clash

Follow Your Bliss and Other Lies about Calling. Bonnie J. Miller-McLemore, Oxford University Press.
© Oxford University Press 2024. DOI: 10.1093/9780190084073.003.0004

of commitments once again: to write *or* be a good companion in the next phase of a lifelong partnership. Maybe Mark was asking: How are we as a couple going to shape our final days ahead?

We do have a lot to figure out. Like where we're going to live. Stay near my ninety-three-year-old mom *or* move closer to the growing families of our sons and their partners? And there again, raising its ugly head, another clash of calling—committed daughter to an aging mother *or* caring parent and grandmother to sons and grandsons? Not to mention other things that I still feel called to do with my "one wild and precious life" besides writing.[1] Is it time to get on with these things before it's too late? It's not that we can't do lots of different things at once; it's just that it's difficult to give multiple callings their due or to follow more than one calling well without a cost or consequence.

Reigning myths about calling obscure this dilemma. It's amazing how often we use the term *calling*, singular, rather than callings, plural. *Purity of Heart Is to Will One Thing* says a book title from an eminent philosopher (I want to shout bull, even though I know he means to will "the Good," capital G, as in what God wills).[2] More popular yet: *What Color Is Your Parachute?* Singular again. This title from the 1970s, for a book that is still going strong, conveys the falsehood that if you read the book, you just might find that *one thing* you're good at.[3] Even the beloved catchphrase, voiced by author Frederick Buechner and repeated ad nauseum—calling as the "place where your deep gladness and the world's deep hunger meet"—can miscommunicate a unity in purpose or a pinpoint in time and space where everything magically coheres. Buechner's longer definition reinforces the message: "There are all different kinds of voices calling you to all different kinds of work," but if you listen to "the voice of God rather than of Society, say, or the Super-ego, or Self-Interest," you won't be lured in such divergent directions.[4]

But life doesn't work out in this nice tidy fashion. There's nothing monolithic about calling. We lie about calling when we don't mention that everyone has multiple desires and faces an ongoing clash of commitments as diverse callings demand our time, attention, care, and energy. Different from missed or blocked callings, the challenge here is not restriction or limitation but abundance, overabundance, and depletion. It's not that we don't know what we want or can't decide; we want too much. We haven't given up a calling or gotten blocked. No, all we've done is add on.

An Explosion of Callings

Conflicted callings arise for nearly everyone in the middle phase of adulthood when demands proliferate and compete for our time. Middle-aged adults aren't just "dually called" to parenthood and career, "balancing" work and family as the problem is often characterized.[5] We're multiply called and often in wildly divergent directions—job entry and advancement, householding, partner relationships, avocational pursuits, parenting, care of parents and close friends, and political or religious commitments to bigger causes. Called to many things, not just one or even two, we can find ourselves overwhelmed, exhausted, burned out, and unable to follow any one of our callings as well as we wish.

Psychologist Matt Bloom describes middle adulthood as "one of the longest stages" of life, running roughly from the mid-thirties to retirement. A profusion of commitments, responsibilities, and social expectations distinguishes this phase from the phases before and after it. Bloom knows this well from experience. Unhappy as an advisor for a financial services company, he didn't dare quit because his wife and two sons depended on him, even if he felt called to more meaningful work. His choices about work, he suddenly realized, were no longer "simply about *my* needs and wants." Rather, "my vocations were deeply intertwined with the lives of my family."[6]

Notice Bloom's use of *vocations* plural here. At least four callings competed for his allegiance: "professional, income-earner, father, life partner." He was the primary earner, but his work as a father played an essential role in his life as did a ten-year marriage, each a highly valued vocation around which he oriented himself. He knew deciding to quit an unsatisfying job to pursue a profession with more appealing aims "would have serious repercussions" for all these vocations.[7]

Those in middle adulthood often experience something researchers call *role proliferation*, a "coterminous, continuous, and additive" accumulation of multiple disparate roles (domestic, occupational, marital, and parental), each one with its own significant commitments.[8] It's not hard to imagine how this comes about. First, we try to discern our own calling, a tough enough mission, and then we bump into someone with whom we fall in love, and we double the complexity. Having children further complicates everything. And we inherit complexity because our vocations are seldom separate from parents, siblings, extended family, and close friends for whom we have important obligations. Paradoxically, as Bloom observes, just as we acquire more *independence* from parents and other authorities, other people become more *dependent* on us. We suddenly see that success in one calling often brings losses in other callings. And we must temper dreams we've harbored about traveling here or there, doing this or that, or even making a difference in the world. As a young parent, I once read a book on prayer that suggested parents should just get up an hour earlier to make time to pray. Right. I posted a cartoon on my office door in which a boss gives employees the following advice for work–life balance: "Review your priorities—family, job, exercise, must-dos, medical, eating, hygiene, sleep, romance, holidays. You have time for three things. Work and holidays are two. You get to pick the third." Right again. More troubling and more serious are conflicts faced by those like the Ukrainian man interviewed on public radio torn between fleeing his war-torn country with his wife and children and staying with parents who couldn't survive the duress of travel.

From everything I see and hear today, life for child bearers and raisers everywhere has only gotten harder. A forty-year-old woman with five kids told me recently that she can't think beyond the immediate moment. I have had moving conversations with the father of two young children who has struggled to commute across state lines to begin a new job while also accompanying his wife through burnout and a new job and attempting to purchase their first home closer to extended family. Another friend agonized for his adult daughter, who can barely care for a two-year-old and manage a high-powered corporate position. Although ours is an era in which we tend to complain proudly about how busy we are, people in this life phase really are busy *and* exhausted. Life feels especially precarious, like it's always "only one small slip-up away from everything crashing down," as Bloom says.[9] Time is "always working against you," newsperson Susan Samberg argued when talking with the author of a group biography on the founding mothers of National Public Radio. Speaking about her effort to raise a child and advance the cause of in-depth news coverage in the 1970s, she remarked, "People who said the juggling was easy were lying. ... There was always something pulling and getting short shrift."[10]

There are all sorts of reasons that conflict between callings in middle adulthood has become more intense—increased work and family expectations, heightened pace of life, and technology's invasion into private space. Behind these diverse pressures lies the cultural domination of Western capitalistic practices and ideals that presume, in the words of German sociologist Ulrich Beck, the "market individual is ultimately a single individual unhindered by a relationship, marriage or family."[11] In a work world that expects single-minded devotion, little space remains for other crucial life callings, especially callings within families, such as care for a partner or spouse, a domicile, children, the elderly, or loved ones who are ill or have special needs. We're still living with a modern split between public and private life that arose alongside Western industrialization. For many people, the "private" vocations of sustaining domestic responsibilities still collide with a "public" work world not structured for and even hostile to homemaking and those who care for homes (often but not only women), a struggle accentuated in the United States for those in the working class by lack of adequate child care and family-unfriendly public policies.[12]

The idea of calling itself is often delimited to paid employment. In fact, businesses have created special programs for employees in which corporate leaders appropriate the term *calling* simply to boost investment in the workplace, using it to refer to a "kind of self-fulfillment through paid work." People assume, argues theologian and business ethicist Christine Fletcher, that "paid employment is the only work that is significant," *and* calling is only about what we get paid to do.[13] Domestic and caring labor aren't factored in or even seen as labor or work, much less callings. They're given little value even if the entire economy depends on them.

In other words, conflicted callings are built into an economic system that divides work from home, creating turmoil *within* people (how do I manage being split between multiple demands?) and tensions *between* people (who's going to do groceries, dinner, laundry, and cleaning?). How can people *not* have conflict over their callings under this kind of economic regime and systemic duress? These inner and outer tensions are so endemic today; isn't it odd that when we extol discerning where "your gladness" and the "world's needs" meet, we seldom talk about the clash of commitments?

You've Come a Long Way, Baby?

Multiplicity and conflict in calling lie especially close to the bone for women. Why? Because over history and up to today, women have been the caretakers of the world, doing the lion's share of cleaning, cooking, caring for kids, and generally "holding up half the sky." A landmark study over thirty years ago by sociologist Arlie Hochschild documented women's "second shift," the "extra month of twenty-four-hour days a year" that women put into unpaid, undervalued, and often invisible domestic labor (e.g., not factored into the GNP).[14] According to a recent study, women still put in two hours or thirty-eight percent more time per day than men on housework and child care, even when women make more money in marriages that are tellingly more precarious as a result.[15] When household demands overflow and women pick up the slack, well, there we have a conflict of callings not only within women's psyches but between people.

Mothers know in a unique way a vocational division internal to their own bodies, bearing children who are at once an intimate part of them and yet not part, growing into an Other, forever connected but separate.[16] Motherhood can be immensely fulfilling, but women's callings can never be fully contained in children from whom they're severed from the start. Women have long felt forced to choose between children and work of one's own, a pressure many men haven't experienced as acutely, even in contexts today where men do more child care and housework. Researchers like economist Rhona Mahony have advocated measures to offset the slippery slope that inclines mothers to assume more and more domestic labor even among couples pledged to mutual responsibility for childrearing and home maintenance, practices like tempering the impulsive "gatekeeping" of mothers over infant care or giving men "extra time with the baby to catch up," what Mahony calls "countertipping."[17] But it's hard to counter centuries of socialization *and* the physical realities of birthing and nursing that draw women more immediately into the orbit of care of children and home.

"I did not foresee," remarks a Catholic mother of two, that while "becoming a parent would strengthen the trust and tie I shared with my husband, it would also erode our relationship as we both suffered exhaustion and frustration." She also didn't expect that her "sacrifice of energy and time to parenting would result in a continually widening gap between my own ability to advance in a financially sustaining career and the comparable ability of my husband

and some of our single women friends." Her effort to return to work surfaced a "constant reassessment" of priorities. "The very ground beneath me seemed to shift and then shift again and again." She explains,

> I had not anticipated that grappling with how to parcel myself out among my new responsibilities would finally demand of me a total reassessment of my identity, my talents, my strengths and weaknesses, and of all my relationships. I never dreamt that this reassessment would require of me nothing less than the clearest truth about my deepest and most protected feelings and hurts.[18]

Combining mothering with paid employment remains for almost all women, in Mary Guerrera Congo's words, "an ongoing and nagging and unresolved puzzle."[19] "To reject the myth of the perfect mother," observes a reporter in an interview with activist and mother Jane Lazarre, "and insist that women's lives are larger than 'being somebody's mother, or somebody's wife'—as Lazarre did when she wrote *The Mother Knot*—was, and still is, a profoundly political act."[20] It's strange: women have been denigrated for wanting to "have it all" when all they have wanted, simply stated, was the expansive view of calling that many men have long presumed.

Conflicted Callings of "Higher" Service

Women don't have a corner on conflict, however. You might think heeding a "higher" calling to serve God or the wider world would lend a unity of purpose that resolves the challenge of conflicted callings. But it doesn't always work that way. Sometimes religious and political callings to the wider community, common good, or matters of social justice only intensify the conflict with other callings and put families, marriages, or paid jobs at risk. Brave, inspiring figures who led incredible political movements to rectify injustices, such as Gandhi and Martin Luther King Jr., were pushed, sometimes against their own desires, to sacrifice important familial relationships and then criticized for such faults. If your calling extends to the welfare of people and other causes—and many people of faith define calling as a deeply relational commitment to neighbors, the wider world, and God—then it's hard to avoid a conflict among callings (think here of the awful story of Abraham called to sacrifice his son Isaac and the disciples asked to follow Jesus and leave their families behind).

Committed Catholic author John Neafsey defines vocation as the call of social conscience. Calling is not only about "you" and your fulfillment, he insists; it's also "about 'us' and the common good."[21] If we listen closely to great leaders, he says, or the still small voice within and the even louder cries of the poor, we will hear a clear and insistent call to resist injustice, inhumanity, and poverty in the world. Those with advantages carry an even *"greater* burden of social responsibility," he insists.[22] *But how do we follow the call to conscience amid other work and family obligations?*

There are "hardly any forums, including church," says Bill Wylie-Kellermann, a United Methodist pastor who is the father of two, "for genuine vulnerable conversation" about such dilemmas. He struggles regularly with how his two girls bear the consequences of his commitments to do ministry in a community torn apart by poverty and lack of public services. When he overheard one daughter explain to her younger sister how to duck when she hears gunshots near their home in southwest Detroit, the family moved, not far but still out of range of the poverty they were committed to relieve. What cost were they as parents "willing to exact" from their kids, Wylie-Kellermann asks, "for the sake of our convictions"? Many children, he acknowledges, face harsh discrimination from birth with far less choice. "Needless to say, I agonize as a father about such stuff."[23] Even baptizing his kids raised a conflict between a calling to protect them and knowledge about the sacrifice demanded by discipleship. What was he doing pledging his own children to take up the cross and follow Christ when he knew what a baptismal vow of "fighting the evil powers of this world" really meant?

"How to be peacemakers both at home and in the larger world is quite a challenge," Catholic parents and peace activists James and Kathleen McGinnis admit on the very first page of the tenth-anniversary edition of their widely read book *Parenting for Peace and Justice*. They refused to see parenting and doing justice as divorced from one another, but for almost twenty years they wrestled with integrating their family life and social ministry. How do parents "act for justice without sacrificing our children and build family community without isolating ourselves from the world"?[24]

That's a question I asked as I raised three boys amid race and class inequities in a predominately White suburb of a major Southern city.[25] Even the question of where to live when we moved raised difficult questions of conscience. Should we live where people of diverse classes, races, and sexual orientations would be our neighbors? Or should we focus on good schools? The fact that we had such a choice was itself a troubling reminder of the injustices we opposed. Moreover, as the McGinnises admit, sustaining commitments to political activism becomes more difficult as children become teenagers and refuse to go to rallies, point out inequities within the family, and develop their own opinions about clothes, shopping, and television.[26] The editors of a more recent book, *Parenting for a Better World*, declare on page 1, "You probably don't need a book to tell you that trying to parent *and* to strive for justice in the world feels overwhelming."[27]

The question of whether families can answer the radical call of the gospel or other demanding religious or moral mandates has a long history of debate in Christianity and other religions. Is it possible for parents "to take seriously Jesus' call to 'turn the other cheek,' share one's wealth," and so forth, asks theology professor Daniel McKanan, "at the same time as one fulfills the responsibilities of marriage and parenthood?"[28] Religions have tended to say no, segregating families from members of monastic communities who renounce family attachments to devote themselves to charity and worship. The Roman Catholic Church, for example, has religious orders with covenants of poverty, chastity, and obedience that are distinct from the duties of families. Other traditions, such as Hinduism, divide up the life cycle, distinguishing a period of life for householding from a later phase in which people can set familial obligations aside and devote themselves entirely to the spiritual life.

There are exceptions, of course. The Catholic Worker, founded in 1933 by Dorothy Day and Peter Maurin, is a prominent example of a twentieth-century movement that tried to unite callings to care for family *and* those on the margins of society. But even here, parents worried about subjecting their children to a range of threats and dangers. "The most challenging thing," in the words of one father McKanan interviewed, "is 'being stretched between the commitments of a Catholic Worker . . . and the responsibilities and commitments to your family. You never feel that anything is done well or enough.'"[29]

This dilemma has origins that go back to the movement's beginnings. Day herself experienced ongoing tensions between her wider call to service and her domestic desire to attend to her daughter Tamar. Practical theologian Claire Wolfteich describes how Day felt "besieged by guilt, constantly failing to measure up to expectations in multiple places at the same time."[30] "At night when visitors came, workers, scholars, priests, laymen, Day left [Tamar] in the bath and all but forgot her," Day admits in her autobiography. "There were plenty who laid claim to my sympathy and loving care," she says, "to the extent of forgetting I had personal family obligations."[31]

Conflicts over callings of service to the wider good also arise for many people in the workplace. "I used to feel like an impostor walking down aisles of book exhibits," remarks academic dean and president Faustino Cruz, "profoundly contrite for 'what I have failed to do.'" A scholar and an academic, he hadn't published a single-authored book. "Worse still," he says, senior colleagues berated him: "'Tito, you have to publish,'" they said, "'It's publish or perish.'

'We need a Filipino voice, write!' " But as he observes, sometimes engaging seriously in one aspect of your calling "works against performing other tasks."[32] He describes the conflict as getting caught between what he knows is right and good on the one hand and what he must do to keep his job on the other. He even encountered the tension as a doctoral student when he had to choose between attending class or going to a Latin American Catholic Bishops conference. Fortunately, his professor seemed to understand. She encouraged him to go: "You would gain more insights from your trip than the class could possibly give you, and the impact of your work... would touch many more lives and communities."[33]

As we have seen, our postindustrial capitalistic economy fosters just such a conflict of values, especially if we're people of faith like Cruz. Its unrelentingly competitive atmosphere encourages the most self-centered of ethics, the "belief... that if I don't look out for myself no one else will," in the words of systematic theologian Kathryn Tanner.[34] In a finance-dominated economy no longer driven by industry or service but by making money off money, people become more and more invisible and expendable. So, it's not surprising that conflicted callings arise whenever we're caught, as Cruz found himself, between "standards by which we must live" to sustain our integrity and "expectations that are generally determined by institutional policies, regulatory boards, and employment contracts."[35]

Cruz's conflict in his professional calling surfaced around the three standards by which faculty are hired and promoted—service, teaching, and scholarship. Not surprisingly, most people neglect service to the institution and wider community because they know it's the "least regarded" area, in Cruz's words. Service is like the caring labor in the home—essential to the welfare of the whole but seldom a step toward self-advancement or a pay raise. The "press of time all too often precludes substantial involvements" in service and care for others, as Jesuit priest and professor Thomas Massaro admits. Early in his own teaching career, he quit volunteering at homeless shelters and participating in political activism so that he could publish, even though he found the situation a "nearly intolerable lacuna." In fact, "as a social ethicist whose work is integrally bound up with issues of *public church* and social justice advocacy," he laments, "I find the gap between what I practice and the values I teach ... and preach ... is one that leaves me dangerously vulnerable to charges of grave hypocrisy!"[36] Someday, he hopes to find a better balance but fears he will always be "ducking" the challenge. He knows other colleagues feel a similar frustrated yearning to reapportion their time but don't feel they can without risking their own security or advancement.

Cruz can't duck his fuller calling, however. Ordering commitments in concentric circles of priority, as Massaro suggests, doesn't work for Cruz. His field of study and his Filipino identity make neglect of service untenable. Trained as a practical theologian, he holds a deep commitment to scholarly reflection that evolves out of action and matters to the wider world. More important, as a Filipino immigrant he has imbibed a powerful imperative to have compassion for others, especially those in his community. He feels a special responsibility to speak out and stand up for marginalized people. Choosing scholarship over service is simply "not an option for persons in minority-related positions," a reality that often unfairly taxes and overextends those who are minoritized.[37]

Even those in monastic communities devoted to God as their sole vocation live with tensions internal to their calling, as author Jonathan Malesic reveals. Caught up in his own struggles with burnout, Malesic searched for those rare places where human worth didn't rest solely on productivity at work, and he found himself studying a couple Benedictine communities. The Rule of Saint Benedict is strict about the hours of daily prayer, but the Benedictines with whom he spoke in two monasteries in Minnesota said, "their daily labor had, at some point in their careers, kept them from making it to every single office" of prayer. One monk, Fr. Nicholas Becker, described the conflict as arising "between an ideal," that of the contemplative life, and the "reality of his position" as full-time faculty and head dorm resident at the university founded by his order. Drawn to monastic life, his active role as professor, mentor, and leader often kept him from participating "fully in the life of his community."[38]

Not Balanced or Centered, Just Ambiguously Abundant

There are plenty of self-help books on balancing work and family, juggling dual careers, time management, burnout, and so forth. But these resources don't really get at the problem of living well amid conflicted callings.

Unfortunately, metaphors like *balancing* and *juggling* oversimplify the challenges and divert attention away from larger forces that create the problems. The modern discipline of time management is, according to journalist Oliver Burkeman, a "depressingly narrow-minded affair."[39] It focuses on techniques, like how to crank through tasks or prepare a week's meals on Sunday, but it seldom considers wider social forces, like hostile work environments and inadequate child care and parental policies, much less deeper questions about calling that lurk behind our conflicts. Burkeman's own life felt out of control, but when he tried tons of procedures to reign it in, he realized that his efforts masked tensions endemic to modern work. He was also avoiding "scary questions" closer to his heart like "what I was doing with my life?"[40] Based on his experience of overwork and unhappiness within the industry of higher education, Malesic critiques popular literature on burnout. The usual remedies, he discovered, seldom challenge assumptions about employment as *the* singular source of personal fulfillment, and they often turn burnout into an individual pathology rather than a cultural problem.[41]

Realism and Imperfection

Gleaning from those who have survived and even thrived amid conflicted callings, the first and perhaps the most important thing to say comes under the general heading of *realism*: Callings conflict. Period. Just saying that feels like a relief. There are no perfect solutions, no one-stop shopping, no one size fits all. We're almost always called in several directions at once, sometimes in more ways than we can manage. Contrary to its popular use in the corporate world and in some college programs, calling isn't just about getting a job. It's about *having a life* in all its fullness. A life of meaning includes more than a job and money; it entails intimate relationships and connections to ultimate hopes and causes. In fact, according to a religion professor who has worked with undergraduates on calling, a "life of integrity and purpose is actually more likely to *occasion* competition and conflict among callings" than not. Jason Mahn encourages educators and parents to quit avoiding the dilemmas and to start helping young adults prepare for what he calls the "anguish (and joy) of willing several things."[42]

Indeed, authenticity doesn't require singularity in focus. Nor does it require perfection or even balance. Balancing and juggling leave the impression that we can arrive at some stable adjustment of obligations, a "greatness," Bloom declares, "that our real lives will never meet." If we achieve balance, it's temporary. "Competing priorities do compete ... ruthlessly ... no matter what we choose." We should recognize that the "best jobs require ... periods of intense work on unfulfilling tasks" and "even the best marriages have rough spells."[43]

Why? Plain and simple: We're limited and finite. "There simply are not enough hours in the day to give proper attention to all of one's vocations," as Bloom says.[44] I like how Burkeman puts it: "Nobody in human history has ever achieved 'work-life balance.'" He is straightforward: "stop berating yourself for failing."

Instead, "let's start by admitting defeat.... That's *excellent* news."[45] It's also "Good News" for Christians who proclaim—in addition to admission of limits—forgiveness, acceptance, and gratitude as essential for the Christian life.

About my life as a mother of three young children and a fulltime job as a professor I finally had to admit: In neither realm was I at my best. Both my husband and I fell short of the standard forty-hour work week, *and* we also cut corners at home, shortchanging our kids and demanding more of them.[46] We spent more time than either of us like to admit negotiating, compromising, even arguing (yes) as we lived amid the costs of multiple responsibilities and the reality of our limitations. *And*—this is key—*it's okay*. Cruz names his situation for what it is, a flat-out "unsolvable conundrum." He uses a plethora of phrases to capture his effort to "live grace-fully the tension"; to "live within and work through" it; to live "between and betwixt, in the conundrum of scholarship and service ... in the midst of turmoil and chaos."[47] A commitment to active engagement with the world also necessitates compromise for the Benedictine sisters and monks. Their "whole adult lives," attests Malesic, "have been a constant negotiation between the Benedictine Rule's ideals of monastic life and the reality of their work."[48] As Fr. Nicholas Becker remarks, "I'm not going to let the job crush me, and I'm not going to give up on the vision of monastic life."[49]

In each case, it isn't a matter of prioritizing (putting one calling ahead of the other), taking turns (my partner gets to make the next major job move; then it's my turn), or making a choice ("perfection of the life, or of the work," as William Butler Yeats says in a poem).[50] We're talking instead about ambiguous abundance and unavoidable imperfection. We need to adopt toward ourselves and others an attitude of leniency, moderation, and compassion as we pursue the elusive middle ground amid tensions and demands.

When Mark and I moved from Chicago to Nashville with three small children, we sometimes joked that we had at least six jobs— two old ones, two news ones, moving, and caring for our kids. These were tasks more than callings, but, still, they bled into what each of us saw as our callings. It wasn't the best time in our lives, but we got through it, partly by giving each demand its necessary due, no less, no more. Certain times of life are more overwhelming than others, and callings evolve over time. Living through conflicts without disaster or irremediable harm is a realistic and sane aim. Several monks and sisters that Malesic interviewed described how their own lives had gradually shifted from a time of intense work in middle adulthood to a slower pace in their later years as they moved into jobs with fewer demands and more contemplative space. Burkeman encourages his readers to adopt a different attitude toward time, waking up to life's brevity and its gift (its "four thousand weeks," as he titles his book, which seems "absurdly, terrifyingly, insultingly short").[51] His "limit-embracing" attitude resembles Stoic philosophy and Christian theology in their recognition of finitude, caution about human hubris, and, in Christianity's case, admission of fallibility and the need for forgiveness and grace.

There is precedence in the Christian tradition for realism about conflicted callings. For sixteenth-century reformer Martin Luther, vocation wasn't a singular duty to which God calls each person. Each of us lives out a primary vocation to love God and neighbor within a variety of what he called "offices" or "estates": as parent, worker, citizen, friend, student, spouse, and so on. Three centuries later, Lutheran pastor and anti-Nazi dissident Dietrich Bonhoeffer understood the inherent complexity of Luther's vision. Because we have several spheres of responsibility—domestic, economic, civic, and spiritual—there will be ambiguity and failure. Given the "unresolved conflict between multiple obligations," Bonhoeffer said, it's impossible to live out our callings perfectly.[52] For Christians, Lutherans especially, we don't earn salvation through our good works anyway. We muddle our way through abundant callings with the help of others and the divine grace that rescues us from relentless lapses. (Indeed, "fractured callings" earns a chapter all its own.)

Reformation of Work and Love

We've gone through social changes that neither Luther nor Bonhoeffer could anticipate, however. Today's experience of conflicted callings suggests that its basic constituents—*work* and *love*—need wholesale redefinition and reformation. Women, for example, should not be forced to choose one vocation (mothering) to the exclusion of others or to choose mothering at all. Motherhood is not a natural or inevitable calling; it can even be a secondary calling for some. In addition, we're no longer willing to live with the conventional stratification and division of major life commitments, assigning work to men, for example, domestic and relational obligations to women, and charity for the poor to the ordained or those in religious communities. Living with conflicted callings can also give rise to new understandings of prayer and the spiritual life—that they might occur in the midst of care of children or laundry or domestic drudgery and not just in the solitude and silence of the mountaintop, desert, or retreat.[53] For Cruz, the experience of conflicted callings also sparked new views of scholarship—that it doesn't need to be separated from service, that we might consider service-oriented scholarship or even service as a form of scholarship.[54]

Conflicted callings also raise huge questions about reforming our economic system of capitalism and how it works. A full response to living well with conflicted callings must go beyond adjusting personal attitudes, feelings, and daily practices and attend directly to flaws in our social and political fabric. Imbibing the values of capitalism not only distort how we think of ourselves but also how we conceive of calling.[55] Not only do we need to reimagine the place of paid work in our lives, demoting it from its absolute reign as source of self-worth; we also need to improve working conditions.[56] Testimony and protest around conflicted callings, it's worth noticing, always have a political and economic edge, and some of our energies must be directed at challenging systemic structures that devalue care of neighbor, children, the environment, and ourselves. Tanner issues a call for committed souls to unite and revamp the system,

Conflicted Callings 83

mounting a "counter-spirit," in her words, equal in power to the "Spirit of Capitalism" that sociologist Max Weber described at the start of the twentieth century. For Tanner, this counter-spirit can come only via something like Christianity, which is "one of the few alternative outlooks" that also has a practical influence over everyday life, an efficacy unearthed by Weber a century ago—what he called the "Protestant work ethic"—but now needed to resist rather than support the way capitalism and the market encroach on all our lives, its "iron cage."[57] But we're a long way from solving the politics and practices that exacerbate conflicted callings, and some people suggest that capitalism and some of its companion ideologies— Western imperialism, nationalism, anthropocentricism—are beyond reformation because their roots are so deeply and globally entrenched.[58]

As this implies, any true response to conflicted callings must be communal and political. Contrary to what finance capitalism would have us believe, calling isn't just about what you do personally with your life but branches out into what other family members do and what social structures sustain or undermine. Solidarity is key, knowing you're not alone, that there are others out there like you from whom you can learn and with whom you might talk, organize, and protest.

Everyday Practices

Every time I spoke about my work on mothering, people wanted to hear what Mark and I did in our everyday lives. How did we divide house chores? Combine or keep our finances separate? Get groceries and meals on the table? Write books *and* care for kids? Communities like religious congregations can provide ballast in the storm, even if they've been slow to aid those struggling to sustain work and family. Exemplars and mentors play a crucial role, as Bloom insists throughout his reflection on calling, showing us a way forward through example and by naming and drawing forth our own gifts. Of course, everyone must find their own pattern, but it helps to glean from others. Just hearing their stories helps. It helped me to hear confirmation from a wide range of theologians, colleagues, and friends that motherhood and other vocations need not be mutually exclusive but, instead, richly expansive.

Sometimes it's the mundane practices, not the big ideas, that matter. Tackle the division of labor early in a relationship, for example. If you wait to figure out how to share domestic responsibility, it'll be too late. Find ways to work against the slippery slope that leads women or mothers to assume more of the caring labor. Take it "bird by bird," author Anne Lamott's sage advice on how to write a big report or book without getting overwhelmed, setting aside the looming challenge and going step by small step. Parenting for justice has "got to be about the piecemeal and the 'good-enough' as well as about high ideals and courage," the editors of *Parenting for a Better World* contend, a "journey where we make mistakes, revise our plans, try again, and discover new strategies." Consider small manageable everyday steps toward social justice within and beyond your family life, they suggest, that "don't have to leave you exhausted or feeling pulled in different directions." The chapters in their collection focus on acts like "meditation, growing vegetables, making collages, singing, giving, eating together, praying, waiting on others, being angry, listening, cultivating kindness along with intimacy and solidarity, joining street protests, and engaging in community organizing."[59]

Finally, there are benefits from living with and through conflicted callings. "By having children," Native American author Louise Erdrich testifies, "I've both sabotaged and saved myself as a writer." She weighs the causalities and gifts:

> With a child you certainly can't be a Bruce Chatwin or a Hemingway, living the adventurer-writer life. No running with the bulls at Pamplona. If you value your relationships with your children, you can't write about them. You have to make up other, less con-

vincing children. . . . But then, having children has also made me this particular writer. Without my children, I'd have written with less fervor; I wouldn't understand life in the same way. I'd write fewer comic scenes, which are the most challenging. I'd probably have become obsessively self-absorbed, or slacked off. Maybe I'd have become an alcoholic. Many of the writers I love most were alcoholics. I've made my choice, I sometimes think: Wonderful children instead of hard liquor.[60]

Erdrich confirms what Mahn suggests—that moral and vocational growth and wisdom can come from bearing rather than resolving the ambiguity of loving more than one thing, "holding onto and negotiating two or more incommensurable callings," in his words.[61] Men benefit, I argue, from investing in children, and children benefit from witnessing parents (including mothers) who love them but also have loves that extend beyond them. Lutheran scholar Katherine Kleinhans offers her own summary of at least four advantages of recovering the "plural dimensions of vocation": it corrects the instrumental view of vocation that associates it primarily with employment; it revalues unpaid vocations and even unemployment; it adheres to the reality of our lives and their change over time; and it frees us from trying to find our one divine calling, the ideal job, the perfect mate.[62]

Standing behind me—as of yesterday—is a new white crib. The day I set aside for final editing of this chapter, it arrived in a slim cardboard box, and I stopped to put it together with Mark. I ordered it a few weeks ago for our two-year-old grandson, who will arrive soon with my son and daughter-in-law for Christmas, and, ironically, the only room that works is my study. So, there it sits, surrounded by four floor-to-ceiling shelves of books. A study-nursery, where the tools of two primary callings abide side by side once again, over thirty years after I first faced serious questions about multiple callings to work and to love. Books and a crib. I'm reminded of a period of my life when I had to keep moving my desk from a spare upstairs bedroom to the downstairs den to right next to Mark's and my bed (talk about a conflict of interest) to provide room for our growing family. I breathed a sigh of relief a decade ago when I reclaimed my oldest son's upstairs bedroom as a study of my own. Now also a nursery. But I see once again: conflicting callings *can* cohere, perhaps not comfortably or perfectly but without crisis or catastrophe.

There is so much more that could be said, but I need to bring this chapter to a close and settle, as best I can, one of my own conflicted callings by eliminating at least one obligation. I wrote this chapter last because I've thought so much about its theme over the last thirty-five years that I wasn't sure what else I had to say. But I'm near the end of the time limit I set for my calling to write, and I'm going to stick to that to preserve my marriage, my sanity, and, of course, my calling to a life beyond the daily grind of turning thoughts into cogent sentences.

Chapter 4

Fractured Callings: I Do Not Do the Good I Want

Merriam-Webster lists over one hundred synonyms for the word *failed*.[1]
So many ways to talk about our foibles.
Not doing "the good we want," Paul says famously in his letter to the Romans; doing instead the "very thing I hate." His words capture so well the wrongs we do despite our best intentions. "I do not understand my own actions.... I can will what is right, but I cannot do it" (7:15, 7:18). The pain is evident in his final plea: "Wretched man that I am! Who will rescue me from this body of death?" (v. 24).
And yet when we talk about calling, we seldom speak about callings that go awry, what we might call *fractured callings*: callings that don't work out or that fall apart not just because something blocked our way but because of something we did or failed to do. Fractured callings arise when we inadvertently or willingly take the wrong path, believing we have gifts or making commitments in our work or relationships, but disappointing ourselves and others through minor or egregious mistakes that hurt and set us back, divert us, and force us to re-evaluate and start again. They differ from blocked callings because we share some of the responsibility. The blame lies as much within as without.

Follow Your Bliss and Other Lies about Calling. Bonnie J. Miller-McLemore, Oxford University Press.
© Oxford University Press 2024. DOI: 10.1093/9780190084073.003.0005

And there's the rub. With this dicey distinction about blame I've waded into muddy philosophical waters. We might not mind admitting we have a blocked calling or any of the other challenges in this book, but few of us want to say we've failed or mistaken our calling. I put off writing this chapter because I was loath to call out other people's mistakes and hesitant to disclose my own. Who was I to talk about dropping out of college or jettisoning a job as vocational breakdowns? Or to label alienation from spouse, parents, or children a failure in a calling to love? I'd inadvertently backed into waters troubled by centuries of debate over the nature of evil and human responsibility.

Here is where you would think religion would help, with its long-term deliberation over right and wrong. You would think. After all, when Paul decries his entrapment in the "body of death," he is speaking about *sin*. But Christianity has a tragic history on sin. Instead of seeing it as a wake-up call for kindness and comfort, which is exactly what we need when we fall short, the Church has often misused the doctrine to discipline and punish individuals and to terrorize whole populations they have wished to control and dominate, whether young children, elementary school students, wives, or colonized and marginalized peoples.

Why have I persisted? And why do I continue to believe it's important to recognize our own fallibility in upsetting our callings? Aren't there many causes? And who's to say what's broken or failed?

Fortunately, other Christians have challenged distorted uses of the doctrine of sin, and my reflection on fractured callings is aligned with this tradition. Sin, as people have redefined it, is systemic as much as personal. Some people describe it as "woundedness" or as "a sign of our brokenheartedness, of how damaged we are."[2] Born vulnerable, we harm others out of the damage we have experienced. Fractured callings, therefore, emerge out of our weakness, vulnerability, and limitation more than out of a willful or prideful bent toward self-promotion, aggression, and destruction. And they occur within entire social and political patterns that influence how we fall short, whether because of manipulative and dysfunctional families or larger-scale sins like racism, homophobia, patriarchy, and imperialism. These patterns narrow and manipulate our choices and fracture our calling to work and love.

Generational and political patterns don't excuse us, but they do help us grasp why we struggle and stray in following our callings. So, when someone like author Ann Patchett says, a "minimum of four generations of my family have failed at marriage," naming divorced aunts, uncles, parents, and siblings, she isn't blaming them; she's only grasping why she entered her marriage with "as much coaching on how to conduct a happy union as a rattlesnake."[3] And when memoirist Mary Karr admits all the misery she has caused her son through alcoholism and neglect *and* simultaneously exonerates herself by seeing the bigger picture, she isn't being contradictory; she's expressing grace. "Just as you're blameless for the scorched parts of your childhood," she tells her son, "I'm equally exonerated for my own mother's nightmare," and she even hopes to show him how she came to absolve her alcoholic father and delusional mother for the harm, fear, and turmoil they caused in her own life.[4] I realize I'm walking a tricky tightrope trying to retain personal responsibility for fractured callings while also recognizing the complexity and nuance, but I think the risk of ambiguity and imprecision is worth the trouble.

My search for the best word for this chapter reflects the challenge and my effort to address it. There are so many words for failure, but none of them seemed entirely right. *Mistaken* or *derailed* didn't embody the pathos of fallibility and culpability that I wanted to explore. But *failed callings* offended a good friend still recovering from a divorce, sounding accusatory to her, especially amid the complicated and even unfathomable reasons behind what we too often label a *failed marriage*. I considered other possibilities like *broken, spoiled,* or *ruined,* but my husband was quick to tell me they didn't work either. These words also sounded harsh and totalizing, suggesting a judgment and hopelessness I didn't intend. People have justifiably protested the phrase *broken families* even more voraciously than *failed marriage*.

I finally landed on *fractured* not because the word is perfect but because it hints at brokenness without weighing it down with undue indictment. The word suggests, I hope, that fractured callings are delicate, morally ambiguous matters whose causes are multiple and whose consequences are ambiguous. There are many reasons why callings go wrong; causation is always complicated, the blame widely shared. We should be extremely cautious in labeling any life experience a *failure*. What might seem like a failure can turn out for the better while good choices in pursuing a calling can quickly or quietly go south. Addiction and divorce may seem like quintessential "I-do-not-do-the-good-I-want" experiences. But do *not* mistake either one as paradigmatic of fractured callings, *especially* when they are already judged too harshly by society. We should only talk about fractured callings carefully, respectfully, and humbly as if we're realigning a bone gently and kindly amid the pain. Finally, and maybe most important, *fractured* also implies the possibility of resetting and healing.

Whatever word we choose, we need to talk about the common human experience of rupture and breakdown. In fact, this may be one of the most important chapters in the book. No one avoids mistakes; they are endemic to life. As one friend put it, "we all end up here." So, we need a way to speak about fractured callings that isn't entirely negative or damning. I know the dangers of the word *sin*, and I have no desire to enter into irresolvable debates over whether human evil is innate, but I have always appreciated how mid-twentieth-century theologian Reinhold Niebuhr describes sin as "inevitable but not necessary"; we fail unavoidably out of the fear that arises from living with finitude and insecurity, even if we're not inherently bad, evil, or bound to fail. He also said the doctrine of sin was the only "empirically verifiable doctrine," the one doctrine that we can witness daily.[5] The stories and examples are as infinite and expansive as there are people in the world; one story opens out to another; and I may even include too many stories in the chapter. But my hope is that readers can find space among them to fill in the twists and turns of your own life or the lives of those you know.

A chief message of this book comes to the foreground here: Readers need to know the hardships of callings, especially the truth that we make mistakes as we figure out our lives. It's even more important to know you can make a mistake without entirely losing your way. Our callings are dynamic and evolving. Some failures are unavoidable; some turn out for the better; and occasionally, so much good comes (or *can* come) that to call our actions and their consequences failures seems totally off base. But before I make the delicate claim that we learn from failures and mistakes, I want to look closer at our flailing.

Blunders in Our Work Callings

Several years ago, in a small seminar that gathered to talk about how vocation evolves over the life cycle, psychologist Matt Bloom spoke about his own fractured calling in work. A childhood spent protecting a sibling with a disability, warding off school bullies, and pleasing stressed parents had shaped his personality and the patterns of self-sacrifice and self-preservation that he carried into adulthood. When dreams of becoming a pediatric physician were dashed in college by too much smoking and poor grades, he decided to major in finance to "make a lot of money," only to find himself in a soul-deadening job that went against his hopes for meaningful work that included care for others besides himself.[6] But how could he turn his life around at this point, now married with responsibilities to his wife and young children? There was no obvious road ahead.

Other people in the group shared stories of their own troubled callings, often influenced by difficult family circumstances or cultural pressures like those Bloom felt about getting the "best job" with the highest salary. Several years before practical theologian

Kathleen Cahalan formed our group, she had had her own powerful awakening to a fracture in her calling. During eight weeks of recovery from back surgery, she couldn't sit more than twenty minutes a day, and she turned to pool exercise to relieve pain, expedite physical healing, and calm her overactive mind. But as she exercised and resumed the practice of reading scripture, meditating on memorized lines from Isaiah 55 ("all you who thirst come to the water"), she discovered the ambitions she harbored within her calling—"to make myself famous," "to become someone great," "to look good and be praised"—betrayed her deepest hopes—to "seek God" (Isaiah 55:6).[7]

This chapter (and the book itself) started right here—amid the confusion and distress each of us in the group felt when we had followed callings that initially seemed right but had led us into unexpected thickets and down dead ends. We began to talk about the double-edged nature of vocation, that callings are good and terribly difficult all at once. As we listened to each other, we discovered how easy it is to lose our way as we try to pursue our callings, especially if our familial and social circumstances push or pull us in bewildering directions.

I've been observing and thinking about fractured callings for a long time, however. My first real exposure came as a college senior when I did an internship in hospital chaplaincy and encountered, in a small supervisory group, several middle-aged men, all previously congregational pastors who had left the church disheartened and were seeking other ways to serve. When I began graduate teaching in the mid-1980s, theological schools were inundated with what they called *second career* students, older adults who often said they'd pursued other jobs for the wrong reasons—money or job security, for example, or, as frequently, pressure from parents and family. "It can be a very disruptive thing for parents to have specific dreams for their kids," notes educator Randy Pausch. "As a professor, I've seen many unhappy college freshmen picking majors that are all wrong for them."[8] Over the course of my career, I've known colleagues and students who entered and then left religious orders, often to marry, sometimes in disenchantment. Perhaps it's wrong to call these fractured callings since people are just making their way through life, but they do reflect a kind of miscalculation and disorientation we all encounter on our way to making a living or following a calling.

It's ironic (and telling) that the founder of my own field of pastoral theology, an area devoted to forming pastors, experienced so much failure in his own calling. From young adulthood, Anton Boisen failed one calling after another in the two areas Freud saw as definitive for adult happiness—to work and to love. In his autobiography, Boisen describes one of his most acute periods of mental illness as a journey through "A Little-Known Country." He had graduated from college in 1897 and, after the first of several psychotic episodes, gone on to earn a forestry degree at Yale. But his career with the Forest Service was short-lived. As was his effort to serve as a congregational pastor after a seminary degree several years later. It didn't help that he had entered ministry for the wrong reason—he wanted to win the heart of a woman with whom he had been smitten since college though she gave no sign of returning his affection. The "failure of this relationship," a biographer observes, "was Anton's deepest sadness and grief for most of his adult life."[9] Boisen faced some unique challenges, but as Glenn Asquith pointed out to his audience of pastoral theologians during a luncheon address, "Everyone in this room has traveled in some little-known country."[10]

From the outside, our paths can look straightforward. But scratch the surface, and the story is usually quite different. My own calling to teaching religion and psychology looks like it follows easily from undergraduate majors in both areas and a doctorate in religion and psychological studies. But I arrived at my calling only after I veered and tacked through three other vocations—hospital chaplaincy, pastoral counseling, and congregational ministry. And I'd veered and tacked before that. As a college senior, I'd applied and been accepted into several schools of social work that I then declined. I'm not sure if I'd call any of these fractured callings, but in each case, I felt a vocational lure and commitment, sought training and education, served in part-time positions, and got paid, only to discover I didn't like the work, wasn't all that good at it, and couldn't imagine doing it every day all day. The closest I had ever come to imagining myself as a professor (until I finally became one) was playing school when I was eight with a third-grade friend. My path to teaching only appears straight looking back: no life-changing upset, no big trauma, no major realignment, *but* plenty of disruptions where I strayed off course and had to make my way back or be pushed back by others around me.

Fractured callings sometimes resemble what we might call *unknown callings* when we just don't know what we want. Desire isn't an easy thing, especially when it comes to calling, even though a huge consumer culture has grown up around eliciting desire. Unfortunately, consumerism only cultivates a hunger for material goods and high-paying jobs that promise to bring the worth and social standing we seek, even though they usually fail. Knowing our deepest desire is much trickier than culture suggests. A close friend tried for years to pursue her love and talent as a violinist, performing and teaching, only to admit midlife and postdivorce that the joy of playing had diminished years ago. She played well enough to substitute for a major city's symphony but not to earn a permanent spot. She had kept playing, auditioning, and doing small gigs because it was what she knew how to do, she had done it so well for most of her life, and her students supplied income. But she'd never really figured out what she wanted for herself as a young adult; then marriage to a well-paid surgeon came along, and the birth of two children kept her from giving further thought to the matter. Life's circumstances and distractions had gradually overshadowed knowing and claiming her hopes and dreams.

Family and social pressures play a role in unknown and fractured callings, causing many women to question or ignore what they want. My violinist friend describes a childhood of benign but damaging neglect by narcissistic parents who didn't listen to her needs, much less affirm them. So how could she know what she wanted or feel good about claiming it? Feminist therapists have repeatedly observed just such a failure or confusion of desire, especially among White women clients who struggle to move out of childhoods in which their mothers actively discouraged them from claiming what they want, trying to prepare them instead for a world in which women must put their needs aside to meet the needs of others.[11]

White women aren't alone, of course, in the suppression of desire when it comes to pursuing our callings. Black authors like Audre Lorde and bell hooks write eloquently of the difficulty and danger of living from your deepest desire. Black women are raised, Lorde observes, "to fear the yes within ourselves, our deepest cravings." To love others, hooks writes, "we must first learn how to respond to inner emotional needs," undoing years of socialization that tell us these needs are unimportant.[12] Nor should we assume that men don't face similar impasses. Recently, a friend who had served the academy for decades told me, "I often wish I had had as much confidence in the academic world as I do preaching and presiding in the world of the church." His calling lay more in the church than the seminary, but he had avoided congregational ministry, despite his passion for it, not wanting to follow his own father, a pastor with whom he had always had a difficult relationship. He went the academic route and never made his way back, not realizing his slightly misplaced calling until he retired.

My friend had had success as a professor, just not the affirmation and happiness he'd hoped for. Sometimes our callings are only fractured in a small way as we discover over the course of our career a great deal about our jobs that doesn't fit our desires, commitments, or abilities. Sometimes our primary callings are right, but key aspects of the calling are wrong, a minor fracturing within a calling. My parents praised a church minister for one-on-one pastoral skills but could barely tolerate the sermons (called to care but not to preach). I felt more called to write than to teach; teaching often felt like something I had to do so I could write. Sometimes, when we manage multiple callings in both work and love, as I explored in the last chapter on conflicted callings, we cannot help but feel we're failing all our callings. Or we succeed with flying colors in the workplace or the public sphere while screwing up our home life.

Even More Painful Ruptures

Fractured callings in work are one thing; rupturing a calling to love is even more painful. I was especially moved by another member of our seminar on calling who described her first two marriages as "big mistakes." Growing up in a fragmented family had made it almost impossible to enter adulthood *without* making multiple mistakes, Jane Patterson said; these mistakes "were going to happen." Her parents were beloved in the community, but they brought a different side to the family, secrets their neighbors never knew. Her father was an alcoholic who had multiple affairs, her mother had multiple sclerosis, and they stayed together "to be honorable," each believing the other needed them. To escape her family, she got married when she was nineteen, but the marriage ended quickly and unsurprisingly, given "all the brokenness we each brought with us."[13] Then, after many years in a second marriage, her husband left. The tumult of these years also affected her ability to discern what she wanted to do in her work until her late fifties, when she returned to school and attempted to restart her life.

Many people who flee troubled families to marry find themselves immersed in fractured callings. Another friend married her high school sweetheart to get away from duplicities in her family caused in part by her father's identity as a closeted gay man. Her marriage ended shortly thereafter, leaving her with two young children, and she began a long journey through three more marriages (and two more divorces) as she sought (and finally found) a secure and loving long-term relationship.

Fractured callings can devolve over long stretches of adulthood, as in these cases, and they can also crystalize in a flash. One of the more disheartening moments in my own calling as spouse and parent came one summer when our extended family was gathered for a few days to celebrate three birthdays—what my younger brother dubbed the 30/60/90 party as my nephew turned thirty, his dad sixty, and my mom ninety. The second morning, my oldest son Chris asked my husband Mark and me if he could join us on our walk. Supported by his middle brother Matt, he told us that when we (Mark and I) argue it's upsetting, evoking scary memories from childhood (that was awful to hear), tainting our time together, and setting a poor example as they nurture new marriages. On another vacation, Matt had already asked us to quit sniping at each other when Mark and I sparred over a card game, with me criticizing him for causing me to lose, and him harassing me for gloating and overanalyzing the play. I've always wished we had a more peaceable marriage, and we usually do. But our bickering increases when we travel and on holidays, times we often spend with our kids (we have all sorts of excuses). I listened, sickened and upset, and yet also ready to explain what they didn't understand about our relationship or the demands of our lives, travel, or being with family, but realizing more clearly than ever before the harm that our foibles and selfishness had caused. This floundering as mother and wife didn't deter me from these callings, but I knew I had threatened vocations to which I felt deeply called (the most precious callings I have), and I had received a startling, disconcerting signal to change my ways.

Novelist Elisabeth Strout excels in capturing how we mess up vocations as parents and spouses, telling truth through fiction in a profound and gentle way. Her unflinching look at human fallibility earned her a Pulitzer for *Olive Kitteridge*, now an HBO miniseries. A review describes Olive as an unlikeable character who "is as bad as you'd be if you let yourself."[14] When we first meet her, she is a gruff, opinionated, middle-aged woman who makes things difficult for her husband Henry and her son Chris while still somehow gracing the lives of those more troubled in the small coastal town around her. Nearly everyone in Crosby, Maine, it seems, has floundered in their callings in some way or other, betraying a spouse, child, employee, or other party—*except* perhaps her husband Henry, whose kindness only irritates Olive.

But it is Strout's return to Olive in *Olive, Again* and Olive's connection with widower Jack Kennison that offer a quintessential reckoning with the casualties of fractured callings. Henry is dead, and Olive, now in her seventies, realizes she soured their marriage with her disgruntlement while also straining her relationship with her son. The tragedy sinks in after a visit from Chris and his second wife, Ann. Things didn't go well. Mundane yet annoying missteps tainted the visit. But it was when Ann yelled at Chris in front of everyone, treating him like a child, as Olive had done too often with docile Henry, that Olive woke up:

> It came to her then with a horrible woosh of the crescendo of truth: She had failed on a colossal level. She must have been failing for years and not realized it. . . . She could not understand what it was about her, but it was about her. . . . And it had to have been there for years, maybe all her life.[15]

She's not sure why she has acted as she has—"she felt as though she had lived her life as though blind"—but Jack seems to understand, perhaps because he has affection for her grumpiness but also because he is reckoning with his own bungled marriage and alienated daughter Cassie, a lesbian whose sexuality he has stubbornly refused to accept.

Sometimes we don't do the good we want, and we don't know why. It's something about us, as Olive suspects, the temperaments with which we're born, what we're given to work with for good and for ill. Ornery, argumentative, competitive, introverted, awkward, laid-back, high-strung, disorganized, or any number of traits that mark our characters. I've always "talked back," something that got me in trouble growing up, and each of my own children emerged with their own annoying quirks and beauties. But it's also things that have happened to us, pivotal moments like Olive's father's suicide when she was young, or a pervasive family atmosphere like Patterson's tumultuous home life. For all sorts of complicated reasons, we mistreat the very people we're supposed to love. Parents inevitably harm their kids, but it still hurts to recognize the ways we've done so. For Olive, it was Henry's very proximity and likeability that made it even harder for her to be kind to him in the most mundane interchanges of daily life.

As with our callings in work, we often don't know how our callings in love will go until we're deep into them; we don't know our limitations until we're in over our heads. When Jack finally recognizes all the damage he has done through his shabby marriage and opinionated rejection of his daughter, he calls her up. After a few stilted interchanges, he breaks the rising silence, "Listen, Cassie, . . . I just wanted to say I know I'm a shit. I know that. Just so you know. I *know* that I'm a shit."[16] And what is she supposed to say? Not surprisingly, after years of distance she is disinclined to receive his belated, ineffectual apology.

Feeling like Shit

Fractured callings make us feel like shit. They carry a visceral gut punch, a sickening akin to losing something precious, except the loss is more disturbing because we feel partly to blame. We wallow in a "body of death," as Paul says eloquently in his letter to the Romans, from which we struggle to extricate ourselves.

This body of death includes shame and guilt. Historically, obsession with guilt has overshadowed shame as an equally powerful result of disgrace. But for years, therapists and pastoral counselors have helped clients recover from childhood trauma by distinguishing the two, suggesting that guilt arises because of something we did whereas shame runs deeper, touching on who we are, not our doing but our very being. One psychologist simplifies the difference by suggesting that guilt pertains to actions done to others, and shame to feelings about ourselves and how we appear to others and ourselves.[17] Shame is that awful feeling that something is wrong with us, our *whole* selves, damage we can't change, for which we have little explanation and over which we have limited control. It's hard to tell ourselves we're valued if we've received the opposite message for too long.

Moderating self-esteem is one of *the* biggest modern challenges, according to some analysts, and many people swing from grandiosity to insecurity, or they compensate for low self-esteem by erring toward one extreme or the other—exaggerated grandiosity or self-denigration.[18] Exaggerated feelings of superiority or of deep unworthiness can permeate and distort our ability to pursue our callings in both work and love, sometimes impacting us in more hidden and deceptive ways than guilt, causing us to lord it over others *or* keeping us from knowing and owning our gifts, gaining confidence in the value of our contributions, and forging ahead with our callings. In some cases, shame can become, as one expert suggests, "a widespread existential issue that renders life unbearable."[19]

Fractured callings, however, can activate both shame and guilt. On one hand, failure nauseates us; it makes us want to hide; we don't want to tell people; we don't want to see ourselves or be seen; we can even feel a kind of self-loathing. But on the other hand, we bare some modicum of responsibility, even if we can rationalize our actions and find persons and circumstances to blame. I felt exposed in front of my own kids and even embarrassed as I recount the story here *and*, at the same time, convicted as charged about actions that clearly caused harm. My recently divorced friend hid the discord at the heart of her thirty-year marriage from everyone for years *and*, at the same time, eventually had to assume responsibility for ending the marriage and announcing the news. In *Olive, Again,* Jack believes, true or not, that he deserves the misfortune that has come his way: a daughter who doesn't want to speak to him, a wife who was furious with him as she died, and even his prostate cancer and padded underwear.

Remorse and disappointment also permeate fractured callings. When Jack looks back over his life, laying his "thoughts out before him like a large piece of cloth," he "feels unbearable regret for all the mistakes." How has he gone from a good-looking, admired Harvard professor strutting across campus to "just an old man with a sloppy belly" who jeopardized his relationship with his wife and daughter? He never really gave himself to the marriage or gave his daughter a chance. "How does one live an honest life?" he wonders.[20]

How *does* one live honestly? Alongside shame, guilt, and regret, there is in fractured callings a kind of self-deception or disingenuousness that drags us down. Bloom and Cahalan both knew their work callings were coming apart when they noticed hypocrisy in their rationale and aims. Bloom felt he wasn't doing any good for anyone despite financial success in his job. When Cahalan resumed work after her recovery from surgery, she found she "had no idea why I was teaching what I was teaching. There was something profoundly inauthentic about what I was doing," she concedes. "I had become an actor on a stage, delivering my lines."[21]

Sometimes we delude ourselves the moment we enter a calling. When the Catholic priest asked Ann Patchett and her fiancé during premarital counseling if their marriage would be "dissolved only by death," she immediately replied "Yes" even though she knew *in that very moment* that it would end otherwise. But she couldn't jump off the "runaway train" of her engagement, "and so I lied."[22] Sometimes our whole lives can feel as if they're filled with duplicity. Mary Karr titled an entire book on her life, *The Liar's Club,* and opened her bestseller *Lit* with this line: "Any way I tell this story is a lie."[23] Hiding addiction from oneself and others may be one of the more insidious acts of covering over fractured callings. Science fiction and horror author Stephen King describes his lying about his drug and alcohol abuse as a "Hemingway Defense": "I am a very sensitive fellow, but I am also a man, and real men don't give in to their sensitivities. Only *sissy*-men do that. Therefore I drink. How else can I face the existential horror of it all and continue to work?"[24] The cover-up of his fractured calling as husband and father was so effective it went almost wholly undetected by the outside world that only witnessed the amazing success of his calling as an incredibly prolific writer.

Mending Fractured Callings

We fracture our callings in egregious and painful ways, sometimes from the very beginning of a commitment. The pain is real because we know, even if it's hard to admit, that we've damaged callings to which we're profoundly obligated, and we've hurt people most directly connected to these callings, the very people about whom we care deeply, including ourselves. And we can't completely undo the damage by the time we realize or admit what we've done, even if we can find remedies and alternative avenues for going forward. But how do we go forward? What kind of amendments are possible?

Truth-Telling

Telling the truth is an important first step. Some of the most powerful narratives arise from broken callings in which people come clean about the untruths they've lived. Patchett says point-blank about her first husband and herself, "We were not helpful to each other. We were not kind. These are the facts."[25] In *Olive, Again*, Jack is blunter than Olive: "My point here is—Children. Your son. My daughter. They don't like us, Olive," he declares.[26] The same openness characterized the conversation among the group of friends with whom I met who shared our struggles with our callings. "What I found, quite honestly," Cahalan admits after months of reflecting on her ambitions while repeating lines from Isaiah 55, "was a fairly self-driven person who stood at the center of the world." She'd written a dissertation several years earlier on how prayer forms the moral life but now sees how "very little" she really knew about it. "Actually, I think forming students in my image," not Christ's, "was my deeper motive."[27]

Truth-telling is horribly uncomfortable but also liberating. Sometimes seeing the bigger picture makes it easier to understand and absolve other people and ourselves. Karr wants to recount the "whole tale as I know it" to her son even though he knows her failures with an accuracy she can't match. Why? Because admitting the misery she caused relieves guilt and shame, and understanding the systemic family failures behind her behavior partly explains and exonerates, even if it doesn't justify the neglect, tumult, and alcoholism that nearly destroyed her childhood, then his childhood, and her calling as his mother.[28]

There's a kind of confession going on, as people process fractured callings, and a leveling or humility and humbling of self. As King crawled out of the hole he had dug through his addictions, he got rid of the huge monolith of a desk he had placed at the center of a spacious loft where he had sat for six years, like a captain on a small ship, "either drunk or wrecked out of my mind," spewing out books he couldn't remember writing. He got a small desk and pushed it into the corner under the eave, leaving room for couches, a Turkish rug, and pizza with his kids. His very first piece of writing advice is good counsel for following a calling: "Put your desk in the corner, and every time you sit down there to write, remind yourself why it isn't in the middle of the room."[29] He had, in essence, discovered a more modest, less grandiose view of himself. As Jack says to himself in *Olive, Again* as he reviews his life, "You not much, Jack Kennison," a remark reminiscent of what Olive had said to brush aside discomfort caused by a woman in town, "She's not much."[30]

Those who have weathered major fractures, in fact, have a humility and wisdom sometimes lacking among those of us spared such trials. In recovery stories that use honesty and humor to lighten the load, the humor often comes at the expense of the author or speaker, and we laugh along because it reveals a silliness, pettiness, and childishness with which we can all identify. It's a relief to laugh at ourselves. We're ridiculous sometimes.

Turning Failure to Good

Many memoires and narratives are popular not just for their honesty, humility, and humor but because they turn failure to good or at least show how brokenness can be woven back into the larger fabric of a life. On my wall hangs artwork from an artist friend who survived sexual abuse as a child partly by incorporating her recovery into her art, the abuse becoming another piece in the puzzle of her calling. The picture weds fabric, beads, lace, wire, a shell, and a rough-edged note with the message "I am strong in the broken places."

Years ago, computer programming professor Randy Pausch created the "Best Failure Award" to encourage creativity among his students. He had to change the name because "failure has so many negative connotations that students couldn't get past the word itself." Redubbed "Best Penguin Award" after the notion of penguins testing water for predators ("somebody's got to be the first penguin"), the award went to those who took the greatest risk and experienced "glorious failure."[31] The idea, in the words of a former student now directing a project Pausch created at Carnegie Mellon, "was that failure, if done in the spirit of trying something new and bold, should be celebrated."[32] Pausch claims he "got more from pursuing [a] dream and *not* accomplishing it than I did from many of the ones I did accomplish." Experience, he remarks, is "what you get when you didn't get what you wanted."[33] Of all the pithy advice in his "last lecture," which went viral after news that his pancreatic cancer had spread to his liver, it's his reinterpretation of failure that has had staying power. In his view, "failure is not just acceptable, it's often essential."[34] Indeed, failure isn't always accompanied by shame, guilt, disappointment, and remorse. Sometimes failure comes with relief and even a sense of liberation.

Not to present too cheery a picture, but fractured callings can become fodder for the road ahead, providing wisdom and self-awareness that can deepen calling in a new form. "Good things came from my mistakes," Patterson told me. "From fractured callings," she went on, "come beautiful shards," like the daughter from her second marriage or Patterson's return to school in New Testament and a current job helping congregations talk about vocation. A "fracture can break open to other things," insisted Bloom. He eventually quit his unsatisfying job, went back to school, and for the last decade has been doing extensive research on what makes callings to work meaningful, an interest that grows straight out of his own early meanderings.[35] My violinist friend discovered late in life, after years of questioning and self-doubt, a deep passion for helping other people get through their own suffering and now has a vibrant counseling practice and a strong second marriage.

Fractured callings can get us to a place we might not have reached otherwise. "Perhaps there was no other way for me to learn this lesson but by being brought low," says Cahalan about the reorientation of her calling.[36] It took derailing the forward motion of a career bent on success and accomplishments to get back on track. "Every single thing" about her happier marriage, Patchett insists, rests on divorce. Divorce is the "history lesson, . . . the rock upon which this church is built." Over time, lots of time, she "came to see that there was something liberating about failure and humiliation."[37] Boisen created a whole new system of clinical pastoral education out of his most traumatic and longest period of psychiatric institutionalization in the 1920s. Based on his illness and healing, he advised physicians to attend to religion, and he urged seminary colleagues to integrate hospital fieldwork into theological education, putting chaplaincy on the map as an important ministry. His framework remains integral to medicine and seminaries almost a century later.[38]

In other words, sometimes we get second chances. Even Strout's book title reflects reprise, *Olive, Again*. Callings are more like a "stream of water flowing down a mountain," as Asquith says while ruminating on Boisen's career and his own; they never "flow in a straight, uninterrupted line."[39] King portrays the evolution of his calling as a "disjointed growth process."[40] Patchett likens her recovery from her unwise marriage to living through a German-style fairy tale where the heroine and hero travel through dank forests and must enter, as she did, the "darkest part of my unhappiness, after which there began to be less darkness."[41] She includes in the same collection as her essay on divorce an essay on her "Story of a Happy Marriage" *and* another essay on her worst fight with her happy-marriage husband. In other words, she seems to say, there are multiple narratives on (happy) marriage or (happy) callings, not just *one* way to tell the story. Our callings may be more like a collection of essays that correct and nuance each other than a plot line where everyone lives happily ever after.

Families, Friends, and Forgiveness

King credits "ambition, desire, luck, and a little talent" for shaping his calling as an author.[42] But as we read on, there are developments he doesn't mention that played a pivotal role, especially when he almost lost everything because of substance abuse—factors that are also apparent and essential in all stories of recovery from fractured callings. To secure safe passage, we need friends and family and, perhaps most important, a suspension of judgment, vanquishing of shame and guilt, and reception of forgiveness, all offering a new lease on life.

On some level, King knew as early as when he wrote *The Shining*, published in 1975, that he was an alcoholic (the book "just happens to be about an alcoholic writer and ex-schoolteacher").[43] But it didn't break through his consciousness until his silence turned into a "scream for help," not just through fictional monsters that resembled the tormented mind on drugs but through his wife, family, and friends, who intervened in 1985.[44] His wife was pivotal. Years earlier, she had pulled the pages of *Carrie*, his first success, out of the trash, and later, with support of family and friends, she refused to stand by and watch him kill himself.

Absent from King's story but abundant in most accounts of amended callings is the role of self-forgiveness and the gradual painstaking banishment of shame, guilt, and judgment. Strout makes clear that solace amid the guilt and shame comes primarily through human connection. In her novel, Olive and Jack's companionship rests on their mutual loneliness, nonjudgmental understanding of each other's failures and disappointments, and comfort in the other's presence, even though their first marriages remain their dearest life experiences despite the ways they ruined them. When Patchett walked out on her first marriage, it was her mother and grandmother who received her with grace. Divorce deserves to be named an "eighth sacrament," she argues, because it paves the way for forgiveness and another start on life. "If we fail at marriage," we are assured by divorce that "we don't have to fail with the force of our whole life."[45] Hear that—whatever the fracture in a calling, *you do not fail with the force of your whole life*. As she concludes, "Family, friends, God, whoever loves us forgives us, takes us in again. They are thrilled by our life, our possibilities, our second chances. They weep with gladness that we did not have to die" to absolve our marriage or any other calling where we fall short.

Despite religion's damaging history on sin, the idea of sin gives us a word for an important reality and expands our grasp of the dynamics behind fractured callings, how they emerge, and how we might best respond—again, with kindness, comfort, and companionship, not judgment or damnation. Religious traditions have many rituals for letting go of callings that fall apart because of "what we have done and by what we had left undone," as some Christians say in the Church's prayer of confession. Confession makes space for sorrow over our failure to love God and our neighbors as ourselves. The only authentic response is a healing of hearts. Healing includes the difficult step (absent from some of the memoirs but there between the lines) of going to those wronged by our actions to admit our mistakes. Forgiving others (or being forgiven), a good friend has reminded me, requires empathy and compassion for everyone involved, a realistic assessment and humility about faults, and gratitude for the gift of mercy when offered. In the Jewish tradition, if we confess once, twice, three times, the other person is obliged to grant absolution.

I'm not just talking about being forgiven by others, however, but also about forgiving ourselves. We speak often about forgiving others, but what seems to have been forgotten is how to forgive ourselves. We don't talk enough about self-forgiveness, especially when it comes to fractured callings. Forgiveness is necessary, as Patchett qualifies, "not so much because we've done wrong as because we feel we need to be forgiven."[46] Amending fractured callings requires reprieve and affirmation; other people (and God) help release us from dwelling on our limitations and accept us for who we are.

Restrain Judgment

I return to an essential point that I labored to make as I began: We need to acknowledge the complicated nature of fractured callings *and* to refrain from knee-jerk judgment of others and ourselves. In many cases, we're not sure how we landed where we landed, but here we are, despite our intentions. We "don't understand our actions," to paraphrase Paul. "I find it to be a law that when I want to do what is good," he says, "evil lies close at hand" (Rom. 6:21). He's not saying he's evil. No, evil just lies close by. For all of us.

When Olive asks Jack why their kids don't like them, he proposes, "You were a crummy mother? Who knows." And perhaps to make her feel better he adds, "He could have just been born that way too."⁴⁷ Who really knows? And why did living side by side with Henry bring a "kind of hard-heartedness," Olive wonders, leading her to repel his affection as he grew needier? "But why? What crime had he been committing, except to ask for her love?"⁴⁸ Why did Patchett marry when she knew she and her husband weren't happy, people frequently ask her? All she can say is "I didn't know how not to."⁴⁹ The momentum of a two-and-half-year relationship? The difficulties and unknowns of extricating herself? Fatigue? Indecision? Public shame? All of the above and more. At some point, we just need to say we don't know.

Those who beat the odds and sail through their callings—stay happily married, make it through college, avoid job disruptions, drugs, and whatever else brings us down—should refrain from judgment. "There can be something cruel about people who have had good fortune. They equate it with personal goodness," observes Patchett.⁵⁰ But the happily married do not stand on higher ground. Neither do those who manage to avoid substance abuse or any other stumbling block that has damaging consequences for our callings. "Luck is a greater factor," insists the protagonist in Alice Elliott Dark's novel *Fellowship Point*, "than anyone who succeeds even wants to admit."⁵¹ As Patchett argues, the "marriages and divorces of other people are deeply private things. Both the successes and the failures are based on an unfathomable chemistry and history that an outsider has no access to." The same could be said about other disappointments and accomplishments. After her own divorce, she "made it a point to wish every marriage well, and to feel a moment of sorrow for any divorce, and that was all."⁵² End of discussion. We would do well to follow her advice in responding to fractured callings.

Plus, you never know. So-called failures may be the best thing that ever happened. It would be simplistic and silly to say people are happier after being broken. But many people who have flunked out; married for the wrong reasons; left religious orders; weathered mid-career job burnout; or survived divorce, addiction, and a myriad of other mishaps in pursuit of callings are better off in the long run. No one would wish fractured callings on anyone. Getting through them requires ruthless honesty, humility, and even humiliation. And confession and self-examination. But many people live to tell the story of a calling that has gone awry, acutely painful in the short run but amended over the long haul. Sometimes failure is the only way we learn. Sometimes mistakes offer a kind of grace.

Chapter 5

Unexpected Callings: With Great Power Comes Lots of *Work*

As I weighed my options, a bell at the Abbey Church began to toll, its heavy resonance marked more by the long lull between strikes than the peal itself. A group of twelve of us and a consultant were nearing the end of a five-day writing retreat, and I had little to show for our time together, despite wonderful colleagues and the tranquility of prairie, wetlands, and hardwood forest surrounding me on the campus of St. John's University. And I faced a dilemma: After dinner that night, we were supposed to share writing excerpts. What was I going to read? I hadn't written anything.

I'd been stumbling for a while, "stuck on the verge of a book for several years," as I wrote in my retreat proposal, but unable "to take the next step." I listed not one but four possible projects, including the book you're reading, and asked for help figuring out "where to put my energies" in the seven or so years remaining before I retired. It wasn't that I couldn't write or hadn't published, but I'd been distracted by many things. I had too much on my plate. *And* I felt the pressure of limited time, a perverse desire to do all four projects somehow keeping me from doing any one of them. So, I dithered over which project and how to start but hadn't written *anything* for the book you're holding. I'd come to the retreat for expert writing advice, but what I really needed was vocational counseling.

I churned with vocational questions. I was nearly in tears (okay, I *was* in tears) talking with a friend about my resistance to writing, my inability to sit still, and my confusion about which of the many demands and projects I should focus on for the last leg of my years teaching. So, I avoided the next step. I boiled water for tea, turned on music, hoping it would help, turned music off, hoping it would help, and made more tea.

You'd think I would've gotten past this uncertainty. After all, I have a *curriculum vitae* (the fancy academic word for what everyone else calls a *resume*), and it doesn't lack for accomplishments. You might think, "She's old(er)" (sixty marks the beginning of later adulthood in my mind, at least), and we expect older adults to have gotten their act together. It was ironic, even funny in my case: I'd set off to do a book on the hardships of calling, writing about the equivocations (everyone *else's*, of course), and here I was, equivocating about whether I was called to do this? Come on. God must have been laughing.

It was like being back in my twenties trying to figure out what I wanted to do with my life, but with two big exceptions: diminishing time *and* a pile of accumulated baggage (literally and figuratively). The reality of life's brevity and escalating demands as I advanced in my profession had only confused and overwhelmed me.

Then I heard the bell. The pause between its peals was poignant, clear, and a bit forlorn, leaving me listening for the next appeal to stop and remember. I knew from morning worship that an elderly monk who had devoted his life to the community had died. Halfway through morning prayer, I'd suddenly seen his body next to the altar. "Oh my God," I thought, "There's an open casket up there." Sleepily ensconced in my high-walled dark-wood pew in the last row of the apse, I hadn't noticed, even though we were reading from— duh—the Common for the Dead. Forever a low-church Protestant. I hadn't thought twice about it. Until that moment. Peering through the pews, I could see forehead, nose (a face?!), hands folded, a black Benedictine robe. *Now I was awake.*

The monk's body had come to rest at the heart of the sanctuary, soon to be carried by his Benedictine confrères across the campus to the cemetery overlooking Lake Sagatagan. The bell tolled for his life. And it reminded me of the limits of my own.

Maybe this is why I've been in turmoil about what to write, I thought—it's a foil for my real angst: that I and the ones I love are finite. Or maybe I should say this straight up: We die (flat out, not just pass away), and, with us, all our plans for tomorrow and the next day and the next day ad infinitum. I turned sixty this past fall, and I ponder life's endings more regularly these days in ways I couldn't anticipate at twenty-five. We're the walking dead, all of us, dying as we live or, as advocates of hospice like to say, living as we die. Consciousness of life's endings heightens pressure on how we use time, upping the ante on making good choices and living wisely into them. Vocation is all about time; it's about what we do with the gift of our lives in time. *Live well with the time you are given.* Now *that's* vocation. A genuine ultimatum.

The bell eventually stopped, but its questions rang on: Is this (this book or whatever else) my *joy*, my *talent*, my *service*—the vocational trinity? Is this what I love to do? Is this my gift? Will this matter to the world?[1] We *want* to *matter*. But now, as I entered my seventh decade, I had questions I never imagined in my twenties. Not just have I spent my life well, but two practical questions that stand at the heart of this chapter: How do I manage all the unexpected demands that have accrued as I pursued my callings, some of which I don't feel drawn to at all even if I'm well positioned and equipped? And how should I use the (possibly few) years that remain?

This chapter takes us back to where we began—the road not taken—but with the unexpected twist of time and detritus. As we age, we amass obligations that radiate out, like a pebble dropped into a pond casting ripples we didn't envision—aging parents, financially insecure adult children, rapidly growing grandchildren, hard-earned knowledge in our jobs and life needed by those around us. I have taught graduate school half my lifetime (that's a scary thought), and never did I foresee the pile up of obligations—former students and junior colleagues to protect and promote, curricula and disciplines to shore up, academic societies to tend and oversee, old obligations and friendships to sustain, new duties and friendships I have less energy to initiate, and a host of things I must now admit I'll never do, see, read, experience, and so on. I may just be in an acute phase, a subcategory of unexpected callings that might better be labeled *accumulated callings*. But even those less encumbered by jobs or family feel the weight of mounting entanglements as our callings evolve.

In fact, as I discovered as I worked on this chapter, unexpected callings can come at any stage of life and with greater trials than I face. There are two sorts of burdens—those that arise toward the end of a productive life of work and love and those that catch us by surprise at any time in the life cycle and are often imposed from the outside. I began this chapter thinking about the first category—the unexpected demands that had piled up for me because of callings I had pursued—but the chapter grew more serious as my understanding expanded to include more extreme examples of unexpected callings that can arise throughout life and are even more unchosen and unwanted. We fall ill; we divorce, remarry, and inherit children; a family member gets seriously ill and new expectations arise for us; or we experience any other misfortune, and our callings shift dramatically. I'll explore both sorts of unexpected callings and then spend the bulk of the chapter on dynamics they share and ways to live well amid the pressures.

In both cases, we must rise to meet demands that we haven't sought or desired but that have come our way nonetheless. Both types result from valuable attachments and commitments and dramatically impact close relationships. We agree to love this or that person, this or that community, and suddenly we find ourselves bearing duties we didn't count on. According to an expert who interviewed scores of people on vocation, caregiving of a spouse, child, parent, or friend over the long haul is *the* "hardest calling."[2] In short, unexpected callings come our way without our intent or full consent, arising in our peripheral vision, landing in our laps, or hitting us on the head when we least expect them. We don't plan for them so much as struggle to deal with them.

The Gift That Keeps on Giving

"With great power comes great responsibility," says Uncle Ben right before he is killed by a carjacker, never knowing the burden he has just laid on his Spider-Boy nephew or the hurdles yet to be faced by young Peter Parker struggling to discern what to do with his newfound abilities to sprout webbing and fly.[3] Uncle Ben recognizes that Peter is changing (and he doesn't know the half of it), becoming the "man he's going to become the rest of his life" (Spiderman), and warns him, "Just be careful what you change into. Just because you can beat [someone] up, doesn't give you the right to." I wish Uncle Ben had added, "With great power also comes *lots of work.*"

Ever since life cycle theorist Erik Erikson envisioned adulthood as a period of continued growth, psychologists have analyzed development over the full life course. But few explore accrued responsibilities and how they cling to us like ocean barnacles on a ship hull. To his credit, Erikson criticized the American optimism that views life as a "one-way street to never ending progress."[4] We must resolve one crisis after another, he argued, right up to the crisis of integrity versus despair in late adulthood.[5] He lauded the bountiful middle years of generativity (versus stagnation), producing and caring for what or who we create, but he didn't say much about the results of all this productivity—expanding obligations—or about how working and loving just begets more work and love. Maybe he was just too young, earning fame before he turned fifty. In a conversation in his eighties, he at least admitted that he had "lacked the capacity then to imagine himself as becoming old" or older.[6]

The older I get the more wary I've become of unexpected callings. Have I refrained, I wonder, from beginning another book because I know the work ahead in a way I never did before, down to the last damn copyediting detail and missing footnote? And then I'll have to publicize the book when I feel completely over it? And in my calling as mother, daughter, and spouse, I sometimes feel as if I'm waiting for the other shoe to drop. My parents are aging but not sick; my kids are fine but unmarried and without children. Are expectations of my parents' decline and expansion of family duties (grandchildren?)— events for which I want to be readily available—making it hard for me to engage the immediate tasks at hand?

As I now see, vocation is a gift that just keeps on giving. A journalist friend once wrote a story about a flood that caused major disruption in a West Coast metropolitan area, complicating its race and class politics. For years after, anytime a major anniversary of the flood or a new event like Hurricane Katrina occurred, media outlets asked him for comment, again and again, even though he had long moved on to other projects.

Academic life was less nerve-wracking once I earned tenure when I was thirty-seven, but never did I picture the growing range of responsibilities in the years to come—literally over the future of people's lives—*and* my own limitations. Several years ago, I acquired enough seniority to earn a place on the university's tenure and promotion committee, and, during one of those years, I also served as my professional school's faculty chair. I could hardly have held more (unpaid) positions of apparent influence and power, and yet I could not control long-established institutional patterns of sexism and racism that likely played a role in the tenure denial of three faculty colleagues (the only person who succeeded that year was a White male). Sitting with several colleagues in the school's refectory as the year ended, I bemoaned, "So much responsibility, so little power." An African American friend smiled at me, glanced at the other African American faculty around the table, and replied, "Welcome to *our* world."

Those in historically oppressed communities have a deep familiarity with the tensions of undesired (even if not wholly unexpected) callings. The phrase "lifting as we climb" captures the paradoxical posture. The National Association of Colored Women adopted the motto in 1896 under civil rights activist Mary Church Terrell's direction in response to the racism, sexism, segregation, and lynching that threatened Black people's lives, welfare, and right to vote. The image evokes the vocational tightrope of looking two ways at once—forward to secure a foothold for justice and backward to shore up those left behind. What a body maneuver, this posture of lifting *and* climbing, climbing *and* lifting. There is a real danger of getting derailed, pulled off balance, and dragged under. The weight can sometimes be deadening, perpetuating a distorted "Strong Black Woman" ideology so pervasive that many womanist pastoral theologians have analyzed and protested it.[7]

We assume power increases as responsibilities grow, but this isn't the case. Decline in influence amid expanding responsibility also characterizes parenting. With each graduation, from elementary to middle to high school, control over a child's playmates, homework, whereabouts, and future drops precipitously. Several years ago, a friend with grandchildren talked about the challenge of sustaining "emotional presence" across "geographical distance" with her two daughters and grandsons.[8] My kids were a decade younger and had not yet moved a two-day drive west. So, I didn't understand the problem. But now I do. Not too long ago, one of my sons spent time in Australia "couch surfing" and hitchhiking (I tried not to imagine the homes and car owners). During that same year, we didn't see our other two young adult sons or meet their girlfriends. And yet we still felt a visceral concern for their well-being, not to mention their cell phone bills, car insurance, and street savvy. And our worries paled next to those who endure far worse patterns of racism, sexism, heterosexism, ethnocentrism, and poverty that threaten their children's survival.

Older adults seldom dwell on the bizarre twists of calling when we talk with young people. Who would want to grow up and respond to a calling if we knew the clutter and exertion ahead? Maybe this explains our attraction to Peter Pan and his unencumbered Never Never Land. Sometimes I also wonder if the frenetic way my husband and I pursued multiple callings (full-time professions, shared parenting, shared housekeeping, etc.) sparked a vocational hesitancy in my own kids. Why would anyone aspire to this, especially the unforeseen ramifications?

To be clear: when I talk about all the work and increasing powerlessness, I am not complaining. Unexpected callings that come from accomplishments or love are not hardships in the same way as blocked or fractured callings. Like the cliché about birthdays as we age, unexpected callings of this sort are "better than the alternative." They grow out of invaluable attachments and commitments, and they can have lasting and gratifying rewards. They are more like what a British theologian calls "overwhelmings," unanticipated occurrences and expectations that are awesome *and* awful all at once.[9] They rain down and threaten to suffocate *and* enlighten us. It's more a matter of keeping up with competing goods than dealing with something bad. But unexpected callings can still feel onerous and taxing because they test our ability to sustain patience, sanity, and grace before escalating obligations; they require endurance; and they have a strong undertow of resistance, frustration, and exhaustion. We can rise to the occasion. Or not. And it's tempting to turn away.

Burdens of a Second Type

"You've led me to do this?" a friend exclaimed recently, talking about God's call and her own internal thoughts as she dealt with the frustration of caring for an aging mother-in-law who had lived longer than predicted and whose care restrained travel, work, weekends, and dinner plans. "Surely, I'm not called to do this!" another friend remarked when she inherited domestic responsibilities for her husband's children. Stepparenting is a quintessential example of an unexpected calling that can come at any time in adulthood. "For many of us," asserts practical theologian and stepmother Dorothy Bass, "it's the hardest thing we've ever done," loaded with minefields, leaving no one in the extended family unscathed or unchanged.[10]

Less frustrating but no less worrisome is the doctoral graduate who took a parish position he never desired when teaching opportunities dried up, just one among many people forced to take jobs to support themselves and their families, unexpected callings to which they feel obliged more than called. One of my colleagues ended up in a career that he didn't intend when his wife died, and he lost their shared calling in overseas ministry. Bereavement of loved ones, especially children, whether in war, drug-related accidents, or other tragedies, throws many mothers into advocacy work they didn't predict. Chronic, debilitating illness also pushes people into unexpected callings. A colleague has spoken poignantly about the bewildering callings caused by Parkinson's. Suddenly, "the world changed, as did my imagined future," writes Allan Cole when a neurologist told him, "I think you are in the early stages of Parkinson's."[11] A social work professor and father of two teenage girls, he was only forty-eight when he heard the news.

Unexpected callings also take us by surprise in our childhood years even if we don't grasp their fuller impact until much later. Two members in a small group on calling shared memories of life-changing demands that arose when they were young. One person spoke about her mother's chronic illness and death, the emotional toll, and the radical reorientation in family roles and workload: cleaning, shopping, cooking, and managing the home. Another explained how the daily efforts to care for a significantly disabled sibling had stretched him and his family, reshaping his personality and career choices.

Sometimes we only grasp the full vocational impact of unforeseen events in retrospect. It took the prodding of a psychologist father-in-law to awaken celebrated filmmaker Ken Burns. When the father-in-law asked, "Who do you think [you're] really trying to wake up?," Burns suddenly realized his abiding investment in historical documentaries—his effort to "wake the dead"—had a great deal to do with his mother's death when he was eleven.[12]

Karen Scheib, a pastoral theologian familiar with the formative influence of childhood narratives, describes how her adolescence and early sense of calling were subverted by care for a mother with an aggressive form of multiple sclerosis, diagnosed when Scheib was only fourteen.[13] Only twenty-five years after her mother's death did she grasp how her mother's ten-year struggle with the disease had played out across her life. Her stepsister sent a box of her mother's personal writing after Scheib's father died. Reading through the yellowed pages, which included her mother's reflections the day she received her diagnosis, Scheib not only gained a richer sense of what her mother had gone through; she also understood her own life trajectory anew—why she had struggled to care for herself through a failed pastorate and marriage, why she pursued a doctorate, and how all this led to midlife burnout and depression. "As I look back on this now, many years later, I am quite convinced that my mother's illness was a significant factor in forming my call."[14]

Expect the Unexpected

I'm not surprised *What to Expect when You're Expecting* has been a bestseller for decades, with its bold promise of dispelling the mysteries of pregnancy. The book served my generation well, and its fifth edition now graces the tabletops of our kids. Who wouldn't want to know *exactly* what to expect? However, I'm afraid the title promises more than it can deliver. The book would sell far fewer copies if it broadcast a more honest appraisal: *Expect the unexpected.* Especially when it comes to calling.

That you never get the child you expect (even if you read the book) is true at a fundamental level. Parents can "decide to conceive 'a' child," as moral theologian Roger Burggraeve observes, "but they can never decide to conceive of 'this' child, the real child as it appears. This unique child escapes their power of decision."[15] And it is *this* child whom they must love regardless of temperament, fit, or circumstance.

Just as children escape the power of our decision, so also do our callings. New parents can't imagine the lifetime commitment they have just birthed (and who in their right mind would want to set them straight?). Nor do most of us anticipate the vocational demands to which we consent when we take up a calling or have a calling foisted upon us. In some cases, I doubt we would accept had we been forewarned. Years ago, when our first son was two, we befriended parents down the street with a toddler the same age who died from brain cancer shortly after we met, a loss that felt utterly unimaginable. Before our first son was born, my younger brother and wife lost their otherwise healthy, nine-pound infant to a heart defect a few days after birth; they suffered greatly in the aftermath. A close family friend has a son who had a benign cyst removed from his spine when he was ten that left him a paraplegic. His parents have devoted themselves to his well-being in the decades since in ways they could never have foreseen. All three families have had to rise to curveball callings that changed their lives forever.

The fact is: We harbor a false assumption that at some point we'll arrive. We'll settle, once and for all, questions that seem so open-ended in early adulthood. But, as unsettling as it may be to hear, the question of what to do with your life is never fully resolved. Calling is more about constantly readjusting to life's shifting boundaries than arriving at some permanent pinnacle. Having to clean, feed, and grieve a mother while still a child goes against what we expect from children, and mourning the death of a child is beyond the pale of any parent's imagining. But calls that we do not desire and cannot predict come along anyway and tax our vocational capacities.

All told, it's not surprising that popular literature ignores unexpected callings. They aren't usually happy occasions, at least on first blush. They demand a difficult extension of self, and they send ripple effects across our lives.

Living with Mediocrity and Regular Triage

One good way to live amid unexpected callings that threaten to engulf us, especially chosen callings whose claims have expanded enormously over the years, is to lower our expectations. Novelist and essayist Barbara Kingsolver captures with whimsy her adjusted disposition in the crossfire of overwhelming obligations: "I'd like to think it's okay to do a lot of different kinds of things, even if we're not operating at genius level in every case."[16] Her comment reflects two related insights that I've touched on when exploring missed, fractured, and conflicted callings.

First, *live with a little mediocrity*. Okay, pursuing mediocrity isn't advice you'd give to a first grader or college freshman. But it's important for those overachievers out there (and sitting right here). I've seen the faces of doctoral graduates and new faculty light up with relief when I tell them it's okay to shift energy over time from research to teaching to administration rather than trying to excel in all three areas at once. The strategy of shifting your focus over time applies to other jobs, even if the specifics differ. I've seen the same relieved expression when I tell parents about *good-enough parenting*, a phrase pediatrician D. W. Winnicott used for parenting that doesn't strive for perfection but, instead, settles for the middle ground between the extremes of anxiously overindulging children (meeting every need immediately) and extreme neglect (disregarding needs selfishly and harmfully).[17] This good-enough middle ground is wide and deep. There are many right ways to respond to children, few reactions (short of either extreme) do permanent harm, and kids are amazingly resilient.

Even more reassuring is psychoanalyst Heinz Kohut's idea that nontraumatic parental mistakes or "failures" are essential to a child's (and a client's) growth. Parents inevitably fail to meet every need, whether for food or emotional reassurance, and, when they fail, the child must find a way to meet the need, creating what Kohut describes as internal structures of solace, self-esteem, and empathy. You can't avoid failure; you can only understand and extend compassion toward yourself and your children (or client) when it happens; indeed, we humans grow precisely as a result of failure. Kohut's examples demonstrate his clinical knack here. We witness how he unpacks his empathic failures with clients and how this understanding becomes *the* most significant moment in their healing and growth. He admits his mistake, how he misunderstood the client by something he did or said or didn't do or say, and then he explores why the failure, what he calls "optimal frustration," was so consequential, how it reminds clients of earlier childhood wounds to which they need to return to recover. "Small-scale, temporary empathic failure," when comprehended and processed, he argues, leads to recovery from early losses and resilience for losses to come.[18]

Second, *sustain practices of discernment*. With unexpected callings, discernment requires asking not only about what brings consolation and desolation, happiness and sadness (as we explored in the chapter on missed callings[19]), but also about what needs are most pressing. What can only be done *now*? What can be postponed or left behind with the least consequence? And what am I most called to do (or what is God calling me to do) at this moment or this point in my life? The medical term *triage* is fitting here: assign degrees of urgency to the incoming calls and live with the fallout.

During the first seven years of my career when I had three kids under five and needed to earn tenure, my teaching was average at best, my institutional service minimal (a generous faculty neighbor told me which nonessential events I could skip), and I included care of kids on my annual faculty report as a civic contribution (a small effort to raise the value of parenting). I had to "publish or perish," so I focused on writing. After I earned tenure, the balance shifted, and I devoted more attention to teaching. In my later years, I paid my dues in administrative service: chairing searches, curricular reviews, and planning grants; leading academic societies, program units, and all that. Like Kingsolver, I'd like to think that having pressing obligations beyond my kids didn't hurt them and maybe even helped them acquire their own resources for self-sustenance, so long as I hit the wide-open space between neglect and overindulgence. In the best of all worlds, living lightly with limitations becomes easier with the passing years.

Is *Duty* a New Four-Letter Word?

Over the past few summers, a pair of swallows have mistaken the pillared portico outside our front door for a barn loft. *Talk about lots of work.* Nearly every time my husband and I pass the front door, we look up through the transom to see if a bird is perched on their mud-and-grass home. And they are inevitably and endlessly there, taking turns for two to three weeks of 24/7 nesting.

And nesting is only half the story. Once the chicks hatch, the real work begins. From dawn to dusk, the babies stretch their tiny heads and white-edged beaks upward, and the parents deliver again and again and again. All day long. For another two to four weeks. And I now grasp the full meaning of "fouling one's own nest." The parents tote away "60–70 bundles a day of fecal sacs"—a polite website term for the poop bag excreted after nearly every feeding. "Usually both parents help with this task."[20] Seems fair enough to me.

I doubt these unassuming birds feel a sense of shared responsibility as we envision it, but something interesting is going on.

Although I'm sure I'm anthropomorphizing and projecting, I see in these dedicated deep-blue swallows qualities needed to survive and thrive amid unexpected callings: patience, endurance, moderation (sometimes the adults soar and leave the eggs and chicks unattended), sacrifice, and gratitude (how can you not see joy in a fork-tailed swallow's swoop?).

We can't always tell who's doing all the work. Swallows from nests across the street glide through our portico and join in the tending and providing. According to the Cornell Lab of Ornithology, even fledglings have a sense of group obligation. Young teens from one round of nesting often hang around and help with the feeding of the next. "These 'helpers at the nest' are usually older siblings from previous clutches, but unrelated juveniles may help as well."[21]

One day last summer, we watched as adult birds coaxed a reluctant neophyte. Its siblings had flown the coop two days before, and the chick sat alone. After nearly two months of nesting, nonstop feeding, and cleaning, we figured the parents were ready to boot this little guy out. Darting, swooping, tempting, and teasing, never delivering the expected food, they invited takeoff—in good-enough-parenting fashion. Finally, the chick took a precarious step over, flew-fell, dropped, and then caught and teetered on the front railing. Launched!

If swallows can tell us a thing or two about challenging callings, so can the zookeepers that we met in the opening chapter—from the article by business professors Stuart Bunderson and Jeffery Thompson that planted a seed for this book.[22] As part of their research on paid work as a calling, they wanted to know why people persevere in unpleasant jobs and decided zookeepers would be a good population to study. They discovered that zookeepers seldom talk about following their bliss, although they do express deep love for and desire to be with animals. Instead, they use what Bunderson and Thompson name "neoclassical" words like *duty, obligation,* and *responsibility,* reminiscent of classical views among sixteenth-century Reformers. There is nothing romantic or directly gratifying about the work, the zookeepers make clear. We are simply "responsible for that [which] we have obtained," one zookeeper said point blank. "That's kind of how I look at it. We obtained these animals... I mean they have no other choice.... They're stuck here. So I have to do what's best for them."[23] As Bunderson and Thompson surmise, quoting Max Weber, the sociologist well known for his hypothesis about the Protestant work ethic behind modern capitalism, a sense of duty still "prowls about in our lives like the ghost of dead religious beliefs," even though the zookeepers may not realize it.[24]

When we talk about following a calling, we often avoid weighty words like *duty, obligation, burden, accountability, restraint,* and *liability*. But these "dead beliefs" are more integrally linked to calling than we realize, especially when we understand the original context of the word within Christian history. Contrary to popular portraits, the longer history and even the everyday thesaurus connect *calling* to *responsibility* as a central synonym.

We might gain a better grasp of the connections if we had a fuller understanding of the term *responsibility*. Mid-twentieth-century Christian ethicist H. Richard Niebuhr designed an entire moral system around the word. He questioned two dominant forms of moral thinking—one based on telos or pursuit of higher aims or ends (doing something because of the good it produces for the individual or society) and the other based on law (doing something not because of an end goal but simply because it's right, such as following the Ten Commandments or the Golden Rule). Niebuhr saw both approaches to moral decision-making as too individualistic, abstract, and ahistorical. He argued instead that moral action based on the idea of responsibility has a more concrete, contextual, and relational dynamic. He imagined responsibility like my pebble in the pond—as having several reverberating concentric circles that begin with our action in response to other people's actions and that depend on how we interpret and respond to these actions within the extended community of actors that surrounds all this, including forces beyond our own lives and, for religiously committed persons, God's own influence.[25]

Writing around the same time, Erikson also favored the word *responsibility* but gave it a psychological spin. He saw the primary task in late adulthood as embracing one's life as "one's own responsibility" in *this* time and *this* place regardless of our history or circumstances.[26] Aging adults must either come to terms with the "one and only life" they have lived "as something that had to be" or suffer remorse, regret, disgust, and depression.[27] Those who successfully navigate this late-life crisis of integrity versus despair acquire the virtue or ego strength of wisdom, which he defined as "detached concern with life itself, in the face of death itself,"[28] an attitude upheld by many religious traditions of loving deeply while also letting go. Although Erikson thought *integrity* lacked "clear definition," his use of the word implies a clarity of purpose or being fully oneself amid life's many tasks and challenges.[29]

Author and activist Rebecca Solnit's appreciation for the life of George Orwell led her to propose a helpful definition of integrity. By reading his lesser-known essays and field trips to his cottage in a rural English village, she discovered a man of immense integrity who tended trees and roses, unbeknown to most people, who only know him as a pessimistic critic of totalitarianism. "The word *integrity*," she concludes, "means moral consistency and commitment, but it also means something whole and unbroken, uninjured, and it's a quality found in many beautiful things."[30] Orwell's love for flowers and his political engagement may seem discontinuous, but, Solnit argues, they are actually two sides of the same coin. Integrity's opposite, she suggests, is not so much despair as disintegration and corruption.

Ken Burns gave a more colloquial portrait of integrity when he addressed college graduates: You must ask yourself who you are "over and over again, unflinchingly" because "inevitable snags will arise [and] nothing is handed to you."[31] But if you "persevere . . . in that effort, in that work," you will find "salvation." As Erikson concludes, "If there is any responsibility in the cycle of life, it must be that one generation owes to the next" this kind of strength. Even though he's talking about demands in life's final stage, his thoughts on integrity and acceptance of one's own life "as something that had to be" also apply to unexpected callings that are foisted upon us at any time over the life cycle and the reception they demand.[32]

Drawing on Niebuhr, Erikson, and Solnit, and of course the swallows and zookeepers, we might say that unexpected callings take many forms, but they all concern responsibility—our response-*ability*. Instead of asking "What rule should I follow?" or "What is my goal?" when callings threaten to overwhelm us, Niebuhr advises us to ask, "To whom or what am I responsible and in what community of interaction am I myself?" What is a "fitting response" to this mess before me?[33] Seek to be what Niebuhr calls a "responsible self" within the reverberating ripples in the pond.

Service, Sacrifice, and Grace

Now we've reached the heart of the matter: People have described calling as evolving out of the intersection of three elements—what brings us joy, what talents or gifts we possess, and what the world needs. But dealing with unexpected callings requires more than discerning our *desire* or *talent*, two aspects that receive so much popular attention. Instead, unexpected callings invite us to turn to the neglected third category—*service*. Callings to service lie farther outside our orbit of control than desire and talent. They're sometimes the *opposite* of what we want to do (our passions and desire) or what we're good at (our talents and gifts).

A *service orientation* isn't our usual go-to idea. *Self-care* is today's buzzword. The first question students ask when I teach pastoral care is not "how can I become a better listener?" but more often "what about self-care?" They're justifiably worried about being exploited by the demands of ministry and the constant need to care for others at their own expense. This is a viable concern for ministers, women, the minoritized, and all those socialized to give endlessly of themselves. But the fixation on self-care is often misplaced, not only for people entering service professions but also for all adults who inevitably accrue responsibilities. As we age (*and* at any age) we gain commitments by default, through the sheer act of living, and we find that we owe something to others from what we've gained, learned, or acquired and because of where we have landed or what has struck us. We can receive this accrual with frustration, discouragement, and bitterness. Or we can find ways to respond in service and gratitude.

Many people exemplify the miracle and mystery of bending unexpected callings into arcs of service. "Stepmothering is not a role I ever imagined," Dorothy Bass says, until she remarried and fell into it.[34] But she found a way to transform the unanticipated work into a calling. In speaking honestly of her failures, jealousies, hurts, and fears, her aim is not simply to heal herself but to help other stepmothers be gentle with themselves and those they love, perhaps thereby avoiding pitfalls and temptations that besiege those who find themselves in unexpected family arrangements. For her, *role* isn't exactly the right word for the complicated and frequently disdained position that she occupies. Instead, she refashions the task as a *calling*, one that has given her purpose and put her in "a place of responsibility," certainly toward her stepdaughter but also toward her husband, her own children, her stepdaughter's mother, and the wider world of stepmothering.[35]

When Allen Cole learned about his Parkinson's, he thought his "life was essentially over."[36] For months, he was unable to tell anyone except his wife. But slowly, with lots of internal work (work he thought he had already accomplished), he used his distress, anxiety, shame, and physical limitation as a foundation for a new mission or calling. Parkinson's became his teacher, and he began sharing what he was learning in advocacy groups, blogs, and books, taking up the mantle of service. Like Bass, Cole writes because it helps him heal *and* because he hopes to help others. He hopes the intimate account of his journey and the way he has lived amid confusing new trials provides testimony to his two daughters that "from personal hardships, whether our own or others', we can learn some of life's most important lessons."[37]

Of course, we should be cautious about justifying arduous callings by saying that suffering and sacrifice make us stronger. This truism has done its fair share of damage. A powerful stream in the Christian tradition has idealized sacrificial love, portraying self-love as prideful or selfish and even suggesting that genuine love of others excludes self-love. These views have had especially damaging consequences for women and those in oppressed communities already at risk for subservience and abuse. If anything, many of us don't love ourselves enough. And "lack of proper self-love can get in the way of loving others and God," Karen Scheib argues. Caring for oneself, as she discovered in her journey, is part of caring for others, *not* opposed to it. In reconceiving her call to ministry several decades after her mother died, she revised her mistaken childhood notion (and truncated Christian assumption) that to save her mother she had to sacrifice herself. "I am pretty sure," she realizes after decades of theological study and personal therapy, "that the biblical text does not place love of God, self, and other in hierarchal arrangement." In fact, as she concludes, "we cannot love God properly if we don't love ourselves."[38]

Indeed, the Golden Rule to love your neighbor as yourself suggests a deep interconnection between love of self and others. Too many people envision love along the lines of Shel Silverstein's popular *The Giving Tree*, in which the central character ends up a stump upon which others sit. We're better off heeding the advice of flight attendants who tell passengers to "put on your own oxygen masks before trying to help the child or dependent next to you." If you can't breathe, you can't help your neighbor. Some of Bunderson and Thompson's zookeepers were vigilant about refusing to let their deep commitment to animals be exploited by the administration, recognizing that their dedication could sometimes obscure their need to protect themselves. Orwell's turn to gardening after fighting in the Spanish Civil War didn't signal an escape or distraction, Solnit argues, but a pursuit of beauty in the world around us as a worthy end in itself, putting a lie to the myth that "there's real work and everything else is self-indulgence or distraction or triviality."[39]

There is still no denying the tension at the heart of unexpected callings. His diagnosis, Cole discloses, "has broken my heart and opened it, taxed my mind and freed it, and bound me to a new kind of life, one full of anticipated limitations *and* unanticipated meaning and joy."[40] Meaningful work, Bunderson and Thompson conclude, is "painfully double-edged." Callings are beautiful and costly at once, bringing joy and meaning while also entailing hardships of "duty, sacrifice, and vigilance."[41] They require, for zookeepers at least, sacrifice of "money, time, and physical comfort or well-being" and even vulnerability to "potential exploitation."[42] Realistically, for the editors of a collection of readings on calling, a "responsible choice" toward a demanding calling often "entails the sacrifice of some personal goods for the sake of a larger public good."[43] In short, contrary to assumptions that callings always entail personal satisfaction (twelve steps to "your personal renaissance," as a contemporary book on "finding your true calling" is titled[44]), callings come with a price. "Balance is not the point," the editors say.[45]

To be clear: In weighing the demands of unexpected callings, it's worth asking yourself some hard questions. The sacrifices should be chosen and motivated by love, not forced or involuntary. They should give life rather than stifle it, bring joy rather than bitterness, and deepen the intrinsic worth of the one who sacrifices rather than tear a person down. These are critical distinctions to make when assessing unexpected callings. In essence: *Are they life-giving?*[46]

Even more important, acts of service and sacrifice should stand within a wider ecology of justice, shared responsibility, and mutual love. At the top of Cole's list of gifts that have made it possible for him to survive are family and work relationships, new friendships, and supportive Parkinson's companions. A loyal spouse and caring networks also run like a through line in Bass's narrative. Her story begins in a remote retreat village in the Cascades, returns to the mountain community for spiritual sustenance, and stops occasionally in their Midwest hometown where stepfamily neighbors pitch in, a summer theater allows her stepdaughter to shine, and her mother helps with her infant twins so Bass has space to be with her emotionally vulnerable stepdaughter.

Bass is also explicit about the necessity of grace that comes from outside her, from a God whose love is stronger than the deeper wounds and little annoyances, from the ultimate responder in Niebuhr's circle of response. God's grace, she says, is the "wellspring" from which springs the compassion, generosity, and hope that make it possible for her to disrupt the "tit for tat" of life, the "zero-sum economics" of love.[47] Scheib is just as adamant about grace as the ground and outer circle. Contrary to self-realization psychologies that stand behind so much literature on calling, happiness and human flourishing don't come from our own individual effort, Scheib believes, but flow out of a *"dwelling and growing in love of God, self, and other."*[48]

All these folks inspire us to pursue our callings wisely amid adverse circumstances, even if we might not be able to rise to the occasion in the way they have. They also demonstrate that cultivating wisdom doesn't happen overnight. It may not be obvious in my retelling, but each person worked hard under difficult circumstances to adjust to unwanted callings. Doing so takes time, practice, self-examination, patience with failure, and forgiveness from others. Only in looking back does Bass see a change in herself; now, she realizes, "a generous response... and a sense of gratitude is easier to summon" in fraught situations that would have set her off before.[49] It took Scheib years to understand the impact of caring for her mother, which had created an "inability to say no" that followed her into her fifties, even after she'd obtained outward signs of vocational success, such as university tenure. Flourishing is a "process, not a fixed state," she underscores.[50] Her desire to care for and save her mother "had turned into a need to care for and save the world." But she was able to revise her story, turning the unexpected calling "shaped by difficult and traumatic events" into a richer life.[51] She writes poignantly about her own process,

> I discovered that I can lose what is most dear to me and not be lost. ... I discovered that being human was enough, that I was enough. I now feel a sense of freedom and joy in my life that I am not sure I have ever felt before. I can now say no, though I still feel the need to do so very politely. I rediscovered my creative abilities and returned to writing poetry, knitting, and other creative pursuits. I enjoy my teaching more now than I have in quite a while.[52]

Our stories of unexpected callings are always works in progress in other words, and, if we're fortunate, they are also littered with moments of grace and glimpses of mercy amid our struggles.

On Our Way

"What should I do?" I implored the writing consultant, seeing clearly that ruminating about my dad's death earlier that month wasn't working all that well in the chapter on blocked callings I envisioned. I had finally committed to working on the book you're holding and was back for a second workshop two years after the first, and I'd wrongly assumed that my problems were behind me just because I had resolved my earlier impasse of where to focus my energies. My dad had just died, and I decided to attend the writing week anyway without realizing how much dealing with his death would impede the writing of a coherent chapter. The consultant considered my distress and, instead of telling me how to get out of the bind (of my writing *and* my life), he simply said, "I think you should go for a walk." That wasn't exactly the advice I wanted to hear.

But, as the sun set later that day, I made my way through the woods, taking a back route through the wildlife preserve on the university campus. The path was barely trodden, overgrown with brambles, hidden under leaves. I couldn't get lost since I only had a short way to go, and I'd eventually bump into the lake in any case. But my shortcut was still unsettling *until* I realized that I simply had to follow the path as far as I could see and then the next leg would become clear. A case where it was more important to focus on the *trees, not* the forest.

With unexpected callings, staying the course may bring us home, tree by tree. By welcoming the hidden gifts, we can divert the fear and frustration of feeling lost and the resentment and fatigue before tasks and challenges we didn't anticipate. Even when the forest threatens to overwhelm us and the path ahead is unclear, we can navigate with grateful acceptance that we are on our way.

On the last day of the first workshop, about an hour and a half after the long slow peals of the Abbey bells announcing the morning funeral, I heard the bells ringing again. This time they came one peal rapidly and joyously after the other—ding, ding, ding, ding, ding, ding, ding. As the funeral procession to the graveyard and internment concluded, the bells celebrated a worthy life and dying as a final act of giving back. Maybe this is how we should receive the unexpected callings that come our way, I thought: with joy, remembrance, and humility before life's limits. A kind of giving back what we've been given.

When the bells finally fell silent, I was relieved. I could rest where I was and join friends for a walleye dinner at a local Minnesota supper club. Eating with friends and getting underway with the next small step in the rest of my life, however long it lasts, for whatever time I have, were bonus enough for one day.

Chapter 6

Relinquished Callings: Riding Off into the Sunset?

Thanks to my grandmother, who gave me novels and often had her nose in one, I've always loved reading. But in graduate school I acquired a serious book appetite, a greediness you might say, to have shelves laden with books like my professors and graduate housemates. By the time I earned my doctorate and a visiting professorship several years later, I'd become a book enthusiast by vocation. Over the next thirty-five years, I amassed over one thousand volumes in my school office alone and another five shelves at home, a book junkie in the academic consumer world.

What was I going to do with all these books as I looked toward retirement? A question I hadn't even thought about along the way. I began asking colleague after colleague what they had done. I got lots of advice, but my friends couldn't really resolve the problem because forsaking my books was all tangled up with a much bigger question: How was I going to relinquish a calling to teach and write that I'd devoted my life to? Books had been constitutive of my calling and my life for nearly a half-century. Popular advice about decluttering, such as organizing guru Marie Kondo's suggestion that we ask whether something "sparks joy,"[1] may prove effective for tossing an unstylish shirt or a dated college textbook, but it wasn't

Follow Your Bliss and Other Lies about Calling. Bonnie J. Miller-McLemore, Oxford University Press.
© Oxford University Press 2024. DOI: 10.1093/9780190084073.003.0007

going to help me figure out what to do with my books. And it certainly doesn't work as we relinquish callings that have grounded and given us great joy.

It's odd: We struggle (sometimes for years) to figure out what to do with our lives, and then we're called to relinquish what we've gained, whether in retirement or at any time of life. Indeed, as I discovered in working on this chapter, many people renounce significant callings at earlier stages, often under greater duress than those of us facing the conclusion of a meaningful career. Other chapters in this book are, in one way or another, about finding, following, and managing callings amid difficulties; it may seem strange to conclude a book focused on *how to follow a calling* with *how to give one up*. But the demand to relinquish our callings, if not along the way, then inevitably at life's end, makes this chapter not only essential but one of the most important. With relinquished callings, we have found a calling and committed ourselves to it, whether briefly or for years, and now we must give it up. Relinquished callings are one last reminder that we don't settle callings once and for all.

As with other chapters, I contemplated the best words to capture this challenge. The idea of *forsaken* callings arose (I have certainly felt at times as if I was forsaking my books, many of which were good friends). But forsaken seemed too dramatic; it captures what it feels like to give up a calling but only at its most extreme. To forsake means "to renounce or turn away from entirely."[2] *Renounced* callings also seemed forbidding and final, as if the calling was rejected as tainted or problematic. I finally landed on *relinquished* because it captures more gently the need to give up willingly and even generously, to let go without rejecting or harming, possibly with a benefit and even a blessing. Many of the words that came to mind as I thought about retirement started with *re*: relinquishment, renunciation, reorientation, *and* relief. Although a nice poetic touch, the alliteration wasn't completely accidental. The Latin prefix *re* means "again" or "again and again" in repetition (as in *retell*) or "back" or "backward motion" (as in *recall*). Relinquished callings, I realized, evoke a review and retelling of one's life, a going backward over life to go forward, a reversal and renewal of calling in a different form and direction. This chapter itself follows the movement of this prefix as it arises in retirement and other relinquished callings, making its way gradually from relinquishment and renunciation to reorientation and relief.

Retirement and Other Callings Let Go

When a colleague told me, "You talk about retirement a lot," she genuinely surprised me. I didn't realize how obsessed I'd been. But then I found a journal entry I wrote in my late fifties where I described myself as "hyper-conscious" about retiring. I pondered the timing; I watched senior scholars, admiring those who ended their careers graciously and questioning those who continued to dominate in conferences and meetings while junior colleagues sat in silence; and I talked with close friends about their own experiences. Why did they choose early or phased retirement? How did they get rid of books?

But still, I wasn't really prepared. I received a temporary reprieve—a two-year research appointment that allowed me to postpone emptying my office and avoid the word *retire*. I'm not sure why the word felt so off-putting. Some people can't wait to retire. They don't like their jobs, or they have physically detrimental or economically unsustainable work that anyone would be hard pressed to turn into a calling. And, I had to admit, I'd grown weary of many aspects of my own job. Yet, for those who experience paid employment as a calling, leaving behind a cherished role is difficult. My dean thought I'd know without a doubt, as her own mother had, when I was ready to vacate my faculty chair. But a sense of certainty eluded me.

The term *retirement* has received plenty of critique. I'm not alone in avoiding it. I noticed when Anthony Fauci announced his retirement after decades as top US infectious disease expert, he insisted he wasn't "retiring" at eighty-two; he was going to write his memoir and do other things. But isn't that retiring? Recently, tennis champion Serena Williams explained the dislike behind her ambivalence: Retiring doesn't "feel like a modern word." She stands among many athletes, like NFL star Tom Brady and NBA legend Michael Jordan, who staged comebacks. Maybe people dodge the word because it sounds as if we're going from doing something to doing nothing. Its synonyms like *cease to work, withdraw to rest*, or *take out of use* just don't capture what's happening. Or they capture the transition in a tainted way. Like riding off into the sunset.

If I'm honest, however, saying *I'm retired* bothered me at a deeper level. Is saying *I'm retired* almost like saying *I'm old*? Does it signal that I am moving one step closer to obsolescence (or death)? Is there something about the term that leads us (or, in all honesty, has led *me*) to discount people? Like their lives are over and done? No one says such things aloud (except about a cow put out to pasture or old codgers who refuse to step down). We prefer to make light of it, like the T-shirt that defines retirement as "1. not working from anywhere; 2. world's longest coffee break; 3. pure joy." Surely an exaggeration. If we're honest, there is something about retirement that signals life's downward turn. And I've known too many people who became seriously ill right after they retired—my predecessor at work, one of my close friends, the person whose office I inherited, and the list goes on. Even if we have the fortune of living another couple decades, we can't avoid recognizing that we're moving into a final phase, and if we have parents still living into their eighties and nineties, we have a picture of what this entails—bodily decline, pain, mental loss, crises, dependency, and, yes, an arduous ending, even under the best of circumstances. Who wants to think about that?

My husband Mark's retirement celebration two years ahead of mine provided an unhappy dress rehearsal. Here's how I handled it: I burst into tears on the car ride home. I hadn't expected that to happen. The celebration of his nearly twenty-five years as dean of a house of students attending a neighboring divinity school had been underwhelming, yes: slim attendance, key members of his wider constituency unaware and absent, his legacy only briefly acknowledged, a gift of an endowed scholarship that honored his name but gave him little to take home. Twenty-plus years of hard work feeling like a wash. Was it all for naught?

And there, perhaps, in these last thoughts lay the source of my distress: He had worked so hard for so long, sometimes sacrificing his own health and well-being, to build up the community; enhance the building; solicit contributions from elusive donors; win grants from foundations; recruit and welcome students and then resolve their conflicts and worries; haggle with local movers, shakers, and politicians who wanted more money in taxes or the land on which the building sat; and negotiate with a divinity school, university, and wider church uncomprehending of the contributions his recruitment and development made to their own welfare and survival. Neither his staff nor board members nor church authorities nor faculty colleagues knew as well as I did the anxieties he had harbored and allayed for over two decades about the survival of a beleaguered institution. There was no way a vegetable tray, homemade pie, and a few nice words could ever measure up. Even a slam-dunk festivity couldn't do that. And if he wanted that, he joked, he would have had to organize it himself.

These relinquished callings pale, however, next to more dire situations. Giving up a calling happens to all of us in late adulthood, but relinquished callings are not limited to retirement. Sometimes our bodies, our very physicality and aging, force relinquishment. When Rebecca Chopp announced she was stepping down from the chancellorship at the University of Denver "because of a 'complex neurological disorder'" (she waited until later to say Alzheimer's), it was a devastating announcement, especially for someone well known for her "stellar memory" and mind, as an article in the *Chronicle of Higher Education* stated. She'd hoped to serve five more years and then return to teaching as "a fitting cap to her career." Suddenly she had to relinquish this well-conceived plan. Once doctors confirmed her diagnosis and encouraged her to stop work to avoid stress and acceleration of the disease, she chose to step down in just three months. When the chair of the board pressured her to serve longer while they completed a search for her replacement, her answer was a firm no. "This has to be it," Chopp told the chair, not only for her sake but also to avoid putting the university at risk. The news seemed especially brutal. As the chair remarked, "For her to know that the way she is going to die, in all likelihood, is going to be by losing the thing that she has valued most her entire life just seemed like such a cruel, cruel twist of fate."[3]

Often, the most painful relinquishments happen in our relational callings to love and care for others. Years ago, a church friend shared with me that no one, including her family, friends, and the minister who visited her in the hospital, grasped the devastating impact of her miscarriage. The wider public has grown more sensitive to the loss of miscarriage, stillbirth, and abortion in the years since, but few people think about these losses as earth-shattering instances of relinquished calling, a calling to parenthood that has been accepted, embraced, and cherished only to be forfeited in the exact moment of exaltation. Suddenly, you are called away from what you wanted so much. To lose a pregnancy means "letting go of all the possibilities of that relationship and that baby," of a new role and identity, and of one's "self-concept as a mother," as a doctoral graduate told me. Pregnancy loss also requires grappling with fears about future steps in the "journey toward parenthood," a path that will always have roots in this first "painful letting go."[4]

Many couples run into life's limits at its beginning. After an ultrasound in the last week of the first trimester of a pregnancy, a close family friend and her husband learned about a chromosome abnormality. The doctors weren't sure but estimated the chances of disability as high. An amniocentesis confirmed the diagnosis but didn't prompt a spontaneous abortion. Ironically, right when the

US Supreme Court was revoking the right of women to determine their callings as parents, these two young adults bore the weight of a horrendous decision with significant ripple effects regardless of what they decided. Whether or not they went forward with the pregnancy, they would find themselves forsaking the child they had hoped for and adjusting to a dramatically different calling.

Memoirist Nadia Owusu gives one of the most graphic portraits of abandonment of a relational calling to care for a child and sibling I have ever encountered. She recounts the travail of her Armenian grandparents as they fled genocide in Turkey in 1915 to immigrate to the United States. They left—abandoned, deserted, forsook— her grandfather's sister Areka three times as they crossed the Syrian Desert: "She was left in the shade of a large rock, under a tree, and on a donkey," the last time in exchange for a goatskin of water. This sounds harsh without knowing the full context. Owusu heard multiple versions. In one, they were delirious from thirst; in another, they did not believe anyone would survive, and no one could stand to carry Areka, too weak to walk, to their death. In a final version, they couldn't suffer her pitiful cries for water, which also threatened the precious quiet required to keep them hidden under cover of darkness. Fortunately, each of her abandonments was reversed by her great-uncles "who could not bear to leave their little sister behind."[5] Choice surrounded my decision about when to retire, but many relinquished callings are forced upon us and might better be called *forsaken*.

Relinquishment and Lament

I don't want to exaggerate the anguish, but I don't want to undersell it either, and we often stray in the latter direction. We underestimate the turmoil of relinquishing a calling, and then we are surprised by it. Letting go of some of our most demanding callings—of paid work, for example, or of children as they go off to college—is wonderful. *In a way*. But to extoll the freedom too quickly bypasses intermediary steps of relinquishment and lament. Whenever we leave behind a calling—voluntarily or by force—something dire is happening: a rending, tearing, giving up. This entire book grapples with the precariousness of callings. But the vulnerability of giving up a calling is especially raw. Here, we come face to face with life's real (and sometimes final) limits.

Unfortunately, although lament seems appropriate as we relinquish callings, it has disappeared from our vocabularies and our understandings of calling.[6] Religion scholars Katie Billman and Daniel Migliore found a striking omission of lament in worshiping communities in their research. Over seventy percent of the psalms omitted from the *Lutheran Book of Worship*, for example, are lament psalms. A similar pattern of exclusion characterizes other books of worship. Amazingly enough, lament psalms are also "noticeably absent from many funeral liturgies." Consequently, we have worship services that are "unrelentingly positive in tone," Billman and Migliore conclude, and "we lose an essential resource in confronting the very emotions that terrify us, in a context where we might receive" help in admitting and coping with them.[7] We worry that lament borders on ungrateful complaint or selfish whining or resentment or lack of faith. They share story after story of people who needed space to lament over callings they've relinquished— people who have lost jobs in downsizing, those displaced by war and natural disasters, and a woman who wrote an entire book of lament psalms after her twenty-one-year-old son died tragically.[8] Those forced to relinquish jobs or forsake a call to parent face real duress. One man who lost his job "was so ashamed," Billman and Migliore observe, "he was afraid to walk in his neighborhood during the day for fear that people would start talking about him," making it almost impossible for him to "ask for help."[9]

We gain from Billman and Migliore's account a deeper understanding of the emotions that surround relinquished callings: anguish, betrayal, anger, protest, and grief. More profoundly, we gain a sense of why these feelings surface. Giving up callings hurts because it undermines the self at its most basic level. It means giving up so much of what we have hoped for, sometimes who we have been from birth. Relinquished callings also require giving up what we have secured through living, sometimes across our life span, and what so intricately comprises our personhood. We are vulnerable, transient creatures who pursue our callings amid so many possibilities for (and the certainty of) casualty. No wonder the word *forsaken* had come to mind.

Part of the challenge in relinquishing a calling to which we've devoted ourselves is a prevailing anxiety about the demise of what we have labored to build up. Mark worried that he was forsaking what he had advanced, *and* he felt forsaken by those who shared and in some ways controlled and stewarded his calling (e.g., his board, the wider denomination, the university divinity school). Even in an institution with a longer legacy, stronger board, and more promising future than the one Mark left, a colleague who recently retired still worried obsessively about several pending decisions, including what seemed like an ill-advised choice for her replacement. A friend who runs a large business told me recently he doesn't want to retire until he has accomplished everything in their five-year strategic plan (good luck with that). Another friend has valid fears she is leaving her workplace in worse shape than she anticipated when several searches floundered as she approached retirement. I spent a major portion of the last twenty-five years building a doctoral area and a program to transform how we educate seminary professors only to end my career watching both efforts dwindle in faculty, students, resources, and focus. Often enough, this kind of negative assessment is distorted by an overblown sense of our own importance. Seeing our workplace thrive without us is surely more gratifying, but oddly enough even success after we leave is a reminder that we are dispensable, replaceable, and quickly forgotten. The world moves on, and we cannot secure what we've accomplished.

People, institutions, and workplaces go on with business as usual. In my husband's last board meeting, members paused to note his retirement and then moved on immediately to discuss a new harassment policy. Talk about anticlimactic. And hurtful. He worried the effort to implement the new policy was an indirect criticism about a recent incident and what he'd failed to do himself. Sometimes people call up after we've departed, as happened for the head officer of a nonprofit, with a request for advice about finances and leadership that my friend needed to refrain from offering because of professional ethics and the possibility of interfering. Harder still and probably more common is when no one contacts us at all.

As we endure relinquished callings, we should refrain, in other words, from extolling the joy or advantages. There is an important place for lament, which differs from grief and bereavement in two interrelated ways. First, it has deep communal and historical roots. There is a long "trajectory of articulating human anguish" in the Jewish and Christian traditions, according to Old Testament expert Jonathan Parker, "one spoken particularly by Israel but universally evocative" and applicable to a "plurality of contexts."[10] From Hebrew lament psalms to their echo in Jesus's final utterance on the cross in two of the Synoptic Gospels, lament has a pivotal role, and this placement situates individual lament in political, historical, *and* spiritual solidarity with others. We owe it to scripture, Parker insists, "to see the anguish there for what it is because this pain is... an invitation for all humanity to hear themselves in the psalmist's suffering and then in Christ's."[11]

Second, and as important, lament is more complicated than grief; it is a compound sentiment with multiple qualities embedded within it. It recognizes the "challenge of the creaturely life" in Parker's words—our contingency, our transience, and our insignificance; it carries a sense of betrayal; it includes justified complaint and anger; and it rests on a bedrock of trust, promise, and recognition of our fleetingness and dependency on a kind of deliverance that can only come from outside ourselves. We cannot raise ourselves up from "dust," as the narrator concludes at the end of one of the most famous laments of forsakenness, Psalm 22 (v. 29); we can only receive the gift of life as something God has already "done" (v. 31).

Renunciation and Reorientation

To say it again, relinquishing callings requires review and retelling of our lives, a going backward over life to go forward, a reversal and renewal of calling in a different form and direction: what Franciscan author Richard Rohr calls "falling upward."[12] As the phrase implies, relinquished callings are counterintuitive. They're not easy; they're ass-backward.

But what does it mean to *fall upward*? The image suggests a giving up of self and possessions that, despite the loss, moves us forward. Influenced by psychologist Carl Jung's comparison of the life span to the rising and setting of the sun, Rohr divides life into two parts. We know about the first half. In fact, we live in a culture obsessed with "first-half-of-life" accomplishments. And with a few exceptions, discussions of calling focus right here—in figuring out what we want to do with our lives, establishing ourselves, our work, our friends, our home, our families. We put so much energy into "going up" that "going down" seems counterintuitive. We "fall into" going down, Rohr believes, through forces outside our first-half-of-life intent that upset and turn the trajectory—failure, loss, suffering, disease, or tragedy. "The supposed achievements of the first half of life have to fall apart and show themselves to be wanting," he suggests, for us to move on. And not everyone does. His riddle for the second-half-of-life journey: "*the way up is the way down*. Or, if you prefer, *the way down is the way up*."[13]

In one of the most fulsome treatments of calling in late adulthood, theologian Kathleen Cahalan invites us to embrace these kinds of reversals, especially the reversal of renunciation. She compares Rohr's basic premise to the Paschal Mystery—the "dying and rising to new life that marks the Christian life." The first part of life, you must "increase so that Christ may increase," she writes, "but the second half of the spiritual journey is relinquishing the self that we have constructed and shifts to the words of John the Baptist in John's Gospel, '*I must decrease so that Christ may increase*' ([John] 3:30)."[14]

The Bible is full of such reversals, big and small. I learned this forcefully on a one-hundred-day virtual retreat that coincidentally (*providentially* might be a better word) began the month I drew my last paycheck. The retreat, run by Cahalan and Catholic sister Margaret Funk, drew on the teachings of the early Christian desert fathers and moved through four renunciations—of our former way of life, our afflictions or temptations, our self-made concepts of God, and our self-made thoughts of ourselves.[15] In one ten-minute audio message, Funk listed the many reversals in the Gospel of Luke, who she called the "master of reversals"—Jesus born in a manger, shepherds and not kings, the little child as the greatest, and so on. At the time, I was working my way through Mark's Gospel as a daily prayer practice, and I could see where Luke got some of his reversals. The reversal or at least the sharp contrast in Mark 9 between quarreling and praying jumped out at me, perhaps because it touched an affliction or temptation about which I was becoming increasingly aware through the retreat—an insistence on my own way, a competitive argumentativeness that did me well in the lecture hall and academic conference but less so in my daily life. The chapter in Mark begins with the disciples arguing with the scribes over the healing of a child and ends with Jesus explaining to his disciples, who had failed to cure the child while bickering, "This kind cannot be driven out by anything but prayer" (v. 29). The inversion of quarreling and praying isn't obvious but struck me at the time; as I relinquish my calling, my way up is my way down, to let go of self-promoting habits that worked on the way up but less so now.

A related but more demanding and central Christian reversal comes a few verses later in Mark 9 when the disciples haggle again over who is the greatest, and Jesus repeats a message we hear elsewhere, "Whoever wants to be *first* must be *last* of all and servant of all" (v. 35). He likens the posture to taking a child up into your arms. Christian calling, it seems, is at its core a dramatic renunciation, a relinquished calling at its most extreme that prepares the way to assume another calling, that of discipleship and service.

A few days before I read this passage and around the time of my retirement, my second grandson was born. I visited a week later and lifted one-week-new-to-the-world Cade Anthony up into my arms. Here lay an ultimate life reversal, an infant who arrives with *nothing*, as I will leave this world. A tangible reminder and an amazing comfort to me. As I held his bare-skin beauty in my arms, I considered the reversals in my life, employed to unemployed, known to unknown, named chair to no chair, young to old. I fell upward. Or at least I felt reoriented.

In holding Cade (and thinking about reversals), I could hardly think of a better portrait of a central virtue that may spring up as we renounce callings, and one of the hardest to sustain: humility. Humility means knowing, admitting, and keeping in front of our face our own foibles and limits before judging the other, yourself, and the world. It requires getting the ego out of the way, as early psychoanalysts labeled it, or, as Cahalan says, a replacement of our afflicted inner chatter, our self-consciousness, with Christ consciousness. Or, as Funk and Cahalan suggest, building on the Benedictine practice of taking the middle way, humility means "having the right estimate of ourselves, not too high, not too low."

The virtue of humility is essential to navigating the demands of relinquished callings. The word shares with *humus* and *human* a closeness to earth, dirt, detritus—"one who is grounded or near to the earth," as a climate spokesperson observes.[16] She joins many environmental activists and novelists who have issued in recent years an even more powerful call to humility, insisting that humans are *not* the center of the universe. Nor are we the center of creation or salvation, according to ecological theologians, especially Native

American scholars and anyone listening to First Nations people. Remembering and knowing our place eases the way as we relinquish and renounce callings. At some strange point, we have to ask impossible but necessary questions: Does dying ever become a calling, a personal and even social calling? The ultimate relinquished calling? How does one die gracefully at the end of a life well lived?

As I made my way through the virtual retreat, a key insight—what should have been obvious to me all along, but I'd missed it—suddenly became clear. The Christian life and the academic life—and for that matter, a great number of professions and jobs to which we are called—do not cohere well. They even oppose one another in crucial ways. The academic life (and many other callings) pushes us to be first, top dog, highest earner, most celebrated, most productive, most published.[17] An inevitable pecking order even arises among those in monastic communities or religious nonprofits. But the Christian calling isn't about moving up or ahead, gaining notoriety, tenure, wealth, status, security, you name it. Far from it: it's about being last, being servant of all. The third-century hermits and ascetics knew the challenge of the Christian calling well, observes spiritual writer Henri Nouwen.[18] Like us, they also lived in a world where success was measured by "money, power, fame, success, influence, and good connections." This way of life, they saw, draws us into a self-perpetuating "spiral of . . . desire for more . . . in the illusion that one day we will arrive." But we never do except, as the desert mothers and fathers suggest, by cultivating practices that thwart compulsions that sustain this self-deception through an encounter with the God of love, a "long and often slow process," Nouwen reminds us, whose intent is not escaping the world but showing a way to liberate it. This is *so* hard to do.

Aging, retirement, and relinquishing a calling give us another chance. Our productivity in work and love, about which we are often so proud, "matter[s] less than we might think," as Trappist monk Thomas Merton once admitted in an imaginary conversation with Karl Barth. Of all the people we might assume would be saved by his productivity it's Barth, Merton reasons, an esteemed dogmatic theologian famous for his multivolume tome, *Church Dogmatics*. But as Merton, famous in his own right, concludes, "Your books (and mine) matter less than we might think"; they will not be the source of "our salvation," an incredibly humbling admission by someone equally esteemed for his impressive literary and spiritual legacy. Instead, Merton suggests, "Trust in Divine mercy," the redemptive spirit that plays out in our lives in more hidden and mysterious ways, even despite ourselves.[19]

I am voicing here what one aging specialist calls the *countercultural role* or *prophetic vocation* that can arise when we reach later life and begin to see the relativity of our work. In aging, writes college chaplain David Maitland, "we have the opportunity to step outside the system by which we have been defined, to recognize, with candor but without bitterness, the provisional, sometimes even dishonest, character of its lures and rewards."[20] And here's something someone wiser should have told me earlier: "Contrary to often-heard religious exhortations on behalf of vocational intensity, the extent of one's diligence in work is often a subtle indicator of how remote one has become from one's calling by God." A great deal of my own busy work has genuinely been for naught, and even at times, done for the wrong purposes (e.g., accolades rather than the good of the world). We now have the capacity to tell those who come after us: Don't "absolutize" the work you do, do not be lured by its false promises. Or, as Maitland remarks: Beware of the "illusory and/or transient nature," the "meaninglessness" of "many of the things" to which you may be drawn to give your life.[21]

Foolish is our worldly wisdom—another reversal, this one in Paul's first letter to Corinth. The term *foolishness* appears five times in six verses "despite the fact that the term (literally 'moron') was as pejorative in Paul's time as it remains today," claims theologian Brian Brock.[22] Yet Paul insists it is what is weak and foolish in the world that saves us. Brocks knows this intimately as a father who has relinquished certain professional aspirations in order to learn from his eldest son, seventeen-year-old Adam, a child on the autism spectrum who has, to Brock's surprise, reoriented him to a different way of living—to wait for the slowest among us, the child and the less abled, what he describes as a "deep practice, one that takes a lifetime to master."[23] Here, quite simply, loss is gain.

Here's what relinquished callings tell us: Hold your calling lightly (as a child might or as you might hold a child). You will be asked to give it up.

Reorientation and Relief

The chair of the University of Denver's Board of Trustees characterized Chopp's Alzheimer's as a "cruel, cruel twist of fate" for someone who had so valued the life of the mind. But Chopp had "long cast her lot with the underdogs," observed a reporter with the *Chronicle of Higher Education*. So, it wasn't surprising that after announcing she was relinquishing her post, she became a spokesperson for early detection, education, and research on dementia, turning her illness into what she calls a "continuation of purpose." She still consults with college leaders, but she also started writing blog posts for Colorado's chapter of the Alzheimer's Association and doing informative videos. People didn't need to talk louder when addressing her, she told her audience, or turn to her husband instead. At least not yet. Her long years of service and leadership equipped her well for this kind of public speaking and advocacy. On the day of her diagnosis, her wise doctor advised, "live with joy" (maybe not the "pure joy" of the retirement T-shirt but good enough). In this endeavor, a supportive spouse remained crucial, accompanying her on her reinvention of a life that now includes time for rest and new adventures like a deep dive into oil painting that just might help "build new neural pathways."[24]

We may relinquish a calling to which we're dedicated, but we never relinquish the sense of ourselves as being called or, as religion professor Paul Wadell says, "as being summoned to find new opportunities to love God and neighbor." In this sense, "we are never *not called*." As he continues, "despite what society often suggests, retirement and old age are not principally a time of leisure, freedom and well-earned self-absorption, but a distinct stage in a life of discipleship in which we continue to be called to live for others."[25] Seeing this age through the "lens of vocation" allows us to redeem the pain of relinquishment, lament, and renunciation. And there is considerable continuity, education professors James Fisher and Henry Simmons suggest, for most people transitioning from middle to late adulthood. Cahalan found further studies that confirm this finding. We build on what came earlier, drawing on prior callings in new ways.[26]

I've been treating older adulthood as if it were one stage, but developmental psychologists now subdivide it into several because of increased life expectancy. Many people today have an extended post-middle-age adulthood (*late* adulthood) before a briefer period of decline, what one epidemiologist labels a "compression of morbidity" (*older* adulthood). That is, the "years of disability are growing shorter even as we live longer." The average person has a decade or more of healthy years after retirement and then spends only a half year to a year and a half in a special care facility at life's end.[27]

This change raises new challenges for calling that even our recent ancestors didn't experience. "People need to prepare for several periods of retirement, each with different goals and levels of autonomy," suggests Fisher. He describes the first of several phases as contiguous with middle age ("middle age sans work") but without the burden of time pressures. This period can last for a while but commonly ends with an event that forces a change, such as the "death of a spouse, the onset of ill-health, or the need to relocate."[28] But in the next phase many people continue to live independently until they enter a final and often briefer phase of acute dependence, frailty, and decline. It's sometimes simpler to think about two phases, the first allowing space to redirect or reinvent our callings and the second characterized by greater disruptions in health, independence, and yet another shift in the "continuation of purpose" that still includes meaningful, even if more limited, callings.[29] My ninety-five-year-old mother is in this phase. Her physical capacities—mobility, hearing, and so forth—have diminished, but she still invests considerable energy in her calling as a grandparent and great-grandparent and as a support person for an extensive network of other aging adults (I try not to worry when my mom's friends see her as their primary driver). In other words, those blessed with extra years after retiring get ample opportunity to turn relinquishment into reorientation.

Sometimes those facing chronic disease at an early age, like Tallu Schuyler Quinn, the older sister of one of my son's close friends, display the most exemplary resilience and reorientation. At age thirty-one, she grew a tiny upstart to a flourishing food ministry that disrupted food deserts and poverty in urban Nashville. Nine years later, when a rapidly spreading brain tumor forced her to relinquish this work, she transformed the diagnosis into a second ministry, writing and sharing her experience.[30] At her memorial service, people who spoke couldn't say enough about how she'd traversed the difficult path from a calling renounced to new life while dying.[31] Vocation, said one person, is so much more than "how we make our living, our professional life, our life's work." Rather, vocation is about "how our living makes us," and Tallu lived vibrantly. Her word for God, her "God-word," another person disclosed, was *bread*, baked and shared as a means for healing community, a word that also captures her calling. From her craft of papermaking arose another metaphor, calling as a *watermark*, the sign within the paper that we can't see but know is there. "There is something about imminent death or illness," she shared in a post, later collected into a book, "that allows us to let what's less important just fall away.... There is so much I have lost, but the falling away of what is worldly, painful, covetous—all of it—is better served cast-off, with new room for life, and life abundant."[32] She testified through her life the radicality of her own claim—how small, ordinary local action "can make a dent of a difference,"[33] doing more through incidental kindness in her forty-some years than many of us accomplish with several more decades.

There are also those at the front end of life who have acute experiences of dramatic reorientation when forced to give up a calling. When mother and author Laura Kelly Fanucci and her husband went to sleep late Saturday night after a C-section, their less-than-two-pound newborn twins Margaret Susan and Abigail Kathleen were fine, but by Sunday morning they were not. Laura and her husband faced the unimaginable trial of relinquishing two premature infants and their calling to parent them. They spent Sunday afternoon "holding Maggie as she died in our arms."[34] But when Monday morning came, and they were called to Abby's room and asked by the nurse if they wanted to hold her before disconnecting tubes, Fanucci broke down. No, she "wanted anything but this." The nurse gently encouraged them, and as Laura tells it, something entirely unexpected happened: as she felt the tiny hearts and lungs flutter against her own, "every last dredge of sadness left my body," and "everything turned inside out." Surely not the end of sorrow, but a transformation all the same. Her story makes no sense, she admits, but she felt called to recount for others what happened without sentimentalizing it: "Right inside what we expected to be the worst day of our lives, we were given the fullness of joy. That as we met death face-to-face, we found it to be life. That when we expected despair, we discovered nothing but love."

Just as I didn't want to undersell the lament earlier in this chapter, I don't want to oversell the joy, love, or relief here. But I do want to notice that sometimes relief and reorientation are possible. They can also come in midlife relinquishments. I lost track of Angela Denise Davis, someone with whom my husband Mark and I'd worked, until he opened his *Ukelele* magazine to her story of relinquishing one calling only to find a way back to another, one she had loved since childhood. People come to the ukulele, the magazine article begins, but few would want to follow Davis's path. An ordained minister and music educator, she had served as our school's admissions officer until her failing vision made the work impossible. She saw her admissions work "as a larger part of my ministry, and when I became blind," she said, "the bottom of my life fell out." The degenerative disease, later diagnosed as optic neuritis, "stopped her whole career."[35] But she went back for a second master's and began work as a vocational counselor for the blind, and as she helped people figure out their lives, she slowly found her own way. She'd always loved music but could no longer play piano. Inspired by a Yo-Yo Ma cello concert, she searched Google for the "easiest instrument to learn," and the ukulele popped up. She "has never looked back." The joy she found in playing the ukulele launched her into several new projects—a community teaching studio, arrangements of spirituals initially played at the bedside of her dying father, grants for a beginning course for LGBT adults and for a small ensemble. Listening to the racially and geographically diverse group learn to play classic spirituals humbled her. "It speaks to how you can put something into the world," she remarks, "but it's not yours alone—you need people to come help you with it. That's the hallmark of the ukulele: the way in which it builds community."[36]

Relief and Rest

One of the first exercises of the spiritual retreat that I began as I transitioned into retirement was to pick some small area of our lives to clean up and put into order as a symbolic and material gesture essential to the longer journey of renunciation. I chose my office books, a Herculean but still focused task. It took me several days to pack and label over thirty-five boxes for donation to three organizations with global outreach to places without ready access to books. I kept in mind a rubric from a friend ("Is the book a classic? Do I love it and reference it frequently? Or is it dear, signed, or written by a mentor or friend?").[37] But in the end, there were few social science or theology books I really wanted or needed anymore. Helped by a deeper call to renounce, I kept only an assorted mix, a book of poetry, another on prayer, several by my doctoral adviser, a few by friends, and one copy of each of my own publications with my scrawled markings. I mourned, but I also felt freed, released, relieved.

So, I've taken care of my books (well, most of them).

But now, what about my academic robe?!

The dark maroon gown with black velvet trim. The robe I first saw a college professor don as he processed into the chapel during opening convocation my freshman year, the professor who became my most admired mentor, and the robe that partly led me to aspire to graduate study with dreams of one day wearing one. *That* robe. The same one I have loved putting on each opening and closing ceremony as semesters begin and end, as students graduate and we celebrate them.

After retiring from the University of Notre Dame, psychologist Matt Bloom told me he didn't know what he should do with his robe, which felt emblematic of a huge amount of doctoral work and a productive career. His mother-in-law suggested cutting it up and turning it into a quilt, an interesting metaphor, I thought, for reorientation. He wore it one last time, he said, making a ritual performance of putting it on, taking it off, and giving it to her with his family surrounding him. She hasn't yet transformed it in a quilt, but that's almost beside the point.[38]

I've found what feels like a good solution for me: I hope to pass my robe on to another graduate from University of Chicago upon whose dissertation committee I sat (after I place a doctoral hood on one final advisee at commencement this spring, I hope). She'll be thrilled to have it, she said, and I'm looking forward to the moment, and even the comfort, of relinquishment. As English farmer James Rebanks said when he toured the farm with his father before he died, as his father turned the baton over to James, "handing on, rather than being sad, or an ending, or defeat, seemed to give him great comfort as he felt he had done what he had set out to do."[39]

Like any treasured possession that serves as an essential tool of a trade, my books and my robe have shaped me in deep ways. Belongings, whether books or other valued objects, often define our callings. They secure our place, our *belonging* in the world. So, giving up the stuff of calling is the underbelly of a more complicated emotional and spiritual task. The "taking apart of a library built up over years is particularly painful," admits historian Esther De Waal, "for here are books that have come to feel almost like an extension of my personality . . . like the loss of an old and cherished friend." Her experience of relinquishment reminded her "just how demanding is [the] attitude of non-possession" that St. Benedict advises. The warning in the Rule of St. Benedict—that possessiveness is "a deep fault line running through our lives"—is *not* a damning of material goods; our belongings are good.[40] This saying is only an invitation to hold our possessions with reverence *and* detachment, as gifts on loan, not acquisitions. As De Waal relinquished a home that had special meaning for her and her family, she went around the house and touched each object, saying, "not mine—only on loan, not mine," giving thanks and letting it go.

The year after I unloaded my office books, I couldn't quite squelch the fear that I had been too rash, keeping only a handful. I couldn't quit thinking about a friend who retired and kept all her books, shipping them from her Toronto office to her Wisconsin cabin. Why didn't I just do that, I asked myself? It helped to envision my books circulating around the world, of use to others. But I couldn't rid myself of this lingering feeling: Did I give away books that I might need or that might have helped me with this book?

Maybe, but I can say now, as I finish the book, that I have only missed a few; I loved drawing on a lifetime of acquired knowledge, of books and authors I already knew; and I found plenty of other ways to find out what I needed to know and to draw on new resources.

More important, as I learned as I wrote this chapter, there is a grace as well as immense gain, a relief, a freedom, and a moderated joy that comes with relinquishing our place and our most cherished goods. Now that I'm *almost* fully retired (there, I said it), I've joined a huge chorus of people lauding a life of a different sort and pace. Relief and rest may be the biggest gifts of this phase, as I tell people what's it's been like. I'm still doing many of the things I loved about my calling, including writing this book, but at a more benevolent tempo and without tasks and pressures I didn't enjoy. Even if a sense of certainty remained elusive initially, a deep gladness has emerged over time. Even if I gave away a few books I should have kept, who cares? There are public libraries and local bookstores that need support. I see the emptied shelves as clearing space for other callings, especially those that connect me to those I love. It's time to be as rash with my life as with my books, learning from people like Chopp, Fanucci, and Davis that giving away is the way to fall up. I'm not sure I'm falling upward, but I'm at least tilting in that direction.

ACKNOWLEDGMENTS

I am deeply grateful for the many people, institutions, and settings that have supported this work and want to thank:

- My colleagues in the Collegeville Institute Vocational Seminar for invaluable conversations (Matt Bloom, Jack Fortin, Joyce Ann Mercer, John Neafsey, Jane Patterson, Katherine Turpin); Project Director Kathleen Cahalan for her wise leadership and Research Associate Laura Kelly Fanucci for her quiet acumen; the staff of the Collegeville Institute for steady support (former Executive Director Don Ottenhoff, Jessie Bazan, Carla Durand, Elisa Schneider, Susan Sink); and Saint John's Abbey and University in Collegeville, Minnesota, for the rich ground on which to engage ideas of calling, the beautiful campus, nature preserve, and Benedictine setting and worship
- Lilly Foundation, Inc., and Vanderbilt University Divinity School for financial support
- Writing consultant Michael McGregor for his kind wisdom, perceptive advice, and deadlines without which the completion of the manuscript wouldn't have happened, and colleagues in writing workshops at the Collegeville Institute

in 2016, 2018, and 2022 for sharing the pain and triumph of getting words on paper
- My companions and friends Dorothy Bass, Kathleen Cahalan, Jim Nieman, and Chris Scharen, who met for years to explore Christian practical wisdom, for reading drafts, sharing your lives and callings, and transforming how I go about my work and life
- My friends and colleagues in New Directions in Pastoral Theology who met annually at Princeton Theological Seminary for your close reading and mind-expanding discussions (Reggie Abraham, Rubén Arjona, Kirk Bingaman, Lee Butler, Nathan Carlin, Richard Coble, Carol Cook, Carrie Doehring, Greg Ellison, Jaco Hamman, Phil Helsel, Jay-Paul Hinds, Ryan LaMothe, Mindy McGarrah-Sharp, Craig Rubano, Carol Schweitzer, Angella Son, Sonia Walters); Bob Dykstra for his seemingly effortless leadership; and Sam Lee and Yolanda Dreyer for helpful comments on two chapter drafts and general encouragement
- My other pastoral and practical theology friends Barbara McClure, Tone Kaufman, Jeanne Stevenson Moessner, Mary Clark Moschella, Phillis Sheppard, and Heather Walton for thinking with me about the subject matter, the title, and lots else
- Several schools and institutions in the United States (Baylor University; Barton College; Louisville Institute; the International Academy of Practical Theology; the Society for Pastoral Theology; Network for Vocation in Undergraduate Education) and in South Korea (Ewha University; Yonsei University; Korea Theological Seminary; Jangshin Presbyterian Seminary; Seoul Women's University) for invitations and forums to speak about calling, and the hosts and participants in these events for sparking all sorts of fresh ideas and insights
- My friends and my divinity and doctoral students and graduates for letting me listen in to your stories of calling

- My mother for living vibrantly even as she enters her tenth decade and for inviting me to write books that everyday people can read and my three sons, their partners, and children for sparking thought about transition into young adult life, letting me use your stories, and setting my own life on a better course
- Mark, my vocational partner in life for listening as I equivocated and enduring my intense focus on the book, broken up by lots of dog hikes, RV travels, and grandparenting

NOTES

Introduction

1. Since the 1990s, the Lilly Endowment, Inc., has given millions of dollars in grant money to schools, institutions, congregations, scholars, pastors, and laypeople for the exploration of vocation and the Christian life. Several of the books I cite were funded by Lilly.

2. Bonnie J. Miller-McLemore, *Also a Mother: Work and Family as Theological Dilemma* (Nashville, TN: Abingdon, 1994). The "crisis of generativity versus stagnation" is a concept used by life cycle theorist Erik Erikson to describe the primary focus of the seventh stage of adulthood in his "eight stages of man." He articulates this theory in numerous places but originally in Erik H. Erikson, *Childhood and Society* (New York: W. W. Norton & Co., 1950; 2nd ed. rev. and enl., 1963).

3. Mark R. Schwehn and Dorothy C. Bass, eds., *Leading Lives That Matter: What We Should Do and Who We Should Be*, 2nd ed. (Grand Rapids, MI: Eerdmans, 2020).

4. Kathleen A. Cahalan, "Towards a Contemporary and Constructive Theology of Vocation" (unpublished Collegeville Institute Seminars paper, May 23, 2011), p. 3. She cites Douglas Schuurman, *Vocation: Discerning Our Callings in Life* (Grand Rapids, MI: Eerdmans, 2004). He begins his book with a question ("Vocation under Assault: Can It Be Salvaged?") and notes the narrow uses of the word (pp. 2–5, 8–16). See also Kathleen A. Cahalan, "Introduction: Finding Life's Purposes in God's Purposes," in *Calling All Years Good: Christian Vocation throughout Life's Seasons*, ed. Kathleen A. Cahalan and Bonnie J. Miller-McLemore (Grand Rapids, MI: Eerdmans, 2017), 2;

and the comments of Research Associate Laura Kelly Fanucci, "Religious Language in the Public Sphere," Bearings Online, May 24, 2018, https://collegevilleinstitute.org/bearings/religious-language-public-sphere.

5. *The Rule of Saint Benedict*, ed. Timothy Fry, OSB (New York: Vintage, 1998). Kathleen Cahalan underscores the setting as essential to the goals of the seminars, providing a "time and place set apart" for guests to "commit to study, prayer, worship, conversation, and writing" ("A Collegeville Institute Seminar: Vocation across the Lifespan," unpublished Collegeville Institute Seminars paper, January 7, 2011, p. 8). The idea of collaborative inquiry in a sustained learning community grew out of earlier gatherings. See the chapter on "Collaborating," in Dorothy C. Bass, Kathleen A. Cahalan, Bonnie J. Miller-McLemore, James R. Nieman, and Christian B. Scharen, *Christian Practical Wisdom: What It Is, Why It Matters* (Grand Rapids, MI: Eerdmans, 2016), 325–333.

6. "The Dark Side of Calling: An Interview with Katherine Turpin," Part 1, September 24, 2016, https://collegevilleinstitute.org/bearings/the-dark-side-of-vocation.

7. See Hans Schmidt, *Maverick Marine: General Smedley D. Butler and the Contradictions of American Military History* (Lexington: University Press of Kentucky, 1998), 231.

8. See Kathleen A. Cahalan and Bonnie J. Miller-McLemore, eds., *Calling All Years Good: Christian Vocation throughout Life's Seasons* (Grand Rapids, MI: Eerdmans, 2017).

9. My study of children's callings for my chapter in *Calling All Years Good* transformed my understanding of calling. We often think of calling as a subjective, individual, interior choice or, in more evangelical Christian terms, a response to God's command. But for children vocation arises in the here and now (not the future) amid interpersonal interaction (not as an inner process) through their impact on the world around them by simply being children who are open, vulnerable (not as a willed act). See Bonnie J. Miller-McLemore, "Childhood: The (Often Hidden yet Lively) Vocational Life of Children," in *Calling All Years Good*, ed. Kathleen A. Cahalan and Bonnie J. Miller-McLemore (Grand Rapids, MI: Eerdmans, 2017), esp. p. 46.

10. J. Stuart Bunderson and Jeffery Thompson, "The Call of the Wild: Zookeepers, Callings, and the Double-Edged Sword of Deeply Meaningful Work," *Administrative Science Quarterly* 54 (2009), 51.

11. Bunderson and Thompson, "The Call of the Wild," 50, my emphasis.

12. Bunderson and Thompson, "The Call of the Wild," 52.

13. Sarah Porter, Vanderbilt Divinity School Voices, Alumni/a News, September 8, 2015, https://my.vanderbilt.edu/vanderbiltdivinity/2015/09/alumniae-tuesday-sarah-porter-mdiv13. Porter finds solace in an essay by Anne Patrick that suggests calling is "ultimately a religious mystery, to be discerned gradually over the course of one's earthly existence." See Anne E. Patrick, "'Framework for Love': Toward a Renewed Understanding of Christian Vocation," in *A Just and True Love: Feminism at the Frontiers of Theological Ethics: Essays in Honor of Margaret Farley*, ed. Maura A. Ryan and Brian F. Linnane, SJ (Notre Dame, IN: Notre Dame University Press, 2007), 306.

14. Deanna A. Thompson, "A Vocation I Didn't Choose," *Christian Century*, July 13, 2022, p. 10. See also Deanna A. Thompson, "Vocation, Deep Sadness, and Hope in a Virtual Real World," in *So All May Flourish: The Aims of Lutheran Higher Education*, ed. Marcia J. Bunge, Jason A. Mahn, and Martha E. Stortz (Minneapolis, MN: Fortress, 2023), 235–252.

15. Frederick Buechner, *Wishful Thinking: A Seeker's ABC* (New York: Harper & Row, 1973), 119; and Thompson, "A Vocation I Didn't Choose," 10, my emphasis. In the first of his four memoirs, *The Sacred Journey*, Buechner talks at length about the impact of his father's suicide, calling it the "formative moment of my life" (see Martin B. Copenhaver's tribute to Buechner, "Frederick Buechner's Many Benedictions," *The Christian Century*, October 2022, p. 51).

16. See, for example, Brenda L. Berkelaar and Patrice M. Buzzanell, "Bait and Switch or Double-Edged Sword? The (Sometimes) Failed Promises of Calling," *Human Relations* 68, no. 1 (2015): 157–178; Ryan D. Duffy, Richard P. Douglass, and Kelsey L. Autin, "The Dark Side of a Calling," in *Being Called: Scientific, Secular, and Sacred Perspectives*, ed. David Bryce Yaden, Theo D. McCall, and J. Harold Ellens (Santa Barbara, CA: Praeger, 2015), 13–25.

17. Harvey Cox, "Theology from the Underside," *Cross Currents* 39, no. 4 (1989–1990): 386.

18. "An Interview with Katherine Turpin."

19. Jason A. Mahn, "The Conflicts in Our Callings: The Anguish (and Joy) of Willing Several Things," in *Vocation across the Academy: A New Vocabulary for Higher Education*, ed. David S. Cunningham (New York: Oxford University Press, 2017), 45–46 (emphasis in the original), 54.

20. Fortunately, more nuanced publications have emerged in recent theology. See, for example, Edward P. Hahnenberg, *Awakening Vocation: A Theology of Christian Call* (Collegeville, MN: Liturgical Press, 2010); Kathleen A. Cahalan and Douglas J. Schuurman, eds., *Calling in Today's World: Voices*

from Eight Faith Perspectives (Grand Rapids, MI: Eerdmans, 2016); Cahalan and Miller-McLemore, eds., *Calling All Years Good*; Kiara A. Jorgenson, *Ecology of Vocation: Recasting Calling in a New Planetary Era* (New York: Lexington Books, 2020); Paul J. Wadell and Charles R. Pinches, *Living Vocationally: The Journey of the Called Life* (Eugene, OR: Cascades, 2021), especially Chapter 6, 128–151; Susan L. Maros, *Calling in Context: Social Location and Vocational Formation* (Downers Grove, IL: Intervarsity, 2022); and three interdisciplinary conference books published as a result of the Network for Vocation in Undergraduate Education (NetVUE), edited by David S. Cunningham and published by Oxford University Press: *At This Time and Place: Vocation and Higher Education* (2015); *Vocation across the Academy: A New Vocabulary for Higher Education* (2017); and *Hearing Vocation Differently: Meaning, Purpose, and Identity in the Multi-Faith Academy* (2019).

21. Jeffery A. Thompson and J. Stuart Bunderson, "Research on Work as a Calling... and How to Make It Matter," *Annual Review of Organizational Psychology and Organization Behavior* 6 (2019): 421–443.

22. This is true even for social scientists who study calling's "darker side." For example, in their article "The Dark Side of a Calling," psychologists Duffy, Douglass, and Autin suggest having a calling is a "bad thing" unless we can "reap" or maximize its benefits (pp. 15, 20), and they conclude their article with "practical suggestions for avoiding calling's potential dark side" (p. 22). Similarly, in "The (Sometimes) Failed Promises of Calling," communication professors Berkelaar and Buzzanell interpret the idea of work as a moral duty as a "failed" use of the word *calling*, a result of religion's destructive legacy, which creates negative outcomes rather than positive benefits. They provide, nonetheless, a helpful critique of the misuse of the idea of calling, including when it's framed so positively we're unable to talk about its shortcomings.

23. For helpful explorations of the distorted impact of capitalism on vocation, see William T. Cavanaugh, "Actually, You *Can't* Be Anything You Want (and It's a Good Thing, Too)," in *At This Time and Place: Vocation and Higher Education*, ed. David S. Cunningham (New York: Oxford University Press, 2015), 25–46; Jason Mahn, "Called to the Unbidden: Saving Vocation from the Market," *The Cresset* 76, no. 1 (Michaelmas 2012): 6–17; Berkelaar and Buzzanell, "Bait and Switch," 161–162, 166–168, 171.

24. For a detailed study of the distinction between special and general callings and its history, see Schuurman, *Vocation*, 17–41.

25. See Cahalan and Schuurman, eds., *Calling in Today's World*.

26. Mahn, "The Conflicts," 60, 61.

27. Wendall Berry, *A World Lost: A Novel* (Berkeley, CA: Counterpoint, 2008), 149.

28. *The Power of Myth*, PBS series, 1988. See also Betty Sue Flowers, ed., *Joseph Campbell and the Power of Myth with Bill Moyers* (New York: Anchor Books, 1991). One of Campbell's most often quoted comments from the interview is "If you do follow your bliss you put yourself on a kind of track that has been there all the while, waiting for you, and the life that you ought to be living is the one you are living."

29. Joseph Campbell, *A Hero with a Thousand Faces* (New York: Pantheon Books, 1949).

30. John Neafsey, *A Sacred Voice Is Calling: Personal Vocation and Social Conscience* (Maryknoll, NY: Orbis, 2006), 88.

Chapter 1

1. Katherine Turpin, "Younger Adults: Exploring Callings in the Midst of Uncertainty," in *Calling All Years Good: Christian Vocation across the Lifespan*, ed. Kathleen Cahalan and Bonnie J. Miller-McLemore (Grand Rapids, MI: Eerdmans, 2017), 95.

2. Turpin, "Younger Adults," 95, 97.

3. William James, *The Will to Believe and Other Essays in Popular Philosophy* (New York: Longmans, Green 1897; repr. Mineola, NY: Dover, 1956), 227.

4. Katherine Robinson, "Robert Frost: 'The Road Not Taken,'" Poetry Foundation, https://www.poetryfoundation.org/articles/89511/robert-frost-the-road-not-taken. According to Robinson, Frost's walking friend Thomas misinterpreted the poem as a call for decisive action and got upset when Frost insisted that the "end of the poem was 'a mock sigh, hypo-critical for the fun of the thing.'"

5. See, for example, Dan P. McAdams, "Personality, Modernity, and the Storied Self: A Contemporary Framework for Studying Persons," *Psychological Inquiry* 7, no. 4 (1996): 315.

6. According to poetry columnist David Orr, the "Road Less Traveled" is the "most misread poem in America"—"almost everyone gets it wrong" ("The Most Misread Poem in America," *The Paris Review*, September 11, 2015, http://www.theparisreview.org/blog/2015/09/11/the-most-misread-poem-in-america/, taken from Orr, *The Road Not Taken: Finding America in the Poem Everyone Loves and Almost Everyone Gets Wrong* [New York: Penguin, 2015]).

7. Maria Popova, "Either/Or: Kiergegaard on Transcending the Tyranny of Binary Choice and Double Regret," *The Marginalian*, https://www.themarginalian.org/2016/05/05/either-or-kierkegaard/.

8. Søren Kierkegaard, *Either/Or*, vol. 1, ed. Victor Eremita; trans. David F. Swenson and Lillian Marvin Swenson (Princeton, NJ: Princeton University Press, 1959), 37.

9. William C. Placher, ed., *Callings: Twenty Centuries of Christian Wisdom on Vocation* (Grand Rapids, MI: Eerdmans, 2005), 144–153.

10. Erich Lindemann, "Symptomatology and Management of Acute Grief," *American Journal of Psychiatry* 101 (1944): 141–148.

11. Lindemann, "Symptomatology," 141.

12. Lindemann, "Symptomatology," 143.

13. See Bonnie J. Miller-McLemore, "Mundane Grief," in *Reflections on Grief and Spiritual Development*, ed. Andrew J. Weaver and Howard W. Stone (Nashville, TN: Abingdon, 2005), 96–104. See also Bonnie J. Miller-McLemore, *In the Midst of Chaos: Care of Children as Spiritual Practice* (San Francisco, CA: Jossey-Bass, 2007), 178–182.

14. Anne Higonnet, *Pictures of Innocence: The History and Crisis of Ideal Childhood* (New York: Thames and Hudson, 1998), 200.

15. Kenneth R. Mitchell and Herbert Anderson, *Our Losses, All Our Griefs: Resources for Pastoral Care* (Philadelphia: Westminster, 1983), 36–46.

16. Melissa M. Kelly, *Grief: Contemporary Theory and the Practice of Ministry* (Minneapolis, MN: Fortress, 2010), 15, emphasis in original.

17. James E. Marcia, "Identity and Psychosocial Development in Adulthood," *Identity: An International Journal of Theory and Research* 2, no. 2 (2002): 9.

18. Atul Gawande, *Being Mortal: Medicine and What Matters in the End* (New York: Henry Holt and Company, 2014), 262.

19. Dennis Linn, Shela Fabricant Linn, and Matthew Linn, *Sleeping with Bread: Holding What Gives You Life* (Mahwah, NJ: Paulist, 1995).

20. Linn, Linn, and Linn, *Sleeping with Bread*, 4.

21. Linn, Linn, and Linn, *Sleeping with Bread*, 19.

22. Frank Rogers Jr., "Discernment," in *Practicing Our Faith: A Way of Life for a Searching People*, ed. Dorothy C. Bass (San Francisco, CA: Jossey-Bass, 2010), 109.

23. Katherine Turpin, "Adolescence: Vocation in Performance, Passion, and Possibility," in *Calling All Years Good: Christian Vocation across the Lifespan*,

ed. Kathleen Cahalan and Bonnie J. Miller-McLemore (Grand Rapids, MI: Eerdmans, 2017), 86–87.

24. Victor Turner, "Betwixt and Between: The Liminal Period in Rites de Passage," in *The Forest of Symbols: Aspects of Ndembu Ritual* (New York: Cornell University Press, 1970), 93–111 (Ch. IV).

25. Victor Turner, "Variations on a Theme of Liminality," in *Secular Ritual*, ed. Sally F. Moore and Barbara G. Myerhoff (Amsterdam: Van Gorcum, 1977), 36.

26. See Arnold Van Gennep, *The Rites of Passage*, trans. Monika B. Vizedom and Gabrielle L. Caffee (Chicago: The University of Chicago Press 1909/1960), 21.

27. Victor Turner, *The Ritual Process: Structure and Anti-Structure* (Chicago: Aldine Publishing, 1969), 95.

28. Turner, "Betwixt and Between," 97, 99.

29. Edwin H. Friedman, *Generation to Generation: Family Process in Church and Synagogue* (New York: Guilford Press, 1985), 22.

30. Friedman, *Generation to Generation*, 34, 296.

31. Friedman, *Generation to Generation*, 27.

32. Friedman, *Generation to Generation*, 296.

33. Orr, *The Road Not Taken*, cited by Adam Plunkett, book review, *The New York Times*, August 20, 2015, http://www.nytimes.com/2015/08/23/books/review/the-road-not-taken-by-david-orr.html?_r = 0.

34. There are important exceptions, of course, especially in biblical narratives (e.g., Paul on the road to Damascus in Acts 9.1–19) or among religious groups (e.g., evangelicals are more likely to say they've heard God's voice than Reformed Protestants).

35. Shawn Copeland, "Saying Yes and Saying No," in *Practicing Our Faith: A Way of Life for a Searching People*, ed. Dorothy C. Bass (San Francisco, CA: Jossey-Bass), 66.

Chapter 2

1. Jesmyn Ward, *Men We Reaped: A Memoir* (New York: Bloomsbury, 2013), 120–121, emphasis in original.

2. Ward, *Men We Reaped*, 121.

3. Benjamin Voigt, "Langton Hughes 101: Understanding a Poet of the People, for the People," Poetry Foundation, https://www.poetryfoundation.org/articles/88972/langston-hughes-101.

4. Langston Hughes, "The Negro Artist and the Racial Mountain," *The Nation*, June 23, 1926, 692–694.

5. "Langston Hughes, 1902–1967," Poetry Foundation, https://www.poetryfoundation.org/poets/langston-hughes.

6. Lorraine Hansberry, *A Raisin in the Sun* (New York: Vintage, 1994), 73.

7. Blair McClendon, "The Many Visions of Lorraine Hansberry," *The New Yorker*, January 17, 2022, https://www.newyorker.com/magazine/2022/01/24/the-many-visions-of-lorraine-hansberry.

8. Hansberry, *A Raisin*, 51.

9. Critical legal race scholar Kimberlé Williams Crenshaw first coined the term *intersectinality* in 1989 to critique the "single-axis framework that is dominant in antidiscrimination law. . . feminist theory and anti-racist politics." She defined intersectionality as "a metaphor for understanding the ways that multiple forms of inequality or disadvantage sometimes compound themselves and create obstacles that often are not understood among conventional ways of thinking." See Kimberlé Williams Crenshaw, "Demarginalizing the Intersection of Race and Sex: A Black Feminist Critique of Antidiscrimination Doctrine, Feminist Theory and Antiracist Politics," *University of Chicago Legal Forum*, Issue 1, Article 8 (1989): 149. The term has since acquired widespread use to capture the challenges of living at the intersection of multiple contextual locations.

10. Virginia Woolf, *A Room of One's Own* (New York: Harcourt Brace Jovanovich, 1929).

11. Reine-Marie Paris, *Camille: The Life of Camille Claudel, Rodin's Muse and Mistress* (New York: Henry Holt and Co., 1988); *Camille Claudel*, directed by Bruno Nuytten (Orion Pictures, 1988).

12. See Susan L. Maros, *Calling in Context: Social Location and Vocational Formation* (Downers Grove, IL: Intervarsity, 2022).

13. Sarah Smarsh, *Heartland: A Memoir of Working Hard and Being Broke in the Richest Country on Earth* (New York: Scribner, 2018), 2.

14. Smarsh, *Heartland*, 44.

15. Amy Frykholm, "Deferred Dreams: Life in Limbo for an Immigrant Teen," *Christian Century*, June 22, 2016, 21.

16. Jonathan Vespa, "The Changing Economics and Demographics of Young Adulthood: 1975–2016," *Current Population Reports*, P20-579 (US Census Bureau, Washington, DC, April 2017), https://www.census.gov/content/dam/Census/library/publications/2017/demo/p20-579.pdf.

17. Kent Haruf, *Our Souls at Night* (New York: Vintage, 2015), 42, 94, 95.

18. Haruf, *Our Souls*, 96.

19. Kent Haruf quoted in Michael McGregor, "An Interview with Kent Haruf," *Writer's Chronicle* 33 (March/April 2001): 38.

20. Ryan D. Duffy, Richard P. Douglass, and Kelsey L. Autin, "The Dark Side of a Calling," in *Being Called: Scientific, Secular, and Sacred Perspectives*, ed. David Bryce Yaden, Theo D. McCall, and J. Harold Ellens (Santa Barbara, CA: Praeger, 2015), 16.

21. Hansberry, *A Raisin*, 25, 85.

22. Heinz Kohut, *How Does Analysis Cure?* (Chicago: University of Chicago Press, 1984), 138.

23. William James, *The Principles of Psychology* (New York: H. Holt & Company, 1890), 292–293, cited by Gregory C. Ellison, *Cut Dead but Still Alive: Caring for African American Young Men* (Nashville, TN: Abingdon, 2013), 1–2.

24. See Charles B. Strozier, *Heinz Kohut: The Making of a Psychoanalyst* (New York: Farrar, Straus and Giroux, 2001); "Heinz Kohut's Struggles with Religion, Ethnicity, and God," in *Religion, Society, and Psychoanalysis: Readings in Contemporary Theory*, ed. Janet Liebman Jacobs and Donald Capps (Boulder, CO: Westview Press, 1997), 165–180; and "Glimpses of a Life: Heinz Kohut (1913–1981)," in *Progress in Self Psychology*, vol. 1, ed. Arnold Goldberg (New York: Guilford Press, 1985), 3–12.

25. See Heinz Kohut, *Self Psychology and the Humanities* (New York: W.W. Norton, 1985).

26. Christie Cozad Neuger, "Women's Depression: Lives at Risk," in *Women in Travail and Transition: A New Pastoral Care*, ed. Maxine Glaz and Jeanne Stevenson Moessner (Minneapolis, MN: Fortress, 1991), 151; Miriam Greenspan, *A New Approach to Women and Therapy* (New York: McGraw-Hill, 1983), cited by Neuger, "Women's Depression," 152.

27. Smarsh, *Heartland*, 282.

28. Smarsh, *Heartland*, 282.

29. Ward, *Men We Reaped*, 131.

30. Ward, *Men We Reaped*, 169, 174.

31. Ward, *Men We Reaped*, 175–176.

32. William H. Grier and Price M. Cobbs, *Black Rage* (New York: Basic Books), 1968.

33. Patrick B. Reyes, *Nobody Cries When We Die: God, Community, and Surviving to Adulthood* (St. Louis, MO: Chalice, 2016), 6.

34. Reyes, *Nobody Cries*, 13.

35. Ward, *Men We Reaped*, 120–121.

36. See Heinz Kohut, "Forms and Transformations of Narcissism," *Journal of the American Psychoanalytic Association* 14 (1965): 243–272.

37. Smarsh, *Heartland*, 286, 287.

38. Ellison, *Cut Dead*, 75.

39. Ellison, *Cut Dead*, 76.

40. Ellison, *Cut Dead*, 18.

41. Reyes, *Nobody Cries*, 17.

42. Smarsh, *Heartland*, 162.

43. Reyes, *Nobody Cries*, 12.

44. Reyes, *Nobody Cries*, 61, 62–63.

45. Reyes, *Nobody Cries*, 62–63.

46. Miguel A. De La Torre, *Embracing Hopelessness* (Minneapolis, MN: Fortress, 2017), 139.

47. Kent Haruf, "The Making of a Writer," *Granta* 129 (2014), https://granta.com/the-making-of-a-writer/.

48. Jeff Baker, "Kent Haruf's Last Novel Is a Beautiful Gift: 'Our Souls at Night,'" *The Oregonian*, July 17, 2015, http://www.oregonlive.com/books/index.ssf/2015/06/kent_harufs_last_novel_is_a_be.html.

49. William Yardley, "Kent Haruf, Acclaimed Novelist of Small-Town Life, Dies at 71," *New York Times*, December 2, 2014, https://www.nytimes.com/2014/12/03/books/kent-haruf-sublime-novelist-of-small-town-life-dies-at-71.html.

50. Barbara Kingsolver, *Small Wonder* (New York: HarperCollins, 2002), 66.

51. "Lorraine Hansberry's Inspirational Words on Being Young, Gifted, and Black," *American Masters*, PBS, http://www.pbs.org/wnet/americanmasters/lorraine-hansberrys-inspirational-words-young-gifted-black/9908/.

52. "About the Film: Lorraine Hansberry: Sighted Eyes/Feeling Heart," *American Masters*, PBS, http://www.pbs.org/wnet/americanmasters/lorraine-hansberry-sighted-eyesfeeling-heart-film/9846/.

53. Ward, *Men We Reaped*, 231.

54. See https://schoolinthewoods.asd20.org/.

NOTES   173

55. Comments by Mark R. Schwehn in "Vocations of the Contributors," in *Vocation across the Academy: A New Vocabulary for Higher Education*, ed. David S. Cunningham (New York: Oxford University Press, 2017), p. xxiii.

56. Elton Trueblood, *The Life We Prize* (New York: Harper & Brothers Publishers, 1951), 58.

57. Henry Van Dyke, *The Story of the Other Wise Man* (New York: Harper and Brothers Publishers, 1923), 72, 74.

Chapter 3

1. From Mary Oliver's poem, "Summer Day," *New and Selected Poems*, vol. 1 (Boston: Beacon Press, 1992), 94.

2. Søren Kierkegaard, *Purity of Heart Is to Will One Thing: Spiritual Preparation for the Office of Confession*, trans. Douglas V. Steere (New York: Harper & Row, 1956).

3. Richard N. Bolles with Katharine Brooks, *What Color Is Your Parachute: Your Guide to Meaningful Work and Career Success* (New York: Ten Speed Press, 2022), described by Brooks as the "bestselling job-hunting book in the world" (p. 2).

4. Frederick Buechner, *Wishful Thinking: The Seeker's ABCs* (New York: Harper & Row, 1973), 95.

5. See, for example, T. S. Sellers, K. Thomas, J. Batts, & C. Ostman, "Women Called: A Qualitative Study of Christian Women Dually Called to Motherhood and Career," *Journal of Psychology and Theology* 33, no. 3 (2005): 198–209. Books on the dual conflict of "work and family" from the late twentieth century to the present are too many to name. For a very small sample, see Claudia Golden, *Career and Family: Women's Century-Long Journey toward Equity* (Princeton, NJ: Princeton University Press, 2021); Joan C. Williams, *Reshaping the Work-Family Debate: Why Men and Class Matter* (Cambridge, MA: Harvard University Press, 2010); and my own *Also a Mother: Work and Family as Theological Dilemma* (Nashville, TN: Abingdon, 1994).

6. Matt Bloom, "Middle Adulthood: The Joys and Paradoxes of Vocation," in *Calling All Year's Good: Christian Vocation throughout Life's Seasons*, ed. Kathleen A. Cahalan and Bonnie J. Miller-McLemore (Grand Rapids, MI: Eerdmans, 2017), 124.

7. Bloom, "Middle Adulthood," 123–124.

8. Frank A. Johnson and Colleen L. Johnson, "Role Strain in High Commitment Career Women," *Journal of the American Academy of Psychoanalysis* 4 (1976): 16.

9. Bloom, "Middle Adulthood," 126.

10. Lisa Napoli, *Susan, Linda, Nini, and Cokie: The Extraordinary Story of the Founding Mothers of NPR* (New York: Abrams Press, 2022), 199.

11. Ulrich Beck, *The Risk Society: Towards a New Modernity* (Newbury Park, CA: Sage, 1992), 116. See also Joan Williams, *Unbending Gender: Why Family and Work Conflict and What to Do about It* (New York: Oxford University Press, 2000), 1; for more on the "ideal worker norm," see Robert W. Drago, *Striking a Balance: Work, Family, Life* (Boston: Dollars & Sense, 2007).

12. See, for example, Anna W. Jacobs, Terrence D. Hill, Daniel Tope, and Laureen K. O'Brien, "Employment Transitions, Child Care Conflict, and the Mental Health of Low-Income Urban Women with Children," *Women's Health Issues* 26, no. 4 (2016), https://www.whijournal.com/article/S1049-3867(16)30038-X/fulltext.

13. Christine M. Fletcher, "Laboring in the Garden: Vocation and the Realities of Work," in *Vocation across the Academy: A New Vocabulary for Higher Education*, ed. David S. Cunningham (New York: Oxford University Press, 2017), 183.

14. Arlie Hochschild with Anne Machung, *The Second Shift: Working Parents and the Revolution at Home* (New York: Viking Penguin, 1989, 2003).

15. Cynthia Hess, Ph.D., Tanima Ahmed, M.Phil, and Jeff Hayes, "Providing Unpaid Household and Care Work in the United States: Uncovering Inequality," Briefing Paper, Institute for Women's Policy Research, January 2020, https://iwpr.org/wp-content/uploads/2020/01/IWPR-Providing-Unpaid-Household-and-Care-Work-in-the-United-States-Uncovering-Inequality.pdf, and Marianne Bertrand, Emir Kamenica, and Jessica Pan, Working Paper, "Gender Identity and Relative Income within Households," *National Bureau of Economic Research*, May 2013, https://www.nber.org/papers/w19023.

16. For a more detailed exploration of the clash of callings as mother, see Miller-McLemore, *Also a Mother*. I have been helped over the years by other efforts among theologians to address the tension between the callings to mother and to have work of one's own. As a small sample, see Nancy J. Duff, "Vocation, Motherhood, and Marriage," in *Women, Gender, and Christian Community*, ed. Jane Dempsey Douglass and James F. Kay (Louisville, KY.: Westminster John Knox, 1997), 69–81; Cynthia L. Rigby, "Exploring Our Hesitation: Feminist Theologies and the Nurture of Children," *Theology Today*, January 2000, 56(4), 540–554; and Janet Martine Soskice, "Love and

Attention," in *Philosophy, Religion and the Spiritual Life*, ed. Michael McGhee (Cambridge: Cambridge University Press, 1992), 59–72.

17. Rhona Mahony, *Kidding Ourselves: Breadwinning, Babies, and Bargaining Power* (New York: Basic Books, 1995), 106.

18. Mary Guerrera Congo, "The Truth Will Set You Free, but First It Will Make You Crazy," in *Sacred Dimensions of Women's Experience*, ed. Elizabeth Dodson Gray (Wellesley, MA: Roundtable, 1988), 78–79.

19. Congo, "The Truth Will Set You Free," 79.

20. Judith Stadtman Tucker, "A Sort of Perfection: An Interview with Writer Jane Lazarre," The Mothers Movement Online, July/August 2005, www.mothersmovement.org/features/05/jane_lazarre/a_sort_of_perfection.htm. See Jane Lazarre, *The Mother Knot* (Durham, NC: Duke University Press, 1976).

21. John Neafsey, *A Sacred Voice Is Calling: Personal Vocation and Social Conscience* (Maryknoll, NY: Orbis, 2006), 1.

22. Neafsey, *A Sacred Voice*, 49, emphasis in original.

23. Bill Wylie-Kellermann, "Lives That Become the Gospel, "*Christian Ministry*, March–April 1998, 15, 17, 24.

24. Kathleen and James McGinnis, *Parenting for Peace and Justice* (Maryknoll, NY: Orbis, 1981, 1995), ix, 1–2.

25. See Bonnie J. Miller-McLemore, *In the Midst of Chaos: Caring for Children as Spiritual Practice* (San Francisco, CA: Jossey-Bass, 2007), 103–104.

26. See McGinnis and McGinnis, *Parenting*, 129–143.

27. Susanna Snyder and Ellen Ott Marshall, eds., *Parenting for a Better World: Social Justice Practices for Your Family and the Planet* (St. Louis, MO: Chalice, 2022), 1.

28. Daniel McKanan, "The Family, the Gospel, and the Catholic Worker," *Journal of Religion* 87, no. 2 (2007): 153.

29. McKanan, "The Catholic Worker," 174.

30. Claire E. Wolfteich, *Mothering, Public Leadership, and Women's Life Writing: Explorations in Spirituality Studies and Practical Theology* (Leiden, the Netherlands: Brill, 2017), 76.

31. Dorothy Day, *The Long Loneliness* (New York: HarperCollins, 1997), 135, 136–137, 140, 239, and 237, cited by Wolfteich, *Mothering*, 75.

32. Faustino M. Cruz, "The Tension between Scholarship and Service," in *Conundrums in Practical Theology*, ed. Joyce Ann Mercer and Bonnie J. Miller-McLemore (Leiden, the Netherlands: Brill, 2012016), 60.

33. Cruz, "The Tension," 66.

34. Kathryn Tanner, *Christianity and the New Spirit of Capitalism* (New Haven, CT: Yale University Press, 2019), 10.

35. Cruz, "The Tension," 63.

36. Thomas J. Massaro, "The Teacher's Career and Life," *Teaching Theology and Religion* 7, no. 4 (2004): 186, emphasis in the original.

37. Cruz, "The Tension," 73.

38. Jonathan Malesic, *The End of Burnout: Why Work Drains Us and How to Build Better Lives* (Oakland: University of California Press, 2022), 182, 183.

39. Oliver Burkeman, *Four Thousand Weeks: Time Management for Mortals* (New York: Farrar, Straus and Giroux, 2021), 4–5.

40. Burkeman, *Four Thousand Weeks*, 28.

41. Malesic, *The End of Burnout*, 11.

42. Jason A. Mahn, "The Conflicts in Our Callings: The Anguish (and Joy) of Willing Several Things," in *Vocation across the Academy: A New Vocabulary for Higher Education*, ed. David S. Cunningham (New York: Oxford University Press, 2017), 45–46.

43. Matt Bloom, "The Illusive Search for Balance," Well-Being at Work, https://wellbeing.nd.edu/assets/169458/life_balance.pdf, p. 2, cited 429.

44. Bloom, "Middle Adulthood," 126.

45. Burkeman, *Four Thousand Weeks*, 14, 32, emphasis in the original.

46. Miller-McLemore, *In the Midst of Chaos*, 12. See also Miller-McLemore, *Also a Mother*, 125, and "Spinning Gold from Straw: A Matter of Multiple Vocations," in *From Midterms to Ministry: Practical Theologians on Pastoral Beginnings*, ed. Allan Hugh Cole Jr. (Grand Rapids, MI: Eerdmans, 2008), 164–178.

47. Cruz, "The Tension," 65, 79, 80–81.

48. Malesic, *The End of Burnout*, 181, 182.

49. Malesic, *The End of Burnout*, 184.

50. William Butler Yeats, "The Choice," in *The Complete Poems of W. B. Yeats* (New York: Macmillan, 1933), 242, included in Mark R. Schwehn and Dorothy C. Bass, eds., *Leading Lives That Matter: What We Should Do and Who We Should Be* (Grand Rapids, MI: Eerdmans, 2020), 412.

51. Burkeman, *Four Thousand Weeks*, 3, 5, 63–64.

52. Bonhoeffer, *Ethics*, vol. 6 (Minneapolis: Fortress, 2006), 292, cited by Kathryn Kleinhans, "Places of Responsibility: Education for Multiple Callings in Multiple Communities," in *At This Time and In This Place: Vocation and Higher Education*, ed. David S. Cunningham (New York: Oxford University Press, 2016), 109–110. See also Kathryn Kleinhans, "The Work of a Christian: Vocation in Lutheran Perspective," *Word & World* 25, no. 4 (2005): 399–400.

53. See Miller-McLemore, *In the Midst of Chaos*, ch. 1 and 2.

54. Cruz, "The Tension," 68–69.

55. For close analysis of this problem, see sociologist Jennifer M. Silva's *Coming Up Short: Working Class Adulthood in an Age of Uncertainty* (New York: Oxford University Press, 2013), and theologian Ryan LaMothe's *Pastoral Reflections on Global Citizenship: Framing the Political in Terms of Care, Faith, and Community* (New York: Lexington Books, 2018).

56. For a similar argument, see Simone Stolzoff, *The Good Enough Job: Reclaiming Life from Work* (New York: Penguin, 2023).

57. Tanner, *The New Spirit of Capitalism*, 8.

58. See Thomas Piketty, *Capital in the Twenty-First Century*, trans. Arthur Goldhammer (Cambridge, MA: Belnap Press of Harvard University Press, 2017), Richard D. Wolff, *The Sickness is the System: When Capitalism Fails to Saves Us from Pandemics or Itself* (New York: Democracy at Work, 2020), and Richard D. Harvey, *The Enigma of Capital and the Crises of Capitalism* (New York: Oxford University, 2010).

59. Snyder and Marshall, eds., *Parenting*, 2, 3.

60. The Writer's Almanac, June 7, 2019, https://www.garrisonkeillor.com/radio/twa-the-writers-almanac-for-june-7-2019/.

61. Mahn, "Conflicts in Our Callings," 45, 60.

62. Kleinhans, "Places of Responsibility," 110–111.

Chapter 4

1. *Merriam-Webster.com Thesaurus*, s.v. "Failed," https://www.merriam-webster.com/thesaurus/failed.

2. Rita Nakashima Brock, *Journeys by Heart: A Christology of Erotic Power* (New York: Crossroad, 1988), 7.

3. Ann Patchett, *The Story of a Happy Marriage* (New York: HarperCollins, 2013), 239–240, 243.

4. Mary Karr, *Lit: A Memoir* (New York: Harper, 2009), 5–6.

5. Reinhold Niebuhr, *The Nature and Destiny of Man* (New York: Charles Scribner's Sons, 1953), 1:150, and *Man's Nature and His Communities: Essays on the Dynamics and Enigmas of Man's Personal and Social Existence* (London: Bles, 1966), 16. Of course, even though I admire Niebuhr's analysis of sin, I'm not arguing here that all mistakes or failures result from any kind of innate brokenness or original sin, a philosophical debate that I don't pretend to resolve in a chapter that simply hopes to explore the incredibly varied ways we bungle our callings.

6. Personal conversation, August 5, 2022, used with permission. Bloom shares some of his story in Matt Bloom, "Middle Adulthood: The Joys and Paradoxes of Vocation," in *Calling All Years Good: Christian Vocation throughout Life's Seasons*, ed. Kathleen A. Cahalan and Bonnie J. Miller-McLemore (Grand Rapids, MI: Eerdmans, 2017), 123–126.

7. Kathleen A. Cahalan, "Swimming: How the Practice of *Lectio Divina* Heals and Transforms," in Dorothy C. Bass, Kathleen A. Cahalan, Bonnie J. Miller-McLemore, James R. Nieman, and Christian Scharen, *Christian Practical Wisdom: What It Is and Why It Matters* (Grand Rapids, MI: Eerdmans, 2016), 48.

8. Randy Pausch, with Jeffrey Zaslow, *The Last Lecture* (New York: Hyperion Books, 2008), 267.

9. "The Biography of Anton Boisen," Association of Clinical Pastoral Education, Inc., https://acpe.edu/docs/default-source/acpe-history/the-biogra phy-of-anton-theophilus-boisen.pdf?sfvrsn%=%f542507_2.

10. Glenn H. Asquith Jr., "Travel in a Little-Known Country," *The Journal of Pastoral Theology* 20, no. 2 (2010): 168. Anton Boisen's autobiography is *Out of the Depths: An Autobiographical Study of Mental Disorder and Religious Experience* (New York: Harper & Brothers, 1960).

11. See Luise Eichenbaum and Susie Orbach, *Understanding Women: A Feminist Psychoanalytic Approach* (New York: Basic Books, 1982, 2012), especially chap. 2, "The Construction of Femininity," and Aída Hurtago, "Relating to Privilege: Seduction and Rejection in the Subordination of White Women and Women of Color," *Signs: The Journal of Women in Culture and Society* 14, no. 4 (1989): 833–855.

12. Audre Lorde, *Sister Outsider: Essays and Speeches* (Berkeley, CA: Crossing Press, 1984), 57, and bell hooks, *Sisters of the Yam: Black Women and Self-Recovery* (Boston: South End, 1993), 137.

13. Personal conversation, August 5, 2022, used with permission.

14. Melissa Bank, "Who Says You Have to Like a Character?," NPR review, *All Things Considered*, December 8, 2008, https://www.npr.org/2008/12/08/97941739/who-says-you-have-to-like-a-character.

15. Elizabeth Strout, *Olive, Again* (New York: Random House, 2019), 91.

16. Strout, *Olive, Again*, 5, emphasis in the original.

17. James Burgo, "The Difference between Guilt and Shame," *Psychology Today*, May 30, 2013, https://www.psychologytoday.com/us/blog/shame/201305/the-difference-between-guilt-and-shame.

18. I refer to the movement of self-psychology begun by Heinz Kohut. See his book *How Does Analysis Cure?*, ed. Arnold Goldberg with the collaboration of Paul Stephansky (Chicago: University of Chicago Press, 1984).

19. Mikkel Gabriel Christoffersen, "Shame as Obstacle or Opportunity? Pastoral Theologies of Shame," *Journal of Pastoral Theology* 31, no. 1 (2021): 24.

20. Strout, *Olive, Again*, 3, 7.

21. Cahalan, "Swimming," 57.

22. Patchett, *Happy Marriage*, 62–63.

23. Mary Karr, *The Liar's Club* (New York: Penguin, 1995), and *Lit*, 1.

24. Stephen King, *On Writing: A Memoir of the Craft* (New York: Pocket Books, 2000), 94.

25. Patchett, *Happy Marriage*, 63.

26. Strout, *Olive, Again*, 35.

27. Cahalan, "Swimming," 48, 56.

28. Karr, *Lit*, 1.

29. King, *On Writing*, 100.

30. Strout, *Olive, Again*, 21.

31. Pausch, *The Last Lecture*, 198.

32. Eric Brown, cited in "'Last Lecture' Keeps Delivering Lessons for Life," Carnegie-Mellon University News, September 15, 2016, https://www.cmu.edu/news/stories/archives/2016/september/last-lecture.html.

33. Pausch, *The Last Lecture*, 53, 197.

34. Pausch, *The Last Lecture*, 199.

35. See Matt Bloom, *Flourishing in Ministry: How to Cultivate Clergy Wellbeing* (New York: Rowman & Littlefield, 2019), and Matt Bloom, Amy E. Colbert,

and Jordan D. Nielsen, "Stories of Calling: How Called Professionals Construct Narrative Identities," *Administrative Science Quarterly* 66, no. 2 (2021): 298–338.

36. Cahalan, "Swimming," 48.

37. Patchett, *Happy Marriage*, 66–67, 240.

38. Pastoral theologian Glenn Asquith suggests Boisen's delusions revealed the "task to which he dedicated the rest of his life"; they provided "a way of salvation—a purpose in life." See Glenn H. Asquith Jr., "Anton T. Boisen and the Study of 'Living Human Documents,'" *Journal of Presbyterian History* 60, no. 3 (1982): 244–265, esp. 254–255. The title of Boisen's autobiography reflects this triumph: *Out of the Depths: An Autobiographical Study of Mental Disorder and Religious Experience* (New York: Harper & Bros., 1960).

39. Asquith, "Little-Known Country," 168, 169.

40. King, *On Writing*, 18.

41. Patchett, *Happy Marriage*, 247.

42. King, *On Writing*, 18.

43. King, *On Writing*, 91, 97.

44. King, *On Writing*, 96, 97.

45. Patchett, *Happy Marriage*, 69, 240.

46. Patchett, *Happy Marriage*, 69.

47. Strout, *Olive, Again*, 35.

48. Strout, *Olive, Again*, 29, 91.

49. Patchett, *Happy Marriage*, 63.

50. Patchett, *Happy Marriage*, 67.

51. Alice Elliott Dark, *Fellowship Point* (New York: Scribner, 2022), 365.

52. Patchett, *Happy Marriage*, 255.

Chapter 5

1. See Michael J. Himes, *Doing the Truth in Love: Conversations about God, Relationships, and Service* (Mahwah, NJ: Paulist, 1995), 55–59; Michael J. Himes, "Three Key Questions," https://www.studocu.com/en-us/document/university-of-san-diego/general-chemistry-i/three-key-questions-practice/22313725; and John Neafsey, *A Sacred Voice Is Calling: Personal Vocation and Social Conscience* (Maryknoll, NY: Orbis, 2006), 43–45.

2. Kathleen A. Cahalan, *The Stories We Live: Finding God's Calling All around Us* (Grand Rapids, MI: Eerdmans, 2017), 105.

3. For a video clip, see TopMovieClips, "With Great Power Comes Great Responsibility," YouTube Video, 2:22, January 30, 2022, https://www.google.com/search?client=firefox-b-1-d&q=spiderman+%E2%80%9CWith+great+power+comes+great+responsibility%2C%E2%80%9D#fpstate=ive&vld=cid:0462l5a4,vid:guuYU74wU70,st:0. The phrase connecting power and responsibility appears in many places historically and in contemporary media, but this scene comes from the 2002 *Spider-Man* film directed by Sam Raimi and produced by Columbia Pictures, Marvel Enterprises, and Laura Ziskin Productions.

4. Erik H. Erikson, *Insight and Responsibility: Lectures on the Ethical Implications of Psychoanalytic Insight* (New York: W. W. Norton, 1964), 132.

5. Erik H. Erikson, *Childhood and Society* (New York: Norton, 1950), 268.

6. James E. Fisher, "A Framework for Describing Developmental Change among Older Adults," *Adult Education Quarterly* 43, no. 2 (1993): 77, citing Elizabeth Hall, "A Conversation with Erik Erikson," *Psychology Today* 17, no. 6 (1983): 22–30.

7. See Teresa E. Snorton, "The Legacy of the African-American Matriarch: New Perspectives for Pastoral Care," in *Through the Eyes of Women: Insights for Pastoral Care*, ed. Jeanne Stevenson-Moessner (Minneapolis, MN: Augsburg Fortress, 1996), 50–65; Beverly R. Wallace, "A Womanist Legacy of Trauma, Grief, and Loss: Reframing the Notion of the Strong Black Woman Icon," in *Women Out of Order: Risking Change and Creating Care in a Multicultural World*, ed. Jeanne Stevenson-Moessner and Teresa Snorton (Minneapolis, MN: Fortress, 2010), 43–56; Chanequa Walker-Barnes, *Too Heavy a Yoke: Black Women and the Burden of Strength* (Eugene, OR: Cascade Books, 2014); and Stephanie Crumpton, *A Womanist Pastoral Theology against Intimate and Cultural Violence* (New York: Palgrave Macmillan, 2014).

8. Pamela D. Couture, "Over the River and through the Woods: Maintaining Emotional Presence across Geographical Distance," in *Mutuality Matters: Family, Faith, and Just Love*, ed. Herbert Anderson, Edward Foley, Bonnie Miller-McLemore, and Robert Schreiter (New York: Rowman & Littlefield, 2004).

9. David F. Ford, *The Shape of Living: Spiritual Directions for Everyday Life* (Grand Rapids, MI: Baker Books, 1997).

10. Dorothy C. Bass, *Stepmother: Redeeming a Disdained Vocation* (Minneapolis, MN: Broadleaf Books, 2022), 8.

11. Allan Hugh Cole Jr., *Discerning the Way: Lessons from Parkinson's Disease* (Eugene, OR: Cascade Books, 2021), xi.

12. "A Conversation with American's Historian, Ken Burns," *MyVU News*, Vanderbilt University, May 8, 2017, https://news.vanderbilt.edu/2017/05/08/a-conversation-with-americas-historian-ken-burns/.

13. Karen D. Scheib, *Attend to Stories: How to Flourish in Ministry* (Nashville, TN: Wesley's Foundery Books, 2018), 11–14.

14. Scheib, *Attend to Stories*, 13. See also pp. 141–144.

15. Roger Burggraeve, "The Ethical Voice of the Child: Plea for a Chaistic Responsibility in the Footsteps of Levinas," in *Children's Voices: Perspectives in Ethics, Theology, and Religious Education*, ed. Annemie Dillen (Leuven, Belgium: Peeters, 2010), 275.

16. Barbara Kingsolver, *High Tide in Tucson: Essays from Now or Never* (New York: HarperCollins, 1995), 132.

17. See D. W. Winnicott, *Playing and Reality* (London: Tavistock, 1971).

18. Heinz Kohut, *How Does Analysis Cure?* (Chicago: University of Chicago Press, 1984), 67.

19. See the section on "Sleeping with Bread," 30–34.

20. "Removing Fecal Sacs," Sialus, http://www.sialis.org/fecalsacs.htm.

21. "All about Birds: Barn Swallow Life History," Cornell Lab, All about Birds, https://www.allaboutbirds.org/guide/Barn_Swallow/lifehistory.

22. See my "Introduction: Double-Edged Callings: Follow Your Bliss (Blisters?)," 6–8.

23. Bunderson and Thompson, "Call of the Wild," 41.

24. Max Weber, *The Protestant Ethic and the Spirit of Capitalism*, trans. Talcott Parsons (London: Routledge, 1930), 124, cited by Bunderson and Thompson, "Call of the Wild," 34. For provocative commentary on the place of duty in calling, see Gordon Marino, "A Life Beyond 'Do What You Love,'" *New York Times*, May 17, 2014, https://archive.nytimes.com/opinionator.blogs.nytimes.com/2014/05/17/a-life-beyond-do-what-you-love/.

25. H. Richard Niebuhr, *The Responsible Self: An Essay in Christian Moral Philosophy* (New York: Harper & Row, 1963), 65.

26. Erik H. Erikson, *Identity, Youth, and Crisis* (New York: W. W. Norton, 1968), 139.

27. Erikson, *Childhood and Society*, 268.

28. Erikson, *Insight and Responsibility*, 133.

29. Erikson, *Childhood and Society*, 268.

30. Rebecca Solnit, *Orwell's Roses* (New York: Viking, 2021), 206–207; see also 208, 228, 232.

31. "A Conversation with Ken Burns."

32. Erikson, *Childhood and Society*, 268.

33. Niebuhr, *The Responsible Self*, 60, 68.

34. Bass, *Stepmother*, 34.

35. Bass, *Stepmother*, 185.

36. Cole, *Discerning the Way*, 3.

37. Cole, *Discerning the Way*, xiii.

38. Scheib, *Attend to Stories*, 97, 100.

39. Rebecca Solnit, quoted in Peter Tonguette, "Q & A with Rebecca Solnit, Author of *Orwell's Roses*," *The Christian Science Monitor*, February 8, 2022, https://www.csmonitor.com/Books/Author-Q-As/2022/0208/Q-A-with-Rebecca-Solnit-author-of-Orwell-s-Roses.

40. Cole, *Discerning the Way*, xii, xvi, his emphasis.

41. Bunderson and Thompson, "Call of the Wild," 50.

42. Bunderson and Thompson, "Call of the Wild," 52.

43. Mark R. Schwehn and Dorothy C. Bass, eds., *Leading Lives That Matter: What We Should Do and Who We Should Be*, 2nd ed. (Grand Rapids, MI: Eerdmans, 2020), 393.

44. Diane Dreher, *Your Personal Renaissance: 12 Steps to Finding Your Life's True Calling* (Cambridge, MA: Da Capo Press, 2008).

45. Schwehn and Bass, *Leading Lives That Matter*, 393.

46. See Bonnie J. Miller-McLemore, "Generativity, Self-Sacrifice, and the Ethics of Family Life," in *The Equal Regard Family and Its Friendly Critics: Don Browning and the Practical Theological Ethics of the Family*, ed. John Witte Jr., M. Christian Green, and Amy Wheeler (Grand Rapids, MI: Wm. B. Eerdmans Publishing Co., 2007), 17–41. I cite several theologians who have written about this, such as Barbara Hilkert Andolsen, "A Page in Feminist Ethics," *The Journal of Religious Ethics* 9, no. 1 (1981): 80; Christine E. Gudorf, "Parenting, Mutual Love, and Sacrifice," in *Women's Consciousness and Women's Conscience: A Reader in Feminist Ethics*, ed. Barbara Hilkert

Andolsen, Christine E. Gudorf, and Mary D. Pellauer (San Francisco, CA: Harper & Row, 1985), 175–191; Brita Gill-Austern, "Love Understood as Self-Sacrifice and Self-Denial: What Does It Do to Women?," in *Through the Eyes of Women: Insights for Pastoral Care*, ed. Jeanne Steven Moessner (Minneapolis, MN: Fortress, 1996), 315; and JoAnne Terrell, *Power in the Blood? The Cross in the African American Experience* (Maryknoll, NY: Orbis, 1998), 124, 142.

47. Bass, *Stepmother*, 135–136.

48. Scheib, *Attend to Stories*, 72; see also 70–71.

49. Bass, *Stepmother*, 160.

50. Scheib, *Attend to Stories*, 72.

51. Scheib, *Attend to Stories*, 44.

52. Scheib, *Attend to Stories*, 45.

Chapter 6

1. "KonMari Method; Fundamentals of Tidying," https://konmari.com/about-the-konmari-method/; see Kon Mari, *The Life-Changing Magic of Tidying Up: The Japanese Art of Decluttering and Organizing* (New York: Ten Speed Press, 2014). For a practical theological critique of the capitalistic values behind the method, see Christy Lang Hearlson, "The Invention of Clutter and the New Spiritual Discipline of Decluttering," *International Journal of Practical Theology* 25, no. 2 (2021): 224–242.

2. Cambridge English Dictionary.

3. Megan Zahneis, "The Reinvention of Rebecca Chopp," *Chronicle of Higher Education*, December 9, 2021, https://www.chronicle.com/article/the-reinvention-of-rebecca-chopp.

4. Jessica Carle Bratt, "Primigravida," *Narrative Inquiry in Bioethics* 12, no. 3 (2022): 198, 199.

5. Nadia Owusu, *Aftershocks: A Memoir* (New York: Simon & Schuster, 2021), 83.

6. As I was checking the copyedited proofs of this chapter, I became aware of important work on lament and calling by Deanna Thompson. See her chapter, "Beyond Deep Gladness: Lamenting Trauma, Injustice, and Suffering in. Service of the Flourishing of All," in *Called Beyond Our Selves: Vocation and the Common Good*, ed. Erin VanLaningham (New York: Oxford University Press, 2024), 44–62.

7. Kathleen D. Billman and Daniel L. Migliore, *Rachel's Cry: Prayer of Lament and Rebirth of Hope* (Cleveland, OH: United Church Press, 1999), 13–14. Their book was inspired by the groundbreaking work on lament of her friend, Old Testament scholar Walter Brueggemann. See also *The Psalms and the Life of Faith: Walter Brueggemann*, ed. Patrick D. Miller (Minneapolis, MN: Fortress, 1995), esp. "The Costly Loss of Lament," 98–111. They also cite Lester Meyer, "A Lack of Laments in the Church's Use of the Psalter," *Lutheran Quarterly* (1993): 69, and Elaine Ramshaw, *Ritual and Pastoral Care* (Philadelphia: Fortress, 1987), 31–32.

8. Ann Weems, *Psalms of Lament* (Louisville, KY: Westminster John Knox, 1995), cited by Billman and Migliore, *Rachel's Cry*, 8–9.

9. Billman and Migliore, *Rachel's Cry*, 12, citing Robert Wuthnow, *The Crisis in the Churches: Spiritual Malaise, Fiscal Woe* (New York: Oxford University, 1997), 113.

10. Jonathan D. Parker, "'My Mother, My God,' 'Why have you forsaken me?': An Exegetical Note on Psalm 22 as Christian Scripture," *The Expository Times* 131, no. 5 (2019): 202.

11. Parker, "'My Mother, My God,'" 201.

12. Richard Rohr, *Falling Upwards: A Spirituality for the Two Halves of Life* (San Francisco, CA: Jossey-Bass, 2011).

13. Rohr, *Falling Upwards*, xviii, xix.

14. Kathleen A. Cahalan, "Late Adulthood: Seeking Vocation Once Again," in *Calling All Years Good: Christian Vocation throughout Life's Seasons*, ed. Kathleen A. Cahalan and Bonnie J. Miller-McLemore (Grand Rapids, MI: Eerdmans, 2017), 163, citing Francis Kelly Nemeck and Marie Theresa Coombs, *The Spiritual Journey: Critical Thresholds and Stages of Adult Spiritual Genesis* (Wilmington, DE: Michael Glazer, 1986), 41; emphasis in the original.

15. The retreat drew on books in a *Matters Series* by Mary Margaret Funk on thoughts, tools, humility, lectio, and discernment. E.g., see *Thoughts Matter: Discovering the Spiritual Journey* (Collegeville, MN: Liturgical Press, 2013).

16. Brenna Davis, "Humus, Humans and Humility," *Earth Beat: Stories of Climate Crisis, Faith and Action*, February 26, 2020, https://www.ncronline.org/news/earthbeat/humus-humans-and-humility.

17. See also Bonnie J. Miller-McLemore, "Theological Protest and the Spiritual Life," in *A Spiritual Life: Perspectives from Poets, Prophets, and Preachers*,

ed. Allan Hugh Cole Jr. (Louisville, KY: Westminster John Knox, 2011), 161–172, where I explore related tensions between the intellectual life of the mind and the spiritual life of faith and mystery.

18. Henri J. M. Nouwen, "Introduction," to Yushi Nomura, *Desert Wisdom: Sayings from the Desert Fathers* (New York: Image Books, 1984).

19. Thomas Merton, *Conjectures of a Guilty Bystander* (New York: Image Books, 1965), 3–4.

20. David J. Maitland, *Aging as Counterculture: A Vocation for the Later Years* (New York: Pilgrim Press, 1990), 122.

21. Maitland, *Aging as Counterculture*, 120–121.

22. Brian Brock, "Wait for One Another," in *Parenting for a Better World: Social Justice Practices for Your Family and the Planet*, ed. Susanna Snyder and Ellen Ott Marshall (St. Louis, MO: Chalice, 2022), 78–79.

23. Brock, "Wait for One Another," 82.

24. Zahneis, "The Reinvention of Rebecca Chopp."

25. Paul J. Wadell, "Discipleship and Aging: The Call Goes On," *Christian Century*, April 19, 2011, p. 11.

26. James C. Fisher and Henry C. Simmons, *A Journey Called Aging: Challenges and Opportunities in Older Adulthood* (New York: Routledge, 2006), 20, and "Working after Retirement: The Gap between Expectations and Reality," Pew Research Center, September 21, 2006, https://www.pewresearch.org/social-trends/2006/09/21/working-after-retirement-the-gap-between-expectations-and-reality/, cited by Cahalan, "Late Adulthood," 154–155.

27. George E. Vaillant, *Triumphs of Experience: The Men of the Harvard Grant Study* (Cambridge, MA: Belknap Press, 2012), 225, 228, citing James Fries, "Aging, Natural Death, and the Compression of Morbidity," *New England Journal of Medicine* 303 (1980): 130–135, and John W. Rowe and Robert L. Kahn, *Successful Aging* (New York: Dell Publishing, 1998).

28. James E. Fisher, "A Framework for Describing Developmental Change among Older Adults," *Adult Education Quarterly* 43, no. 2 (1993): 76, 82.

29. See commentary on this distinction in Cahalan, "Late Adulthood," 153–154.

30. Blake Farmer, "Nashville Food Project Founder Tallu Schuyler Quinn Remembered for Her Ordinary Goodness," https://wpln.org/post/nashvi

lle-food-project-founder-tallu-schuyler-quinn-remembered-for-her-ordinary-goodness/.

31. Tallu Schuyler Quinn, "Celebration of Life," YouTube video, February 22, 2022, https://www.youtube.com/watch?v=lXsBJFoh9pg.

32. Tallu Schuyler Quinn, "Tallu's Story," Caring Bridge, journal entry, August 17, 2021, https://www.caringbridge.org/visit/talluquinn. See also Tallu Schuyler Quinn, *What We Wish Were True: Reflections on Nurturing Life and Facing Death* (New York: Convergent Books, 2022).

33. From an August 2019 newsletter, quoted in The Nashville Food Project, "Celebrating the Life of Our Founder Tallu Schuyler Quinn," February 18, 2022, https://www.thenashvillefoodproject.org/blog/2022/2/18/celebrating-the-life-of-our-founder-tallu-schuyler-quinn.

34. Laura Kelly Fanucci, "This Is the Story I Have to Tell You," Mothering Spirit: Everyday Parenting as Spiritual Practice, March 3, 2016, https://motheringspirit.com/2016/03/this-is-the-story-i-have-to-tell-you.

35. Angela Denise Davis, cited by Blair Jackson, "Spiritual Journey," *Ukulele*, Summer 2022, p. 54.

36. Davis, cited by Jackson, "Spiritual Journey," 55.

37. Christian Scharen, personal email correspondence, May 11, 2022.

38. Personal conversation, August 5, 2022, used by permission.

39. James Rebanks, *Pastoral Song: A Farmer's Journey* (New York: Mariner Books, 2020), 210.

40. Esther de Waal, *The White Stone: The Art of Letting Go* (Collegeville, MN: Liturgical Press, 2021), 29, 31.

BIBLIOGRAPHY

"About the Film: Lorraine Hansberry: Sighted Eyes/Feeling Heart." *American Masters*. PBS. http://www.pbs.org/wnet/americanmasters/lorraine-hansberry-sighted-eyesfeeling-heart-film/9846/.
Andolsen, Barbara Hilkert. "A Page in Feminist Ethics." *The Journal of Religious Ethics* 9, no. 1 (1981): 69–83.
Asquith, Glenn H. Jr. "Anton T. Boisen and the Study of 'Living Human Documents.'" *Journal of Presbyterian History* 60, no. 3 (1982): 244–265.
Asquith, Glenn H. Jr. "Travel in a Little-Known Country." *The Journal of Pastoral Theology* 20, no. 2 (2010): 165–177.
Baker, Jeff. "Kent Haruf's Last Novel Is a Beautiful Gift: 'Our Souls at Night.'" *The Oregonian*, July 17, 2015, http://www.oregonlive.com/books/index.ssf/2015/06/kent_harufs_last_novel_is_a_be.html.
Bank, Melissa. "Who Says You Have to Like a Character?" NPR review of *Olive Kitteridge* by Elizabeth Strout. *All Things Considered*. PBS. December 8, 2008. https://www.npr.org/2008/12/08/97941739/who-says-you-have-to-like-a-character.
Bass, Dorothy C. *Stepmother: Redeeming a Disdained Vocation*. Minneapolis, MN: Broadleaf Books, 2022.
Bass, Dorothy C., Kathleen A. Cahalan, Bonnie J. Miller-McLemore, James R. Nieman, and Christian B. Scharen. *Christian Practical Wisdom: What It Is, Why It Matters*. Grand Rapids, MI: Eerdmans, 2016.
Beck, Ulrich. *The Risk Society: Towards a New Modernity*. Newbury Park, CA: Sage, 1992.
Benedict. *The Rule of Saint Benedict*. Edited and translated by Timothy Fry, OSB. New York: Vintage, 1998.

Berkelaar, Brenda L., and Patrice M. Buzzanell. "Bait and Switch or Double-edged Sword? The (Sometimes) Failed Promises of Calling." *Human Relations* 68, no. 1 (2015): 157–178.

Berry, Wendall. *A World Lost: A Novel*. Berkeley, CA: Counterpoint, 2008.

Bertrand, Marianne, Emir Kamenica, and Jessica Pan. Working Paper, "Gender Identity and Relative Income within Households," National Bureau of Economic Research, May 2013. https://www.nber.org/papers/w19023

Billman, Kathleen D., and Daniel L. Migliore. *Rachel's Cry: Prayer of Lament and Rebirth of Hope*. Cleveland, OH: United Church Press, 1999.

Bloom, Matt. "The Illusive Search for Balance." Well-Being at Work, 2011, 1–7, https://wellbeing.nd.edu/assets/169458/life_balance.pdf.

Bloom, Matt. "Middle Adulthood: The Joys and Paradoxes of Vocation." In *Calling All Year's Good: Christian Vocation throughout Life's Seasons*, edited by Kathleen A. Cahalan and Bonnie J. Miller-McLemore, 123–147. Grand Rapids, MI: Eerdmans, 2017.

Bloom, Matt. *Flourishing in Ministry: How to Cultivate Clergy Wellbeing*. New York: Rowman & Littlefield, 2019.

Bloom, Matt, Amy E. Colbert, and Jordan D. Nielsen. "Stories of Calling: How Called Professionals Construct Narrative Identities." *Administrative Science Quarterly* 66, no. 2 (2021): 298–338.

Boisen, Anton. *Out of the Depths: An Autobiographical Study of Mental Disorder and Religious Experience*. New York: Harper & Brothers, 1960.

Bolles, Richard N., with Katharine Brooks. *What Color Is Your Parachute: Your Guide to Meaningful Work and Career Success*. New York: Ten Speed Press, 2022.

Bonhoeffer, Dietrich. *Ethics*, vol. 6. Minneapolis, MN: Fortress, 2006.

Brock, Brian. "Waiting for One Another." In *Parenting for Better World: Social Justice Practices for Your Family and the Planet*, edited by Susanna Snyder and Ellen Ott Marshall, 73–84. St. Louis, MO: Chalice, 2022.

Brock, Rita Nakashima. *Journeys by Heart: A Christology of Erotic Power*. New York: Crossroad, 1988.

Brueggemann, Walter. *The Psalms and the Life of Faith: Walter Brueggemann*. Edited by Patrick D. Miller. Minneapolis, MN: Fortress, 1995.

Buechner, Frederick. *Wishful Thinking: A Seeker's ABC*. New York: Harper & Row, 1973.

Bunderson, J. Stuart, and Jeffery Thompson. "The Call of the Wild: Zookeepers, Callings, and the Double-Edged Sword of Deeply Meaningful Work." *Administrative Science Quarterly* 54 (2009): 32–57.

Burggraeve, Roger. "The Ethical Voice of the Child: Plea for a Chiastic Responsibility in the Footsteps of Levinas." In *Children's Voices: Perspectives in Ethics, Theology, and Religious Education*, edited by Annemie Dillen, 271–301. Leuven, Belgium: Peeters, 2010.

Burgo, James. "The Difference between Guilt and Shame." *Psychology Today*, May 30, 2013, https://www.psychologytoday.com/us/blog/shame/201305/the-difference-between-guilt-and-shame.

Burkeman, Oliver. *Four Thousand Weeks: Time Management for Mortals*. New York: Farrar, Straus and Giroux, 2021.

Cahalan, Kathleen A. "Late Adulthood: Seeking Vocation Once Again." *Calling All Years Good: Christian Vocation throughout Life's Seasons*, edited by Kathleen A. Cahalan and Bonnie J. Miller-McLemore, 150–170. Grand Rapids, MI: Eerdmans, 2017.

Cahalan, Kathleen A. *The Stories We Live: Finding God's Calling All around Us*. Grand Rapids, MI: Eerdmans, 2017.

Cahalan, Kathleen A., and Bonnie J. Miller-McLemore, eds. *Calling All Years Good: Christian Vocation throughout Life's Seasons*. Grand Rapids, MI: Eerdmans, 2017.

Cahalan, Kathleen A., and Douglas J. Schuurman, eds. *Calling in Today's World: Voices from Eight Faith Perspectives*. Grand Rapids, MI: Eerdmans, 2016.

Campbell, Joseph. *A Hero with a Thousand Faces*. New York: Pantheon Books, 1949.

Carle, Jessica Bratt. "Primigravida." *Narrative Inquiry in Bioethics* 12, no. 3 (2022): 197–199.

Cavanaugh, William T. "Actually, You *Can't* Be Anything You Want (and It's a Good Thing, Too)." In *At This Time and Place: Vocation and Higher Education*, edited by David S. Cunningham, 25–46. New York: Oxford University Press, 2015.

Christoffersen, Mikkel Gabriel. "Shame as Obstacle or Opportunity? Pastoral Theologies of Shame." *Journal of Pastoral Theology* 31, no. 1 (2021): 1–15.

Cole, Allan Hugh Jr. *Discerning the Way: Lessons from Parkinson's Disease*. Eugene, OR: Cascade Books, 2021.

Congo, Mary Guerrera. "The Truth Will Set You Free, but First It Will Make You Crazy." In *Sacred Dimensions of Women's Experience*, edited by Elizabeth Dodson Gray. Wellesley, MA: Roundtable, 1988.

"A Conversation with American's Historian, Ken Burns." MyVU News, Vanderbilt University. May 8, 2017. https://news.vanderbilt.edu/2017/05/08/a-conversation-with-americas-historian-ken-burns/.

Copeland, Shawn. "Saying Yes and Saying No." In *Practicing Our Faith: A Way of Life for a Searching People*, edited by Dorothy C. Bass, 59–74. San Francisco, CA: Jossey-Bass, 2010.

Copenhaver, Martin B. "Frederick Buechner's Many Benedictions." *The Christian Century*, October 2022, 48–53.

Couture, Pamela D. "Over the River and through the Woods: Maintaining Emotional Presence across Geographical Distance." In *Mutuality Matters: Family, Faith, and Just Love*, edited by Herbert Anderson, Edward Foley, Bonnie Miller-McLemore, and Robert Schreiter, 137–152. New York: Rowman & Littlefield, 2004.

Cox, Harvey. "Theology from the Underside." *Cross Currents* 39, no. 4 (1989–1990): 385–390.

Crenshaw, Kimberlé Williams. "Demarginalizing the Intersection of Race and Sex: A Black Feminist Critique of Antidiscrimination Doctrine, Feminist Theory and Antiracist Politics." *University of Chicago Legal Forum*, Vol. 1989, Issue 1, Article 8, 139–167.

Crumpton, Stephanie. *A Womanist Pastoral Theology against Intimate and Cultural Violence*. New York: Palgrave Macmillan, 2014.

Cruz, Faustino M. "The Tension between Scholarship and Service." In *Conundrums in Practical Theology*, edited by Joyce Ann Mercer and Bonnie J. Miller-McLemore, 60–89. Leiden, the Netherlands: Brill, 2016.

Cunningham, David S., ed. *At This Time and Place: Vocation and Higher Education*. New York: Oxford University Press, 2015.

Cunningham, David S., ed. *Vocation across the Academy: A New Vocabulary for Higher Education*. New York: Oxford University Press, 2017.

Cunningham, David S., ed. *Hearing Vocation Differently: Meaning, Purpose, and Identity in the Multi-Faith Academy*. New York: Oxford University Press, 2019.

Dark, Alice Elliott. *Fellowship Point*. New York: Scribner, 2022.

Davis, Brenna. "Humus, Humans and Humility." *Earth Beat: Stories of Climate Crisis, Faith and Action*, February 26, 2020, https://www.ncronl ine.org/news/earthbeat/humus-humans-and-humility.

Day, Dorothy. *The Long Loneliness*. New York: HarperCollins, 1997.

De La Torre, Miguel A. *Embracing Hopelessness*. Minneapolis, MI: Fortress, 2017.

Drago, Robert W. *Striking a Balance: Work, Family, Life*. Boston: Dollars & Sense, 2007.

Dreher, Diane. *Your Personal Renaissance: 12 Steps to Finding Your Life's True Calling*. Cambridge, MA: Da Capo Press 2008.

Duff, Nancy J. "Vocation, Motherhood, and Marriage." In *Women, Gender, and Christian Community*, edited by Jane Dempsey Douglass and James F. Kay, 69–81. Louisville, KY: Westminster John Knox, 1997.

Duffy, Ryan D., Richard P. Douglass, and Kelsey L. Autin. "The Dark Side of a Calling." In *Being Called: Scientific, Secular, and Sacred Perspectives*, edited by David Bryce Yaden, Theo D. McCall, and J. Harold Ellens, 13–25. Santa Barbara, CA: Praeger, 2015.

Eichenbaum, Luise, and Susie Orbach. *Understanding Women: A Feminist Psychoanalytic Approach*. New York: Basic Books, 1982, 2012.

Ellison, Gregory C. *Cut Dead but Still Alive: Caring for African American Young Men*. Nashville, TN: Abingdon, 2013.

Erikson, Erik H. *Childhood and Society*. New York: W. W. Norton & Co., 1950; 2nd ed. rev. and enl., 1963.

Erikson, Erik H. *Insight and Responsibility: Lectures on the Ethical Implications of Psychoanalytic Insight*. New York: W. W. Norton 1964.

Erikson, Erik H. *Identity, Youth, and Crisis*. New York: W. W. Norton, 1968.

Fanucci, Laura Kelly. "This Is the Story I Have to Tell You." Mothering Spirit: Everyday Parenting as Spiritual Practice. March 3, 2016. https://motheringspirit.com/2016/03/this-is-the-story-i-have-to-tell-you/.

Fanucci, Laura Kelly. "Religious Language in the Public Sphere." Bearings Online. May 24, 2018. https://collegevilleinstitute.org/bearings/religious-language-public-sphere/.

Farmer, Blake. "Nashville Food Project Founder Tallu Schuyler Quinn Remembered for Her Ordinary Goodness." WPLN News. February 18, 2022. https://wpln.org/post/nashville-food-project-founder-tallu-schuyler-quinn-remembered-for-her-ordinary-goodness/.

Fisher, James E. "A Framework for Describing Developmental Change among Older Adults." *Adult Education Quarterly* 43, no. 2 (1993): 76–89.

Fisher, James C., and Henry C. Simmons. *A Journey Called Aging: Challenges and Opportunities in Older Adulthood*. New York: Routledge, 2006.

Fletcher, Christine M. "Laboring in the Garden: Vocation and the Realities of Work." In *Vocation across the Academy: A New Vocabulary for Higher Education*, edited by David S. Cunningham. New York: Oxford University Press, 2017.

Flowers, Betty Sue, ed. *Joseph Campbell and the Power of Myth with Bill Moyers*. New York: Anchor Books, 1991.

Ford, David F. *The Shape of Living: Spiritual Directions for Everyday Life*. Grand Rapids, MI: Baker Books, 1997.

Friedman, Edwin H. *Generation to Generation: Family Process in Church and Synagogue*. New York: Guilford Press, 1985.

Fries, James. "Aging, Natural Death, and the Compression of Morbidity." *New England Journal of Medicine* 303 (1980): 130–135.

Frykholm, Amy. "Deferred Dreams: Life in Limbo for an Immigrant Teen." *Christian Century*, June 22, 2016, 20–23.

Funk, Mary Margaret. *Thoughts Matter: Discovering the Spiritual Journey*. Collegeville, MN: Liturgical Press, 2013.

Gawande, Atul. *Being Mortal: Medicine and What Matters in the End*. New York: Henry Holt and Company, 2014.

Gill-Austern, Brita. "Love Understood as Self-Sacrifice and Self-Denial: What Does It Do to Women?" In *Through the Eyes of Women: Insights for Pastoral Care*, edited by Jeanne Steven Moessner, 304–321. Minneapolis, MN: Fortress, 1996.

Golden, Claudia. *Career and Family: Women's Century-Long Journey toward Equity*. Princeton, NJ: Princeton University Press, 2021.

Greenspan, Miriam. *A New Approach to Women and Therapy*. New York: McGraw-Hill, 1983.

Grier, William H., and Price M. Cobbs. *Black Rage*. New York: Basic Books, 1968.

Gudorf, Christine E. "Parenting, Mutual Love, and Sacrifice." In *Women's Consciousness and Women's Conscience: A Reader in Feminist Ethics*, edited by Barbara Hilkert Andolsen, Christine E. Gudorf, and Mary D. Pellauer, 175–191. San Francisco, CA: Harper & Row, 1985.

Hahnenberg, Edward P. *Awakening Vocation: A Theology of Christian Call*. Collegeville, MN: Liturgical Press, 2010.

Hall, Elizabeth. "A Conversation with Erik Erikson." *Psychology Today* 17, no. 6 (1983): 22–30.

Hansberry, Lorraine. *A Raisin in the Sun*. New York: Vintage, 1994.

Harvey, Richard D. *The Enigma of Capital and the Crises of Capitalism*. New York: Oxford University, 2010.

Haruf, Kent. "The Making of a Writer." *Granta* 129 (2014), https://granta.com/the-making-of-a-writer/.

Haruf, Kent. *Our Souls at Night*. New York: Vintage, 2015.

Hearlson, Christy Lang. "The Invention of Clutter and the New Spiritual Discipline of Decluttering." *International Journal of Practical Theology* 25, no. 2 (2021): 224–242.

Hess, Cynthia, Tanima Ahmed, and Jeff Hayes. "Providing Unpaid Household and Care Work in the United States: Uncovering Inequality."

Briefing Paper, Institute for Women's Policy Research, Washington, DC, January 2020. https://iwpr.org/wp-content/uploads/2020/01/IWPR-Providing-Unpaid-Household-and-Care-Work-in-the-United-States-Uncovering-Inequality.pdf.

Higonnet, Anne. *Pictures of Innocence: The History and Crisis of Ideal Childhood*. New York: Thames and Hudson, 1998.

Himes, Michael J. *Doing the Truth in Love: Conversations about God, Relationships, and Service*. Mahwah, NJ: Paulist, 1995.

Himes, Michael J. "Three Key Questions." https://www.studocu.com/en-us/document/university-of-san-diego/general-chemistry-i/three-key-questions-practice/22313725.

Hochschild, Arlie, with Anne Machung. *The Second Shift: Working Parents and the Revolution at Home*. New York: Viking Penguin, 1989, 2003.

hooks, bell. *Sisters of the Yam: Black Women and Self-Recovery*. Boston: South End, 1993.

Hughes, Langston. "The Negro Artist and the Racial Mountain." *The Nation*, June 23, 1926, 692–694.

Hurtago, Aída. "Relating to Privilege: Seduction and Rejection in the Subordination of White Women and Women of Color." *Signs: The Journal of Women in Culture and Society* 14, no. 4 (1989): 833–855.

Jackson, Blair. "Spiritual Journey." *Ukulele*, Summer 2022, 54–56.

Jacobs, Anna W., Terrence D. Hill, Daniel Tope, and Laureen K. O'Brien. "Employment Transitions, Child Care Conflict, and the Mental Health of Low-Income Urban Women with Children." *Women's Health Issues* 26, no. 4 (2016): 366–376. DOI: https://www.whijournal.com/article/S1049-3867(16)30038-X/fulltext.

James, William. *The Principles of Psychology*. New York: H. Holt & Company, 1890.

James, William. *The Will to Believe and Other Essays in Popular Philosophy*. New York: Longmans, Green, 1897; repr., Dover, 1956.

Johnson, Frank A., and Colleen L. Johnson. "Role Strain in High Commitment Career Women." *Journal of the American Academy of Psychoanalysis* 4 (1976): 13–36.

Jorgenson, Kiara A. *Ecology of Vocation: Recasting Calling in a New Planetary Era*. New York: Lexington Books, 2020.

Karr, Mary. *The Liar's Club*. New York: Penguin, 1995.

Karr, Mary. *Lit: A Memoir*. New York: Harper, 2009.

Kelly, Melissa M. *Grief: Contemporary Theory and the Practice of Ministry*. Minneapolis, MN: Fortress, 2010.

Kierkegaard, Søren. *Purity of Heart Is to Will One Thing: Spiritual Preparation for the Office of Confession.* Translated by Douglas V. Steere. New York: Harper & Row, 1956.

Kierkegaard, Søren. *Either/Or*, vol. 1. Edited by Victor Eremita and translated by David F. Swenson and Lillian Marvin Swenson. Princeton, NJ: Princeton University Press, 1959.

King, Stephen. *On Writing: A Memoir of the Craft.* New York: Pocket Books, 2000.

Kingsolver, Barbara. *High Tide in Tucson: Essays from Now or Never.* New York: HarperCollins, 1995.

Kingsolver, Barbara. *Small Wonder.* New York: HarperCollins, 2002.

Kleinhans, Kathryn. "The Work of a Christian: Vocation in Lutheran Perspective." *Word & World* 25, no. 4 (2005): 399–400.

Kleinhans, Kathryn. "Places of Responsibility: Education for Multiple Callings in Multiple Communities." In *At This Time and In This Place: Vocation and Higher Education*, edited by David S. Cunningham, 109–110. New York: Oxford University Press, 2016.

Kohut, Heinz. "Forms and Transformations of Narcissism." *Journal of the American Psychoanalytic Association* 14 (1965): 243–272.

Kohut, Heinz. *How Does Analysis Cure?* Edited by Arnold Goldberg with the collaboration of Paul E. Stepansky. Chicago: University of Chicago Press, 1984.

Kohut, Heinz. *Self Psychology and the Humanities.* New York: W.W. Norton, 1985.

LaMothe, Ryan. *Pastoral Reflections on Global Citizenship: Framing the Political in Terms of Care, Faith, and Community.* New York: Lexington Books, 2018.

Lazarre, Jane. *The Mother Knot.* Durham, NC: Duke University Press, 1976.

Lindemann, Erich. "Symptomatology and Management of Acute Grief." *American Journal of Psychiatry* 101 (1944): 141–148.

Linn, Dennis, Shela Fabricant Linn, and Matthew Linn. *Sleeping with Bread: Holding What Gives You Life.* Mahwah, NJ: Paulist, 1995.

Lorde, Audre. *Sister Outsider: Essays and Speeches.* Berkeley, CA: Crossing Press, 1984.

"Lorraine Hansberry's Inspirational Words on Being Young, Gifted, and Black." *American Masters.* PBS. http://www.pbs.org/wnet/amer icanmasters/lorraine-hansberrys-inspirational-words-young-gifted-black/9908/.

Mahn, Jason A. "Called to the Unbidden: Saving Vocation from the Market." *The Cresset* 76, no. 1 (Michaelmas 2012): 6–17.

Mahn, Jason A. "The Conflicts in Our Callings: The Anguish (and Joy) of Willing Several Things." In *Vocation across the Academy: A New Vocabulary for Higher Education*, edited by David S. Cunningham, 44–66. New York: Oxford University Press, 2017.

Mahony, Rhona. *Kidding Ourselves: Breadwinning, Babies, and Bargaining Power.* New York: Basic Books, 1995.

Maitland, David J. *Aging as Counterculture: A Vocation for the Later Years.* New York: Pilgrim Press, 1990.

Malesic, Jonathan. *The End of Burnout: Why Work Drains Us and How to Build Better Lives.* Oakland: University of California Press, 2022.

Marcia, James E. "Identity and Psychosocial Development in Adulthood." *Identity: An International Journal of Theory and Research* 2, no. 2 (2002): 7–28.

Mari, Kon. *The Life-Changing Magic of Tidying Up: The Japanese Art of Decluttering and Organizing.* New York: Ten Speed Press, 2014.

Marino, Gordon. "A Life Beyond 'Do What You Love.'" *New York Times*, May 17, 2014, https://archive.nytimes.com/opinionator.blogs.nytimes.com/2014/05/17/a-life-beyond-do-what-you-love/.

Maros, Susan L. *Calling in Context: Social Location and Vocational Formation.* Downer's Grove, IL: Intervarsity, 2022.

Massaro, Thomas J. "The Teacher's Career and Life." *Teaching Theology and Religion* 7, no. 4 (2004): 230–237.

McAdams, Dan P. "Personality, Modernity, and the Storied Self: A Contemporary Framework for Studying Persons." *Psychological Inquiry* 7, no. 4 (1996): 295–321.

McClendon, Blair. "The Many Visions of Lorraine Hansberry." *The New Yorker*, January 17, 2022, https://www.newyorker.com/magazine/2022/01/24/the-many-visions-of-lorraine-hansberry.

McGinnis, Kathleen, and McGinnis, James. *Parenting for Peace and Justice.* Maryknoll, NY: Orbis, 1981, 1995.

McGregor, Michael. "An Interview with Kent Haruf." *Writer's Chronicle* 33, March/April (2001).

McKanan, Daniel. "The Family, the Gospel, and the Catholic Worker." *Journal of Religion* 87, no. 2 (2007): 153–182.

Merton, Thomas. *Conjectures of a Guilty Bystander.* New York: Image Books, 1965.

Meyer, Lester. "A Lack of Laments in the Church's Use of the Psalter." *Lutheran Quarterly* 7, no. 1 (1993): 45–66.

Miller-McLemore, Bonnie J. *Also a Mother: Work and Family as Theological Dilemma*. Nashville, TN: Abingdon, 1994.

Miller-McLemore, Bonnie J. "Mundane Grief." In *Reflections on Grief and Spiritual Development*, edited by Andrew J. Weaver and Howard W. Stone, 96–104. Nashville, TN: Abingdon, 2005.

Miller-McLemore, Bonnie J. "Generativity, Self-Sacrifice, and the Ethics of Family Life." In *The Equal Regard Family and Its Friendly Critics: Don Browning and the Practical Theological Ethics of the Family*, edited by John Witte Jr., M. Christian Green, and Amy Wheeler, 17–41. Grand Rapids, MI: Eerdmans, 2007.

Miller-McLemore, Bonnie J. *In the Midst of Chaos: Caring for Children as Spiritual Practice*. San Francisco, CA: Jossey-Bass, 2007.

Miller-McLemore, Bonnie J. "Spinning Gold from Straw: A Matter of Multiple Vocations." In *From Midterms to Ministry: Practical Theologians on Pastoral Beginnings*, edited by Allan Hugh Cole Jr., 164–178. Grand Rapids, MI: Eerdmans, 2008.

Miller-McLemore, Bonnie J. "Theological Protest and the Spiritual Life." In *A Spiritual Life: Perspectives from Poets, Prophets, and Preachers*, edited by Allan Hugh Cole Jr., 161–172. Louisville, KY: Westminster John Knox, 2011.

Miller-McLemore, Bonnie J. "Childhood: The (Often Hidden yet Lively) Vocational Life of Children." In *Calling All Years Good*, edited by Kathleen A. Cahalan and Bonnie J. Miller-McLemore, 38–62. Grand Rapids, MI: Eerdmans, 2017.

Mitchell, Kenneth R., and Herbert Anderson. *Our Losses, All Our Griefs: Resources for Pastoral Care*. Philadelphia: Westminster, 1983.

Napoli, Lisa. *Susan, Linda, Nini, and Cokie: The Extraordinary Story of the Founding Mothers of NPR*. New York: Abrams Press, 2022.

Neafsey, John. *A Sacred Voice Is Calling: Personal Vocation and Social Conscience*. Maryknoll, NY: Orbis, 2006.

Nemeck, Francis Kelly, and Marie Theresa Coombs. *The Spiritual Journey: Critical Thresholds and Stages of Adult Spiritual Genesis*. Wilmington, DE: Michael Glazer, 1986.

Neuger, Christie Cozad. "Women's Depression: Lives at Risk." In *Women in Travail and Transition: A New Pastoral Care*, edited by Maxine Glaz and Jeanne Stevenson Moessner, 146–161. Minneapolis, MN: Fortress, 1991.

Niebuhr, H. Richard. *The Responsible Self: An Essay in Christian Moral Philosophy*. New York: Harper & Row, 1963.

Niebuhr, Reinhold. *The Nature and Destiny of Man*, vol. 1. New York: Charles Scribner's Sons, 1953.

Niebuhr, Reinhold. *Man's Nature and His Communities: Essays on the Dynamics and Enigmas of Man's Personal and Social Existence*. London: Bles, 1966.

Nomura, Yushi. *Desert Wisdom: Sayings from the Desert Fathers*, with an introduction by Henri J. M. Nouwen. New York: Image Books, 1984.

Orr, David. "The Most Misread Poem in America." *The Paris Review*, September 11, 2015, http://www.theparisreview.org/blog/2015/09/11/the-most-misread-poem-in-america/.

Orr, David. *The Road Not Taken: Finding America in the Poem Everyone Loves and Almost Everyone Gets Wrong*. New York: Penguin, 2015.

Owusu, Nadia. *Aftershocks: A Memoir*. New York: Simon & Schuster, 2021.

Paris, Reine-Marie. *Camille: The Life of Camille Claudel, Rodin's Muse and Mistress*. New York: Henry Holt and Co., 1988.

Patchett, Ann. *The Story of a Happy Marriage*. New York: HarperCollins, 2013.

Patrick, Anne E. "'Framework for Love': Toward a Renewed Understanding of Christian Vocation." In *A Just and True Love: Feminism at the Frontiers of Theological Ethics: Essays in Honor of Margaret Farley*, edited by Maura A. Ryan and Brian F. Linnane, SJ, 303–337. Notre Dame, IN: Notre Dame University Press, 2007.

Pausch, Randy, with Jeffrey Zaslow. *The Last Lecture*. New York: Hyperion Books, 2008.

Piketty, Thomas. *Capital in the Twenty-First Century*, trans. Arthur Goldhammer. Cambridge, MA: Belnap Press of Harvard University Press, 2017.

Placher, William C., ed. *Callings: Twenty Centuries of Christian Wisdom on Vocation*. Grand Rapids, MI: Eerdmans, 2005.

Plunkett, Adam. Review of *The Road Not Taken* by David Orr. *The New York Times*, August 20, 2015, http://www.nytimes.com/2015/08/23/books/review/the-road-not-taken-by-david-orr.html?_r = 0,.

Popova, Maria. "Either/Or: Kiergegaard on Transcending the Tyranny of Binary Choice and Double Regret." The Marginalian. https://www.themarginalian.org/2016/05/05/either-or-kierkegaard/.

Quinn, Tallu Schuyler. *What We Wish Were True: Reflections on Nurturing Life and Facing Death*. New York: Convergent Books, 2022.

Ramshaw, Elaine. *Ritual and Pastoral Care*. Philadelphia: Fortress, 1987.
Rebanks, James. *Pastoral Song: A Farmer's Journey*. New York: Mariner Books, 2020.
Reyes, Patrick B. *Nobody Cries When We Die: God, Community, and Surviving to Adulthood*. St. Louis, MO: Chalice, 2016.
Rigby, Cynthia L. "Exploring Our Hesitation: Feminist Theologies and the Nurture of Children." *Theology Today* 56, no. 4 (2000): 540–554.
Robinson, Katherine. "Robert Frost: 'The Road Not Taken.'" Poem Guide, *Poetry Foundation*. https://www.poetryfoundation.org/articles/89511/robert-frost-the-road-not-taken.
Rogers, Frank, Jr. "Discernment." In *Practicing Our Faith: A Way of Life for a Searching People*, edited by Dorothy C. Bass, 103–116. San Francisco, CA: Jossey-Bass, 2010.
Rohr, Richard. *Falling Upwards: A Spirituality for the Two Halves of Life*. San Francisco, CA: Jossey-Bass, 2011.
Rowe, John W., and Robert L. Kahn, *Successful Aging*. New York: Dell Publishing, 1998.
Scheib, Karen D. *Attend to Stories: How to Flourish in Ministry*. Nashville, TN: Wesley's Foundery Books, 2018.
Schmidt, Hans. *Maverick Marine: General Smedley D. Butler and the Contradictions of American Military History*. Lexington: University Press of Kentucky, 1998.
Schuurman, Douglas. *Vocation: Discerning Our Callings in Life*. Grand Rapids, MI: Eerdmans, 2004.
Schwehn, Mark R., and Dorothy C. Bass, eds. *Leading Lives That Matter: What We Should Do and Who We Should Be*, 2nd ed. Grand Rapids, MI: Eerdmans, 2020.
Sellers, T. S., Thomas, K., Batts, J., & Ostman, C. "Women Called: A Qualitative Study of Christian Women Dually Called to Motherhood and Career." *Journal of Psychology and Theology*, 33, no. 3 (2005): 198–209.
Silva, Jennifer M. *Coming Up Short: Working Class Adulthood in an Age of Uncertainty*. New York: Oxford University Press, 2013.
Smarsh, Sarah. *Heartland: A Memoir of Working Hard and Being Broke in the Richest Country on Earth*. New York: Scribner, 2018.
Snorton, Teresa E. "The Legacy of the African-American Matriarch: New Perspectives for Pastoral Care." In *Through the Eyes of Women: Insights for Pastoral Care*, edited by Jeanne Stevenson-Moessner, 50–65. Minneapolis, MN: Augsburg Fortress, 1996.
Snyder, Susanna, and Ellen Ott Marshall, eds. *Parenting for a Better World: Social Justice Practices for Your Family and the Planet*. St. Louis, MO: Chalice, 2022.

Solnit, Rebecca. *Orwell's Roses*. New York: Viking, 2021.
Soskice, Janet Martin. "Love and Attention." In *Philosophy, Religion and the Spiritual Life*, edited by Michael McGhee, 59–72. Cambridge: Cambridge University Press, 1992.
Stolzoff, Simone. *The Good Enough Job: Reclaiming Life from Work*. New York: Penguin, 2023.
Strout, Elizabeth. *Olive, Again*. New York: Random House, 2019.
Strozier, Charles B. "Glimpses of a Life: Heinz Kohut (1913–1981)." In *Progress in Self Psychology*, vol. 1, ed. Arnold Goldberg, 3–12. New York: Guilford Press, 1985.
Strozier, Charles B. "Heinz Kohut's Struggles with Religion, Ethnicity, and God." In *Religion, Society, and Psychoanalysis: Readings in Contemporary Theory*. Edited by Janet Liebman Jacobs and Donald Capps, 165–180. Boulder, CO: Westview Press, 1997.
Strozier, Charles B. *Heinz Kohut: The Making of a Psychoanalyst*. New York: Farrar, Straus and Giroux, 2001.
Tanner, Kathryn. *Christianity and the New Spirit of Capitalism*. New Haven, CT: Yale University Press, 2019.
Terrell, JoAnne. *Power in the Blood? The Cross in the African American Experience*. Maryknoll, NY: Orbis, 1998.
Thompson, Deanna A. "A Vocation I Didn't Choose." *Christian Century*, July 13, 2022, 10–11.
Thompson, Deanna A. "Vocation, Deep Sadness, and Hope in a Virtual Real World." In *So All May Flourish: The Aims of Lutheran Higher Education*, edited by Marcia J. Bunge, Jason A. Mahn, and Martha E. Stortz, 235–252. Minneapolis, MN: Fortress, 2023.
Thompson, Deanna A. "Beyond Deep Gladness: Lamenting Trauma, Injustice, and Suffering in. Service of the Flourishing of All." In *Called Beyond Our Selves: Vocation and the Common Good*, edited by Erin Van-Laningham, 44–62. New York: Oxford University Press, 2024.
Thompson, Jeffery A., and J. Stuart Bunderson, "Research on Work as a Calling . . . and How to Make It Matter." *Annual Review of Organizational Psychology and Organization Behavior* 6 (2019): 421–443.
Tonguette, Peter. "Q & A with Rebecca Solnit, Author of *Orwell's Roses*." *The Christian Science Monitor*, February 8, 2022, https://www.csmonitor.com/Books/Author-Q-As/2022/0208/Q-A-with-Rebecca-Solnit-author-of-Orwell-s-Roses.
Trueblood, Elton. *The Life We Prize*. New York: Harper & Brothers Publishers, 1951.

Tucker, Judith Stadtman. "A Sort of Perfection: An Interview with Writer Jane Lazarre." The Mothers Movement Online. July/August 2005. www.mothersmovement.org/features/05/jane_lazarre/a_sort_of_perfection.htm.
Turner, Victor. *The Ritual Process: Structure and Anti-Structure*. Chicago: Aldine Publishing, 1969.
Turner, Victor. *The Forest of Symbols: Aspects of Ndembu Ritual*. New York: Cornell University Press, 1970.
Turner, Victor. "Variations on a Theme of Liminality." In *Secular Ritual*, edited by Sally F. Moore and Barbara G. Myerhoff. Amsterdam: Van Gorcum, 1977.
Turpin, Katherine. "The Dark Side of Calling," Part 1. Interview by Janel Kragt Bakker. Bearings Online, Collegeville Institute. September 24, 2016. https://collegevilleinstitute.org/bearings/the-dark-side-of-vocation/.
Turpin, Katherine. "Adolescence: Vocation in Performance, Passion, and Possibility." In *Calling All Years Good: Christian Vocation across the Lifespan*, edited by Kathleen Cahalan and Bonnie J. Miller-McLemore, 67–91. Grand Rapids, MI: Eerdmans, 2017.
Turpin, Katherine. "Younger Adults: Exploring Callings in the Midst of Uncertainty." In *Calling All Years Good: Christian Vocation across the Lifespan*, edited by Kathleen Cahalan and Bonnie J. Miller-McLemore, 95–118. Grand Rapids, MI: Eerdmans, 2017.
Vaillant, George E. *Triumphs of Experience: The Men of the Harvard Grant Study*. Cambridge, MA: Belknap Press, 2012.
Van Dyke, Henry. *The Story of the Other Wise Man*. New York: Harper and Brothers Publishers, 1923.
Van Gennep, Arnold. *The Rites of Passage*. Translated by Monika B. Vizedom and Gabrielle L. Caffee. Chicago: The University of Chicago Press 1909/1960.
Vespa, Jonathan. "The Changing Economics and Demographics of Young Adulthood: 1975–2016." Current Population Reports P20-579, Washington, DC: U.S. Census Bureau, April 2017. https://www.census.gov/content/dam/Census/library/publications/2017/demo/p20-579.pdf.
Voigt, Benjamin. "Langton Hughes 101: Understanding a Poet of the People, for the People." Poetry Foundation. https://www.poetryfoundation.org/articles/88972/langston-hughes-101.
Wadell, Paul J. "Discipleship and Aging: The Call Goes On." *Christian Century*, April 19, 2011, 11–12.

Wadell, Paul J. and Charles R. Pinches. *Living Vocationally: The Journey of the Called Life.* Eugene, OR: Cascades, 2021.

Walker-Barnes, Chanequa. *Too Heavy a Yoke: Black Women and the Burden of Strength.* Eugene, OR: Cascade Books, 2014.

Wallace, Beverly R. "A Womanist Legacy of Trauma, Grief, and Loss: Reframing the Notion of the Strong Black Woman Icon." In *Women Out of Order: Risking Change and Creating Care in a Multicultural World,* edited by Jeanne Stevenson-Moessner and Teresa Snorton, 43–56. Minneapolis, MN: Fortress, 2010.

Ward, Jesmyn. *Men We Reaped: A Memoir.* New York: Bloomsbury, 2013.

Weber, Max. *The Protestant Ethic and the Spirit of Capitalism.* Translated by Talcott Parsons. London: Routledge, 1930.

Weems, Ann. *Psalms of Lament.* Louisville, KY: Westminster John Knox, 1995.

Williams, Joan C. *Unbending Gender: Why Family and Work Conflict and What to Do About It.* New York: Oxford University Press, 2000.

Williams, Joan C. *Reshaping the Work-Family Debate: Why Men and Class Matter.* Cambridge, MA: Harvard University Press, 2010.

Winnicott, D. W. *Playing and Reality.* London: Tavistock, 1971.

Wolff, Richard D. *The Sickness is the System: When Capitalism Fails to Saves Us from Pandemics or Itself.* New York: Democracy at Work, 2020.

Wolfteich, Claire E. *Mothering, Public Leadership, and Women's Life Writing: Explorations in Spirituality Studies and Practical Theology.* Leiden, the Netherlands: Brill, 2017.

"Working after Retirement: The Gap between Expectations and Reality." Pew Research Center. September 21, 2006. https://www.pewresearch.org/social-trends/2006/09/21/working-after-retirement-the-gap-between-expectations-and-reality/.

Woolf, Virginia. *A Room of One's Own.* New York: Harcourt Brace Jovanovich, 1929.

Wuthnow, Robert. *The Crisis in the Churches: Spiritual Malaise, Fiscal Woe.* New York: Oxford University, 1997.

Wylie-Kellermann, Bill. "Lives That Become the Gospel." *Christian Ministry,* March–April 1998, 15–17.

Zahneis, Megan. "The Reinvention of Rebecca Chopp." *Chronicle of Higher Education,* December 9, 2021, https://www.chronicle.com/article/the-reinvention-of-rebecca-chopp.

INDEX

For the benefit of digital users, indexed terms that span two pages (e.g., 52–53) may, on occasion, appear on only one of those pages.

adulthood
  elderly adulthood, 4, 28–29, 69–70, 150–51
  middle adulthood, 11–12, 65–66, 67–70, 80–81
  young adulthood, 4–5, 19, 20–21, 28–29, 35–36, 50, 79
accumulated callings, 112, 113–14
aesthete, 25–26
affirmation, 53, 57–58, 108
Also a Mother (Miller-McLemore), 174–75n.16
ambiguity, 23, 29–30, 35, 81, 85, 89
Anderson, Herbert, 28
Asquith, Glenn, 93, 106, 180n.38

Barth, Karl, 148–49
Bass, Dorothy, 118–19, 129–30, 131–33
Becker, Nicholas, Fr., 77–78, 80
being seen and heard, 57–59
belonging, 54, 156
Berkelaar, Brenda, 166n.22

Benedictine Rule, 80
Berry, Wendall, 13
Best Penguin Award, 104–5
Bible, 146
Billman, Katie, 142–43
Black Rage (Grier and Cobbs), 56
blame, 87–89, 90, 99, 100–1
blocked callings
  addressing of, 56–64
  being seen and heard and, 57–59
  communal dimensions of, 47–48, 59–60
  deferred dreams and, 43–49
  definition of, 43
  denial and, 53–54, 56–57, 59–60
  depression and, 53, 54–56
  false promises and, 60–61
  grandmothering and, 60
  hope and, 43–45, 46, 50–51, 53, 60–61
  intergenerational addressing of, 61–64
  as interrupted callings, 62–63

205

blocked callings (cont.)
  lack of simple answers on, 56–57
  less dire obstructions and, 49–52
  living (well) despite limits and, 56–64
  narcissistic injury and, 54, 57–58
  obliterated callings and, 43, 60
  overview of, 42–43
  popular culture's influence on, 50–51
  prisoner rehabilitation and, 58–59
  race and, 43–49, 53–54, 57, 58, 61–63
  rage as result of, 53–54, 58–59
  recompense and, 60
  scientific findings on, 52–56
  self-hatred and, 53, 54–56
  shame and, 54–56
  survival and, 57
  suspended deferrals and, 51–52
  thwarting of callings and, 52–56
  as underside of undersides, 43
  women and, 45–47, 54–56
Bloom, Matt, 67–69, 79–80, 83–84, 91–92, 101, 105, 155
Boisen, Anton, 93, 105–6
Bonhoeffer, Dietrich, 81–82
Bowen, Murray, 38
Brady, Tom, 137–38
Brock, Brian, 149–50
Brown, Michael, 53–54
Buechner, Frederick, 8, 10–11, 66, 165n.15
Bunderson, Stuart, 6, 125–26
Burggraeve, Roger, 121
Burkeman, Oliver, 78
Burns, Ken, 120, 127–28
Buzzanell, Patrice, 166n.22

Cahalan, Kathleen, 2, 3–4, 91–92, 101, 102–3, 105–6, 145–46, 147, 150–51, 163–64n.4, 164n.5
calling. *See also* blocked callings; conflicted callings; fractured callings; missed callings; relinquished callings; unexpected callings
  Christian tradition of, 1–2, 3, 11, 14–15
  common good and, 10–11
  communal dimensions of, 4–5, 7
  conflicts inherent within, 9
  as deeply grounded, 5
  definition of, 1–3, 10–11, 14–15
  as developing over a lifetime, 4
  dilemmas of, 11–14
  as double-edged sword, 7–9
  follow your bliss and, 15–16
  forms of, 11–14
  generativity and, 2–3
  good life and, 2–3
  increased interest in, 9–10
  joy, talent, and service and, 11
  limitations of theological discussions on, 9–10
  meaningful lives and, 3–4
  mothering and, 3
  motivation for current volume on, 1–8
  neoclassical views of, 6–7
  overview of, 1–16
  previous works by author and, 2–3
  public understanding of, 3–4
  race and, 4–5
  reclaiming of, 4, 11–12
  sacred dimensions of, 14–15

INDEX   207

structure of current volume on,
    11–14
suffering as part of, 8–9
superficial views of, 2
terminology of, 1–3, 8–9
undersides of, 7–9
vocation's relation to, 1, 3, 11
zookeepers as example of, 6
Calling All Years Good (Cahalan
    and Miller-McLemore),
    164n.9
Calvin, John, 3
capitalism
    calling's relation to, 4–5,
        82–83, 125–26
    corporate business and, 10–11
    economics of love and, 132
    finance capitalism, 76, 83
    market and, 47–48
    money and, 7, 11, 43, 51, 55,
        70–71, 76, 79, 91, 148
    Wall Street and, 4–5
Camille Claudel (film), 46
Campbell, Joseph, 15–16, 167n.28
Catholic Worker movement, 75
Chopp, Rebecca, 139–40, 150
children, 4–5, 17–18, 27–28, 32–33,
    57–58, 68, 71, 73–75, 84–85,
    88, 119, 122–23
Christian tradition
    academic life and, 148
    calling and, 1–2, 3, 11, 14–15
    colonialism and, 14–15
    conflicted callings and, 74–75,
        79–80, 81
    counter-spirit and, 82–83
    duty and, 126
    families and, 74–75
    finitude and, 80–81

fractured callings and, 88–
    89, 107–8
relinquished callings and, 145–48
sin and, 88–89, 107–8
unexpected callings and,
    126–27, 130
Church Dogmatics (Barth), 148–49
Claudel, Camille, 46
Cole, Allan, 119, 129–30, 131–32
communal dimensions of calling, 4–
    5, 7, 36–39, 47–48, 59–60, 83
conflicted callings
    ambiguously abundant nature of,
        78–86
    Catholic Worker movement and, 75
    causes of, 67–70
    Christian tradition and, 74–75,
        79–80, 81
    communal dimensions of, 83
    dependence and
        independence in, 68
    everyday practices and, 83–86
    explosion of callings and, 67–70
    families and, 69–70, 72–78
    "higher" service and, 72–78
    metaphors for understanding, 78
    middle adulthood roles and, 67–70
    mothering and, 71–72, 82
    myths about calling and, 66
    ordering of commitments and, 77
    overview of, 65–67
    race and, 74
    realism and imperfection and,
        79–81
    reformation of work and life and,
        82–83
    role proliferation and, 67–70
    service and activism and, 74–77
    women and, 70–72

INDEX

Congo, Mary Guerrera, 72
consolation and desolation,
 31–33, 123
Crenshaw, Kimberlé Williams 64
Cruz, Faustino, 75–77, 80, 82

Davis, Angela Denise, 153–54
"Dark Side of a Calling, <The>"
 (Duffy, Douglass, and Austin),
 166n.22
Day, Dorothy, 75
Dedeaux, Joshua Adam, 62
deferred dreams, 43–49
De La Torre, Miguel, 60–61
denial, 53–54, 56–57, 59–60
depression, 53, 54–56, 120, 127
desire, 33, 49, 50, 54–55, 57–58,
 60, 64, 72–73, 94–96, 117,
 121–22, 128, 148
De Waal, Esther, 156
disappointment, 8, 14, 20–21, 101,
 104–5, 107, 109
discernment processes, 30–34, 123
divorce, 19, 28, 74, 89–90, 96–98,
 100–2, 105–6, 107, 109, 120
duty, 6–7, 8–9, 54–55, 81, 124–28

Ellison, Greg, 54, 58–59
elderly adulthood, 4, 28–29,
 69–70, 150–51
emotional toll of callings
 depression and, 53, 54–56,
  120, 127
 fractured callings and, 99–102
 guilt and, 8, 75, 100–1, 104–
  5, 106–7
 rage and, 53–54, 58–59
 remorse and, 26, 101, 104–5, 127
 self-hatred and, 53, 54–56
 shame and, 54–56, 99–101, 106–7

end of life decisions, 29–30, 153
environment, 4–5, 82–83, 147–48
 climate change and, 4–5, 147–48
 ecology and, 131–32
Erdrich, Louise, 84–85
Erikson, Erik, 28–29, 35–36,
 55–56, 115–16, 127, 163n.2
Evangelical Protestantism, 1,
 82–83, 125–26
everyday practices, 83–86

families, 69–70, 72–97, 106–8, 119
Fanucci, Laura Kelly, 153
Fauci, Anthony, 137–38
Fellowship Point (Elliott), 109
finitude and finite, 11, 14, 79–81,
 90–91, 113
Fisher, James, 150–52
follow your bliss advice, 15
follow your blisters advice, 15–16
forgiveness, 79–81, 96–97, 106–8
fractured callings
 blame and, 87–89, 90, 99, 100–1
 blunders in our work callings
  and, 91–96
 Christian tradition and,
  88–89, 107–8
 definition of, 87–90
 delusion and, 101–2
 development of, 97
 emotional toll of, 99–102
 families, friends, and forgiveness
  and, 96–97, 106–8
 honesty and, 104, 105–6
 guilt and, 100–1, 107
 meaning of, 87–90
 mending of, 102–8
 mothering and, 94–95
 overview of, 87–91
 personal relationships and, 96–99

race and, 95
remorse and disappointment
    and, 101, 104–5, 107, 109
responsibility for, 89
restraining of judgment and,
    108–10
ruptured love callings and,
    96–99
self-esteem and, 100
self-forgiveness and, 107–8
shame and, 99–101, 106–7
shared experience of, 90–91
sin and, 88–89, 107–8
truth-telling and, 102–4
turning failure to good and,
    104–6
unknown callings as similar to,
    94
women and, 94–95
Freud, Sigmund, 54–55
Friedman, Edwin, 37–38
friendship, 96–97, 106–8, 113–
    14, 131–32
Frost, Robert, 22, 40

Gandhi, 72–73
Gawande, Atul, 29–30
gender. *See* mothering;
    parenting; women
generativity, theories of, 2–3,
    28–29, 115–16
Giving Tree, The (Silverstein),
    130–31
grandmothering, 4–5, 60
grief, 14, 26–28, 93, 142–45
guilt, 8, 75, 100–1, 104–5, 106–7

Hansberry, Lorraine, 44–46, 61–62
Harlem Renaissance, 43–44
Haruf, Kent, 50–51, 52–53, 61

Higonnet, Anne, 27–28
hindsight, 19, 34
Hinduism, 74–75
Hochschild, Arlie, 70–71
honesty, 58–59, 104, 105–6
hooks, bell, 95
hope, 43–45, 46, 50–51, 53, 60–61
Hughes, Langston, 43–45, 53, 54–55
humility, 103–4, 107–8, 134, 147–48

Ignatius of Loyola, 30–33
integrity, 9, 28–29, 76, 79, 115–
    16, 127–28
irrevocable decisions, 18–22

James, William, 22, 54
Jonah, biblical story of, 2
Jung, Carl, 145

Karr, Mary, 89, 103
Kathleen, Abigail, 153
Kelly, Melissa, 28
Kierkegaard, Søren, 25, 54–55
King, Martin Luther, Jr., 72–73
King, Stephen, 99, 101–2, 106–7
Kingslover, Barbara, 61–62, 122
Kohut, Heinz, 53–54, 57–58, 123

lament, 14, 29–30, 62, 76–77, 141–45
Lamott, Anne, 84
Liar's Club, The (Karr), 101–2
Lilly Endowment, Inc., 163n.1
Lindemann, Erich, 26–27
Linn, Dennis, 30–31
Linn, Matthew, 30–31
Linn, Sheila Fabricant, 30–31
"Little-Known Country, A"
    (Boisen), 93
Lizana, Ronald Wayne, 56
Lorde, Audre, 95

Luther, Martin, 3, 81–82
Lutherans, 81, 85, 142

Mahn, Jason, 9, 11–12, 85
Mahony, Rhona, 71
Maitland, David, 149
Malesic, Jonathan, 77–78
Marcia, James, 28–29
marriage
 calling's relation to, 19, 35–36, 45, 63, 70–71, 74–75, 79
 divorce and, 19, 28, 74, 89–90, 96–98, 100–2, 105–6, 107, 109, 120
 failed marriages, 89–90
 second marriages, 61, 96, 105–6
Mark 9, 146
Maros, Susan 47–48
Massaro, Thomas, 76–77
Maurin, Peter, 75
McAdow, Samuel, 37
McGinnis, Kathleen, 74
McKanan, Daniel, 74–75
Men We Reaped (Ward), 42
Merton, Thomas, 148–49
middle adulthood, 11–12, 65–66, 67–70, 80–81
Migliore, Daniel, 142–43
miscarriage, 140
missed callings
 aesthetic and moral life and, 25–26
 ambiguity and, 29–30
 becoming an adult and, 19–22
 communal dimensions of, 36–39
 complexity of decision-making and, 19
 components of loss and, 28–29
 definition of, 18–22
 differentiation and, 38
 discernment processes and, 30–34

 end of life and, 29–30
 engaging youth and, 32–33
 epiphanies and, 33–34
 grief and, 26–28
 hindsight and, 19
 irrevocable decisions and, 18–22
 learning to count your days and, 26–30
 living in vocational liminality and, 34–36
 mothering and, 19, 27–28
 overview of, 17–18
 parental role in calling and, 19–21
 race and, 38–39
 recognition and support and, 28
 redemption despite loss and, 39–41
 regret and, 24–26
 road less traveled and, 23, 39–40
 road not taken and, 18, 22–23, 39–40
 self-reflection and, 33
 sleeping with bread and, 30–34
 vocational insight and, 32–33
 vocational stories and, 24–26
Mitchell, Kenneth, 28
money, 7, 11, 43, 51, 55, 70–71, 76, 79, 91, 148
mothering
 blocked callings and, 60
 calling and, 3
 conflicted callings and, 71–72, 82
 double-burden and, 72, 82
 fractured callings and, 94–95
 grandmothering, 4–5, 60
 missed callings and, 19, 27–28
 stepmothering, 129
Mother Knot, The (Lazarre), 72
Moyers, Bill, 15

Myrtle Alice Lee McAdow portrait, 36–38

narcissistic injury, 54, 57–58
National Association of Colored Women, 117
Neafsey, John, 73
neoclassical views of calling, 6–7, 125–26
Niebuhr, H. Richard, 126–27, 128, 132
Niebuhr, Reinhold, 90–91, 178n.5

obliterated callings, 43, 60
organizational psychology, 6
Olive, Again (Strout), 98, 100–1, 102–3, 106
Olive Kitteridge (Strout), 97–98
Orr, David, 40, 167n.6
Orwell, George, 127, 130–31
Our Souls at Night (Haruf), 50–51, 61
Owusu, Nadia, 141

parenting, 19–21, 71–72, 74, 117–18, 119, 122–23. See also mothering
Parenting for a Better World (Snyder, Susanna and Marshall), 74, 84
Parenting for Peace and Justice (McGinnis and McGinnis), 74
Parker, Jonathan, 144
Paschal mystery, 145
Patchett, Ann, 89, 101–3, 105–6, 107–9
Patrick, Anne, 165n.13
Patterson, Jane, 96, 98–99, 105
Paul, 87–88, 99, 108, 149–50
Pausch, Randy, 92–93, 104–5
political patterns and dimensions of calling, 4–5, 7, 38–39,
47–48, 60, 72–73, 74, 82–83, 88–89, 144
Porter, Sarah, 165n.13
prophetic vocation, 149
Psalm 22, 144–45
Psalm 90, 27
psychology, 3, 10–11, 53–54, 93–94
organizational psychology, 6
social sciences and, 10–11, 154–55
Purity of Heart Is to Will One Thing (Kierkegaard), 66

Quakers, 31, 63–64
Quinn, Tallu Shuyler, 152–53

race
blocked callings and, 43–49, 53–54, 57, 58, 61–63
calling and, 4–5
conflicted callings and, 74
fractured callings and, 95
missed callings and, 38–39
unexpected callings and, 116–18
racism, 4–5, 42, 43–45, 88–89, 116–18
rage, 53–54, 58–59
Raisin in the Sun, The (Hansberry), 44–45
regret, 7, 18, 22–26, 39–40, 43, 101, 127
religion. See also theology
Bible, The, 27
calling's relation to, 10–11, 24–25, 47–48, 63–64, 88, 93–94, 107–8
Evangelical Protestantism, 1, 82–83, 125–26
Hinduism, 74–75
Lutherans, 81, 85, 142
progressive Christianity, 1
Roman Catholicism, 3, 74–76

relinquished callings
  belonging and, 156
  Christian tradition and, 145–48
  definition of, 136–37
  falling upward and, 145
  grief and, 144–45
  humility and, 147–48
  lament and, 141–45
  overview of, 135–37
  prophetic vocation and, 149
  relief and, 150–57
  renunciation and reorientation and, 145–50
  rest and, 154–57
  restoration and, 150–54
  retirement and other callings let go and, 137–41
  terminology of, 136–37
remorse, 26, 101, 104–5, 127
Reveles, Cristina, 48–49
Reyes, Patrick, 57, 59–60
road less traveled, 23, 39–40
Road Less Traveled, The (Peck), 22–23
road not taken, 18, 22–23, 39–40
"Road Not Taken, The" (Frost), 22, 24–25
Robinson, Katherine, 167n.4
Rodin, Auguste, 46
Rogers, Frank, 32
Rohr, Richard, 145–46
role proliferation, 67–70
Roman Catholicism, 3, 74–76
Room of One's Own, A (Woolf), 45–46
Rule of Saint Benedict, 15, 77–78, 80, 156

Samberg, Susan, 69
Scheib, Karen, 120, 130
Schwehn, Mark, 63

scripture
  religion, 92, 144
  self-esteem, 54–55, 100, 123
  self-forgiveness, 107–8
  self-hatred, 53, 54–56
  self-reflection, 31, 33
  service, 11, 74–77, 128–33
  sexism, 45, 116–18
  shame, 54–56, 99–101, 106–7
  Shining, The (King), 106–7
  sickness and illness
    calling's relation to, 5, 35–36, 54–55, 93, 105–6, 119–20, 150, 152–53
    Alzheimer's, 139–40, 150
    brain tumors, 121, 152–53
    cancer, 8, 29–30, 61–62, 100–1, 104–5, 121
    Parkinson's, 119, 129–30, 131–32
  Simmons, Henry, 150–51
  sin, 88–89, 107–8
  Sleeping with Bread (Linn and Linn), 30–32
  Smarsh, Sarah, 48, 55–56, 57–58, 59–60
  social sciences, 10–11, 154–55
  Solnit, Rebecca, 127
  Spiritual Exercises, The (Ignatius of Loyola), 30–32
  Story of the Other Wise Man, The (Van Dyke), 51–52, 64
  Strout, Elisabeth, 97–98
  suffering as part of calling, 8–9, 52–53, 105, 130
  Susan, Margaret, 153
  "Symptomatology and Management of Acute Grief" (Lindemann), 26–27

Tanner, Kathryn, 76
Terrell, Mary Church 117

Thompson, Deanna 156–57
time, 4, 7, 11, 13, 21, 35–36, 45–46, 67, 111–12
  gift of, 11
theology. *See also* religion
  calling's relation to, 8–10, 24, 80–81, 93, 154–55
  discussions of, 9–10
  liberation theology, 8–9
  pastoral theology, 28, 54–55, 93, 117, 120
  theologians, 1, 2, 8–9, 28, 93, 117, 147–48
Thompson, Jeffrey, 6, 125–26
thwarting of callings, 52–56
Turner, Victor, 34
Turpin, Katherine, 20–21, 32–33

unexpected callings
  accumulated callings and, 113–14
  burdens of a second type and, 118–20
  Christian tradition and, 126–27, 130
  development of, 119–20
  duty and, 124–28
  expect the unexpected and, 120–22
  families and, 119
  gift that keeps on giving and, 115–18
  integrity and, 127
  life-giving sacrifices and, 131
  lifting as we climb and, 117
  living with mediocrity and, 122–24
  looking forward from, 133–34
  overview of, 111–15
  race and, 116–18

regular triage and, 122–24
responsibility and, 127
service, sacrifice, and grace and, 128–33
stepparenting and, 118–19
women and, 116–18

Van Dyke, Henry, 64
vocation. *See* calling
vocational insight, 32–33
vocational liminality, 34–36
vocational stories, 24–26
vulnerability, 5, 14, 88–89, 131, 141–42

Wadell, Paul, 150–51
What Color Is Your Parachute? (Bolles), 66
What to Expect when You're Expecting (Murkoff), 120–21
Williams, Serena, 137–38
Winnicott, D. W., 122–23
Wolfteich, Claire, 75–76
women. *See also* mothering
  blocked callings and, 45–47, 54–56
  conflicted callings and, 70–72
  double-burden and, 72, 82
  fractured callings and, 94–95
  second shift of, 70–71
  unexpected callings and, 116–18
Woolf, Virginia, 45–46
Wylie-Kellermann, Bill, 73–74

Yeats, William Butler, 80
young adulthood, 4–5, 19, 20–21, 28–29, 35–36, 50, 79
Younger, Walter Lee, Jr., 44–45

www.ingramcontent.com/pod-product-compliance
Lightning Source LLC
Chambersburg PA
CBHW071833290825
31867CB00003B/120